Language Teachir  **ts**

Language Teaching in Blended Contexts

Edited by

Margaret Nicolson, Linda Murphy
and Margaret Southgate

DUNEDIN

Published by
Dunedin Academic Press Ltd
Hudson House
8 Albany Street
Edinburgh EH1 3QB
Scotland

ISBN 978 1 906716 20 2

British Library Cataloguing in Publication Data
A catalogue record for this book is available from the British Library

Typeset by Makar Publishing Production
Printed in Great Britain by CPI Antony Rowe

Contents

Contributors

The editors and contributors all work in the Faculty of Education and Language Studies in The Open University (OU) in various parts of the UK. They are all experienced members of teams who work on language course development and teaching, student support and the professional development of OU language teachers. They all write and research in the area of language, language education and/or teacher development.

Helga Adams is Senior Lecturer and Staff Tutor in Languages in the OU in Yorkshire and the OU in the North of England.

María-Rosa Amoraga-Piqueras is an Associate Lecturer in Spanish for the OU in the South of England.

Vikki Atkinson is an Associate Lecturer in English and Education for the OU in the South and the East of England.

Bärbel Brash is an Associate Lecturer in German for the OU in Scotland.

Anna Comas-Quinn is Lecturer in Spanish at the OU in Milton Keynes.

Annette Duensing is Senior Lecturer and Staff Tutor in Languages at the OU in the East of England.

Matilde Gallardo is Senior Lecturer and Staff Tutor in Languages at the OU in the East of England.

Hannelore Green is Lecturer and Staff Tutor in Languages at the OU in the West Midlands.

Felicity Harper is Lecturer and Staff Tutor in Languages at the OU in the South West of England.

Sarah Heiser is Lecturer and Staff Tutor in Languages at the OU in London.

Stella Hurd recently retired from her post as Senior Lecturer in French at the OU in Milton Keynes.

Loykie Lominé is an Associate Lecturer in French for the OU in the South of England and also teaches at Winchester University.

Linda Murphy is Senior Lecturer and Staff Tutor at the OU in the South of England.

Lynda Newcombe is an Associate Lecturer in Welsh for the OU in the South of England and also teaches at Cardiff University.

Margaret Nicolson is Senior Lecturer and Staff Tutor in Languages at the OU in Scotland.

Helen Peters is Lecturer and Staff Tutor in Languages at the OU in London.

Elke St.John is an Associate Lecturer in German for the OU in the North West of England.

Lijing Shi is an Associate Lecturer in Chinese for the OU in the South of England.

Margaret Southgate is Senior Lecturer and Staff Tutor in Languages at the OU in Wales.

Sylvia Warnecke is Lecturer in German at the OU in Milton Keynes and an Associate Lecturer in German and in Education for the OU in Scotland.

Acknowledgements

The Editors wish to thank Dunedin Academic Press for supporting the project and bringing it to publication as well as for their responsive approach to all editorial queries. They also thank the authors for their contributions and for the willingness with which they took on board reviewers' and editors' comments and ideas at each stage of the book's development. The support and patience of Louisa Scott at The Open University in Scotland have also been much appreciated throughout the project. Helga Adams and Felicity Harper are due particular acknowledgement for the significant part they played in the reviewing process. The following reviewers also deserve acknowledgement for their comment on chapters and sections at stages in the book's development: María-Rosa Amoraga-Piqueras, Uwe Baumann, Gillian Beattie-Smith, Bärbel Brash, Christine Brunton, Michel Byrne, Valérie Demouy, Annie Eardley, Beth Erling, Dewi Evans, Jo Fayram, Concha Furnborough, Matilde Gallardo, Lore Gallastegi, Regine Hampel, Christina Healey, Sarah Heiser, Janet Ireland, Nerys Jones, Rachel Leslie, Katie Murray, Maria Luisa Perez Cavana, Helen Peters, Christine Pleines, Stephen Phillips, Paula Rice, Eva Staiger, Uschi Stickler, Hilary Thomas, Mike Truman, Anne Verriès-Wade and Sylvia Warnecke.

Glossary

Activity: the task at the stage when it is undertaken by learners and is subject to variation, depending on what learners do with it, their attitudes and motivations, based on the distinction by Coughlan and Duff (1994) (see also 'Task').

Affordances: the qualities of an online (synchronous or asynchronous), face-to-face or telephone environment that enable particular activities to take place.

Agency: the capacity to act and make choices about action. Learner agency refers to the learner's capacity to take charge of her/his own actions and ultimately responsibility for her/his own learning.

Assessment-framed activities: activities with learning outcomes arising from the assessment structure of the course.

Assessment strategy: a strategy that lays down the number of assessment points, the task types and the standards used in the assessment of a course.

Asynchronous teaching: teaching where teacher and learners do not have to be present at the same time (e.g. in online forums).

Audiographic synchronous conferencing: a multi-user and multi-functional web-based communication tool with audio and visual channels, where all users are online at the same time.

Authentic assessment: a term sometimes used to describe tasks that mirror real-world usage.

Autonomy: the capacity for critical reflection, informed decision-making and independent action.

Beginning-middle-end teaching plan model: a plan where there is movement from beginning to end in terms, usually, of increasing difficulty of content, language and task type, sometimes moving ultimately to a culmination of everything covered in the teaching session.

Blog: an online diary or 'weblog'. Individual entries appear chronologically. Blogs are strictly author-led (see 'Blogger') yet they accommodate interaction through reader comments. They support multi-media elements such as video, audio or images and often focus on specific topic areas of interest to the author.

Blogger: a person who creates and regularly updates her/his own blog or a member of a group involved in writing a blog.

Carousel model of teaching plan: a plan where tasks are to be carried out in rotation by learners in pairs, groups or as individuals, each starting at a different point (see also 'Workstation model').

Circulatory tasks: tasks where learners are required to move round the room, usually to engage in interactive speaking practice.

Collaboration: where two or more people work together to reach a common goal and produce a joint outcome for which all share responsibility, such as a presentation or a text on a specific topic.

Collaborative assessment: where learners work together on an assessment task with a joint outcome, for which a common mark may be awarded to all participants.

Continuous assessment: one or more formal or informal assessment tasks carried out throughout a course rather than at the end, the outcomes of which are added together.

Continuing professional development (CPD): formally presented or individually accessed training to enhance professional skills and competence throughout a person's career.

Co-operation: where two or more people work together or support each other in their learning, even though they may be working towards achieving different independent outcomes.

Co-operative assessment: assessment in which learners carry out a task together, but individual performances are assessed separately.

Communication apprehension: where learners may be anxious about uttering or communicating with others.

Course: a programme, module or unit of study sustained over a period of time.

Criterion-referenced system: an assessment system that measures a candidate's performances against the requirements of the task.

Critical moment: after Pennycook (2004), an incident that can have a major, often detrimental effect in terms of learner comfort and progress.

Diagnostic assessment: see 'Formative or diagnostic assessment'.

Extrinsic motivation: motivation to do something (such as to learn a language or attend a class) stemming from outside forces, such as the need to gain an externally recognised qualification.

Formative or diagnostic assessment: used to diagnose what has been successfully learned by candidates and what needs further revision.

Hook: according to Bentley (1965, p. 229) 'a disturbance of normality [such as] awful mistakes, unfortunate coincidences, extremes of behaviour, embarrassments, secret thoughts and passions' which entice learners to speak/react. In language learning a task, or statement in a task, to encourage participation and engage learners.

Individual skills assessment: assessment that tests only one skill (e.g. reading, listening, speaking or writing) at a time.

Instrumental motivation: motivation to do something for practical purposes or personal gain (e.g. learning a language in order to get a better job).

Integrated skills assessment: assessment that uses one task to test two or more skills through one outcome.

Integrative motivation: in the context of language learning, motivation to learn arising from a desire to integrate with a community of speakers of the language.

Intrinsic motivation: motivation from within (e.g. the desire to learn a language arising from love of the culture it reflects).

Jigsaw task: task in which individuals or groups exchange or pool different pieces of information in order to complete it.

L1: the common language of the learners (mother tongue, first language or lingua franca).

L2: the language being learned, or the target language.

L3: the third language, which is neither L1 nor L2.

Language shock: where learners experience language input in L2 as a barrage of words which they cannot process (Holliday *et al.*, 2004).

Language anxiety: communication apprehension arising from a learner's fear of expressing herself/himself (Horwitz and Young, 1991).

Learners: those engaged in studying/learning the language.

Learner-generated content: material produced by learners which is used by them or by other learners in learning programmes. For example, learners relate language learning experiences from their childhood in L2 for other members of the group to read and comment on. These stories form the basis of a discussion in the group about the influence of particular significant events on views of language learning.

Marketplace tasks/activities: often linked to circulatory tasks/activities where learners collate information from a certain number of individuals on the same topic.

Mediation: ensuring that online codes of conduct are adhered to by all participants.

Mentor: a peer who supports a teacher, often in the early stages of their work within an institution or team.

Metacognitive: related to mental processes. Metacognitive awareness refers to becoming aware of one's own mental processes when acquiring knowledge.

Mode: the teaching environment in use (e.g. face-to-face, online, telephone).

Moderation: overseeing and guiding interactions in an online environment. Also sometimes used in the context of assessment marking, where a second marker checks the mark or grade given by the teacher.

Moderator: the person organising and overseeing the interaction in online environments. In assessment, the person who second-marks the work.

Netiquette: rules that govern online interaction to ensure respect for all participants.

Norm-referenced system: assessment system that compares candidates to one another, seeking to achieve a 'normal' distribution of marks.

Ongoing assessment: see 'Continuous assessment'.

Open source: the practice of making materials and resources freely accessible to anyone who wants to use them.

Particularity: Kumaravadivelu's concept (2006) which aims to base teaching on the particular needs of the group or context.

PDA: personal digital assistant or palmtop computer.

Peer assessment: assessment in which other learners are involved in evaluating an individual's performance, either through giving feedback or allotting all or part of the mark for a task.

Performance-referenced assessment tasks: tasks which test the learner's use of the language (see also 'System-referenced assessments').

Posting: a single, usually written, contribution to an asynchronous communication tool.

Reliability: the extent to which a test measures consistently what it is supposed to measure.

Rolling model of teaching plan: where tasks are planned to gain momentum in a lateral way, i.e. where level of difficulty *per se* or an increasing gradient is not at stake.

Self-assessment: the learner's own evaluation of her/his achievements, which may be guided by checklists or can-do statements.

Self-determination: in relation to learning this relates to the motivation behind the choices that people make which are without any external influence and interference.

Self-regulation: the capacity to regulate one's own activity (e.g. to pace study and maintain motivation over a period of time).

Self-study materials: work that the learner studies independently via course materials in hard copy, recordings or online.

Simulation: similar to role-play in which learners take on roles or pretend to be someone else.

Snowball tasks: tasks that build in terms of content and usually in terms of group number (e.g. learners gather ideas in a pair, exchange and collate these with learners in another pair, then exchange these in groups of fours and so on).

SNS: social networking site, such as Facebook.

Summative assessment: assessment that tests achievement at the end of a unit of study, and is usually concerned with assigning the candidate a grade.

Synchronous teaching: teaching where teacher and learners meet together at the same time whether face-to-face, by telephone or online.

System parameter: performance indicator used to measure a learner's competence (knowledge and skill) in a subject of study (Ramaprasad, 1983). Performance indicators are usually set out in the assessment marking criteria.

System-referenced assessment: tests the learner's knowledge of the linguistic system (e.g. grammar rules, vocabulary).

Task: an exercise designed by the teacher and presented to the learners before they are engaged upon it (Coughlan and Duff, 1994) (see also 'Activity').

Teachers: those who lead, mediate or support the learning.

Teaching mode: refers to the delivery mode of the teaching (e.g. by telephone, face-to-face, online synchronous, online asynchronous).

Teaching session: a session led or mediated by the teacher in a synchronous or asynchronous mode.

Telephone bridging: a teleconferencing mechanism that allows the group to be divided to enable pair or sub-group conversations.

Thread: a strand in an online discussion linked by a common topic or idea.

Tools: in the online context, the individual functionalities within software applications or stand-alone applications such as blogs.

Total Physical Response (TPR): a language teaching/learning method 'relying on physical or kinaesthetic movement accompanied by language practice' (Brown, 2006; Asher, 1988).

ULPAN: an intensive method of teaching Hebrew. A less intensive form has been adopted for teaching Welsh (WLPAN) and Gaelic (ÚLPAN) to adults.

Validity: concerns how well a particular test measures what it is supposed to measure, i.e. whether it is the right task for the job.

Virtual Learning Environment (VLE): an online environment which encompasses a range of tools and resources designed to support teaching and learning.

Washback: The notion that testing influences teaching (Alderson and Wall, 1993).

Workstation model: where learners move from one task to another in rotation and usually in groups, pairs or individually, each with a different starting point (see also 'Carousel model').

Zone of Proximal Development (ZPD): term used by Vygotsky (1986) to describe the situation where the learner can achieve progress by working with other learners or with a teacher who give appropriate 'scaffolded' help.

Abbreviations

AACE	Association for the Advancement of Computing in Education
AFLS	Association for French Language Studies
AILA	Association Internationale de Linguistique Appliquée or International Association of Applied Linguistics
ALL	Association for Language Learning; and Autonomous Language Learning
ASCILITE	Australasian Society for Computers in Learning in Tertiary Education
BAAL	British Association for Applied Linguistics
CALICO	Computer Assisted Language Instruction Consortium
CALL	Computer Assisted Language Learning
CETL	Centre for Excellence in Teaching and Learning
CIDREE/DVO	Consortium of Institutions for Development and Research in. Education in Europe/Department for Educational Development, Flemish Community of Belgium — Curriculum Division
CILT	The National Centre for Languages
CILT Cymru	The National Centre for Languages in Wales
CLT	communicative language teaching
CMC	computer-mediated communication
COLMSCT	Centre for Open Learning of Mathematics, Science, Computing and Technology
EADTU	European Association of Distance Teaching Universities
ESCR	Economic and Social Research Council
EURODL	European Journal of Open, Distance and E-Learning
HEA	Higher Education Academy
IATEFL	International Association of Teachers of English as a Foreign Language
ICT	information and communication technology
JALT	Japan Association for Language Teaching
LASIG	Learner Autonomy Special Interest Group
LATHE	Learning and Teaching in Higher Education
LEAVERAGE	LEArn from Video Extensive Real ATM Gigabit Experiment
LLAS	Languages, Linguistics and Area Studies
L-MO	Language-Mobile

LP	Language Pedagogy
OU	The Open University
PGCE	Postgraduate Certificate of Education
PLUM	Programme of Learner Use of Media
PPT	PowerPoint
RTÉ	Raidió Teilifís Éireann
SALT	Scottish Association for Language Teaching
SCILT	The Scottish Centre for Information on Language Teaching
SLA	Second Language Acquisition
SLE	Sharp Laboratories of Europe
SMO	Sabhal Mór Ostaig
SNP	Scottish National Party
SNS	Social networking sites
TESL	Teachers of English as a Second Language
TESOL	Teachers of English to Speakers of Other Languages
TOOL	Tool for Online and Offline Language Learning
TPR	Total Physical response
UOC	Universitat Oberta de Catalunya
VLE	Virtual Learning Environment
WAP	Wireless Application Protocol
ZPD	Zone of Proximal Development

Preface

Those engaged in language teaching and in the development of language teachers are usually rich in ideas concerning best practice and best learner support. Such ideas have often been honed in a mixture of scenarios: in the teaching situation with groups of learners; in formal and informal discussion with teaching peers, teacher developers and learners; and through engagement with research and scholarship. The reality can often be though that, because of busy working lives, these ideas do not extend beyond the context in which they have been developed. They may in fact remain with an individual teacher or within the confines of a teaching team, a department or an institution. Informal sharing with colleagues elsewhere may occasionally allow their transmission to a wider audience, particularly if teachers and teacher developers have part-time working portfolios and bring ideas developed from one context into another. However, formal sharing may not be engaged in often enough. This book is itself an illustration of all of this in that the idea for it was a good intention long before it became a print reality.

In fifteen years of pioneering development of practice in blended language teaching at The Open University (OU) with an ever-evolving combination of delivery modes, a large bank of creative ideas and good principles had been developed. These had influenced us as OU language teachers and teacher developers in our practice, our support of learners and our development of teaching teams and individuals, as we strived to come to terms with newer and often more complex ways of teaching and supporting learners. Some of these ideas may have been shared informally along the way with colleagues in other institutions or teaching domains, but have not always formally reached the broader audience who might welcome them. It also became clear that, although there is an increase in the number of publications on specific aspects of blended learning, such as online tools or online pedagogy, an all-round book on language teaching in the blended context, which also looked at issues such as the blend of resources or learner diversity, was harder to come by. It seemed the right time to bring together a coherent package so that others might benefit. The willingness of authors to contribute their ideas underlined this, as did the fact that Dunedin Academic Press immediately threw their support behind the project.

Three caveats are perhaps sensible from any editor of such a volume. First, books on practice in teaching can quickly go out of date, depending on the rate of change, which is perhaps faster than we have known it in past decades, not least because of the development in technology. It is hoped, nonetheless, that the core of ideas contained in this book will stand the test of time, for in many ways they represent good tenets of language teaching in any blended context, perhaps, indeed, in any future teaching context. Second, books on practice cannot be all things to all people. It could be argued that each topic in this book deserves a volume in its own right. However, the book has been designed with many readers in mind: those who want to read the chronological whole, covering the gamut of ideas which may be relevant to blended contexts in language teaching; and those who simply want to dip in because they are interested in a particular aspect of it such as learner autonomy or asynchronous online tools. It aims not only to discuss practice for those who seek this alone but also to situate the discussion with reference to research and scholarship work which has usefully informed the field. Third, the specific context in which readers may work cannot possibly be covered in every aspect of this book and readers will have to be prepared to select and amend ideas to suit their own needs. However, all parts of the book try to take account of the differing blends and varying options of delivery that exist in language teaching.

Against that background, then, the book aims to offer an insight into the key discussion areas in blended language teaching. It looks both at the human and the technological, the methodological and the philosophical, the teacher perspective and the teacher developer perspective. It endeavours to keep the learner at the centre, to ensure that the partnership between teacher and learner is a key focus, and to advocate that creativity within teaching and learning and within the development of ideas is paramount.

The editorial team hopes that you will enjoy reading the contributions and that you will find in the book ideas to provoke further thought and new practice in this constantly evolving field.

Margaret Nicolson on behalf of the editorial team

Section 1:
The Learning Context

Chapter 1: **Language Teaching in a Changing World:
Introduction and Overview**

*Margaret Nicolson, Linda Murphy
and Margaret Southgate*

Learning in a changing world

Change is a hallmark of our time. Social, economic and technological development has resulted in rapid change in many areas of life in the United Kingdom as in other parts of the world, and the domain of education has not been exempt. Fundamental differences in employment patterns and social structures (for example, new family groupings and changes in male and female roles, as researchers such as Field and Malcolm (2006) point out) have led to changes in the forms of learning people undertake. Major industrial restructuring in the 1980s and 1990s, combined with fast-moving technological development and global competition, brought a consensus regarding the need for lifelong learning in industrialised nations (Field, 2003) since initial education was deemed no longer sufficient to equip individuals for the changing knowledge and skill requirements they will face during their lifetime. This had already been recognised in the widely quoted preface to a UK Government White Paper in 1999 (DfEE, 1999). Although political interest in lifelong learning has generally been linked to economic change and the need to ensure an appropriately skilled workforce, Field (2006) suggests that social and cultural changes in society at large are also significant in inspiring people to acquire new skills and knowledge. These include increased life expectancy, the longer-term reduction for men and the increase for women in the amount of time spent in paid employment, and the opportunities for informal learning and community action offered by the worldwide web.

Changes in learning patterns give rise to new issues about the financing of lifelong learning. Questions such as who should pay, what the state can afford to support and what the priorities should be are regularly debated. Political changes have favoured accountability by providers and increased choice for learners, all of which places greater onus on individuals to take responsibility for planning and organising their lives within the context of what some have termed a 'risk society' (Beck, 1986 in Jansen and van der Veen, 1996). A major outcome of these changes is the demand for *flexible* learning opportunities. In the UK context in particular, there are several reasons for this. First, reductions in individual financial support from the state, with the focus on loans rather than grants for those participating in higher education at undergraduate and post-graduate level, result in some people making choices based on financial criteria. Seeking out flexible patterns of delivery in university education, for example, may be one of those choices, so that people can fund their learning incrementally, while holding down a full- or part-time job. An unprecedented 34% increase in eighteen to twenty-four year olds undertaking a distance learning degree with the OU, reported by BBC News in August 2010, seems to underline this. Part-time learning may of course mean that individuals take longer to complete degree studies but this is outweighed by the financial safety net they create for themselves. Second, institutions are seeking more flexible forms of delivery to reduce costs at a time when resources are shrinking and likely to continue to be constrained. Third, lack of security in employment, together with changes in the global economy and greater mobility, have led to the need for individuals to take up study opportunities flexibly at various stages of their lives in order to re-skill or up-skill so that they can move between jobs or roles or take advantage of completely new career opportunities. Finally, social and lifestyle changes and expectations of choice are accompanied by a demand for more flexible learning opportunities to suit individual needs and circumstances, so that learning can be fitted in, for example, while undertaking caring responsibilities or while travelling. As a result, learning has become part of the 'consumer culture' (Field, 1996), where individuals want to access programmes of study and learning opportunities in a way that fits their lifestyle, at a time of life that requires it or makes it possible, and without having to travel at set times to a certain place for the purpose.

The policy focus on a lifelong learning agenda has bolstered the need for flexibility in learning for all ages of the adult population, whether or not they are in the labour market, and has allowed for a welcome revision of the more traditional view which tended to associate education with youth. The focus has broadened to include the retired, those needing to change career later in life, and those with specific needs linked to disability or illness. Technological innovation has both driven the demand for and enabled the provision of flexible learning opportunities. It has been crucial in supporting the development of new modes of teaching and learning by virtual means, allowing learning opportunities to be independent of time and place. Coupled with existing self-study and distance learning options, this has greatly enhanced the scope and reach of the part-time education sector in particular.

Blended learning and teaching

Blended learning and teaching is an approach that is felt by many to provide the kind of flexibility required if learning opportunities are to match the demands created by the economic and social changes outlined above. Blended learning (and, by extension, blended teaching) may be defined in a variety of ways. Driscoll (2002) in Oliver and Trigwell (2005, p. 18) identifies four different meanings denoted by this term:

- combining or mixing web-based technology to accomplish an educational goal;
- combining pedagogical approaches (e.g. constructivism, behaviourism, cognitivism) to produce an optimal learning outcome with or without instructional technology;
- combining any form of instructional technology with face-to-face instructor-led training;
- combining instructional technology with actual job tasks.

Oliver and Trigwell (2005) note further definitions and indeed suggest that the variety of definitions and lack of agreement on the nature of blended learning and teaching make the term itself less than helpful. It has nevertheless been widely adopted and is most frequently used to refer to an integrated combination of traditional learning, for example face-to-face or telephone, with web-based, online approaches (ibid., p. 17). Driscoll's third definition above, which refers to the combination of any form of instructional technology with instructor-led training, is also widespread and in fact an approach that has been in existence for many years. Garrison and Vaughan (2008, p. 5) see blended learning as 'the thoughtful fusion of face-to-face oral communication and online learning experiences' and as 'a fundamental redesign that transforms the structure of, and approach to, teaching and learning'. Blended learning, which in their view stems from an understanding of the strengths of face-to-face and online learning so that they can be deployed in an integrated combination, enabling the goals of a programme to be met, is in their words 'multiplicative not additive' (ibid., p. 7).

In *Language Teaching in Blended Contexts*, the terms 'blended teaching' and 'blended learning' refer to a combination of forms of instructional technology, including traditional forms of learning used in conjunction with web-based, online approaches. Technological developments have greatly increased the number and complexity of options that can be integrated in this combination. The exact combination and relative amount of use of each form of technology may also vary widely (Garrison and Vaughan, 2008). Blends may cover a wide spectrum ranging from those at the simpler end combining a couple of delivery options, print materials and telephone conferencing, for example, to more complex combinations, which employ synchronous voice conferencing, asynchronous online forums, self-study print and online written, audio or audiovisual materials along with telephone conferencing and face-to-face sessions. It is therefore possible to argue that the very variety of options is in itself a measure of the flexibility inherent in blended teaching and blended learning.

As noted above, many examples of blended teaching and learning have in fact been operating for some time. In the UK, for example, since the 1970s, the OU has traditionally combined print and audiovisual material with face-to-face or telephone meetings. The National Extension College, founded in 1963, combined print material with telephone teaching. The adult education departments of campus universities, variously termed open learning, continuing education, lifelong learning or extra-mural departments, have offered on-site once-a-week teaching combined with some home study through print or online materials and optional credit-bearing assessments for many years. Further Education colleges and Adult Education institutions have also run programmes that rely on open learning where individuals choose resources to use from a resource base, and have access to a teacher for consultation or support every so often.

In recent years many institutions have taken advantage of technological developments to offer new teaching and learning delivery methods and to improve communication with and between learners and teachers. For example, some have introduced a Virtual Learning Environment (VLE) which provides channels of communication such as forums and noticeboards and a platform for online teaching. Others have begun to use text alerts sent to mobile phones to remind learners about assessment deadlines or to provide 'bite-size' learning. Many are keen to exploit the flexibility of mobile phones and similar handheld electronic devices in the delivery of teaching as well, and as a result there has been a growth in the number of private web-based companies who provide the facilities to support this development.

Blends in language learning and teaching

In language learning, blends have to a large extent developed to meet a variety of needs and to support the learning of languages in a manner that allows flexibility and yet offers support that goes beyond teach-yourself materials or self-study only options. The reasons for demand for flexible language study at different times of life may be varied. Employers may require their employees to acquire knowledge of a particular language so they can develop more fruitful business contacts with colleagues and customers. This can range from operating in the language at a basic courtesy level, such as using and responding to greetings and polite phrases, for example, to acquiring a fluency level that allows professional discussions to take place in the language. The need to learn a language can also arise because an individual wants to live in or visit another country, perhaps because they have family members who live there. The ability to operate in the language enables people to be better integrated when they are resident or visiting. Language knowledge required for a hobby or interest, such as film or literature, may motivate others, while some may quite simply love language learning *per se* and seek opportunities for adding new languages or improving their existing language skills at different points in their lives.

Blended programmes for language learning have also been in existence for some time. The precise composition of the blend can vary, and different components may be selected as the focus for new teaching input or as the opportunity for learners to practise what they have learned. For example, in some cases, conventional classroom teaching of new material is complemented by opportunities for practice through online activity. In others, particularly in distance and open settings, new material may be presented in self-study resources, while language practice and reinforcement are offered via teacher-facilitated sessions either online or in a face-to-face classroom.

Examples of blended provision include the OU's language programme, in operation in the UK and parts of Europe since 1995 and, at the time of writing, offering courses in French, German, Spanish, Italian, English, Welsh and Chinese. In this case, a blend based on print and audiovisual material with classroom tutorials has gradually moved to a fairly complex multi-modal blend, supporting teaching and learning in all language skills. Print and audio self-study materials continue to form the mainstay of the provision, supported by synchronous online, face-to-face and telephone tutorials, asynchronous forums, individual written or spoken feedback on assessments and academic support from a personal tutor. Telford College in Edinburgh used a blended programme to support the teaching of Scots Gaelic in the 1980s and 1990s to those who were distant from campus. Weekly one-to-one teaching by telephone supported the home study being carried out via print and recorded materials, with teacher–learner dialogue also occurring in cassette recordings. Sabhal Mòr Ostaig, the Gaelic college on Skye, developed a blended distance Gaelic language course in the late 1990s, incorporating print and audio with telephone conferencing and occasional face-to-face teaching sessions in geographical centres appropriate to learner clusters. European Union Socrates-funded projects have more recently developed blended learning programmes for lesser-taught languages, such as the Autonomous Language Learning (ALL) project (www.allproject. info) for learners of Turkish, Romanian, Bulgarian and Lithuanian and the Tool for Online and Offline Language Learning (TOOL) project (www.toolproject.eu) for learners who want to continue their study of Dutch, Estonian, Hungarian, Maltese and Slovene. Both of these programmes employ a mix of face-to-face and online teaching and see blended learning as combining 'the inspiration and motivation of traditional classroom teaching and the fun and flexibility of eLearning to create courses that are accessible and motivating for today's adult students' (www.allproject.info accessed 9 October 2010).

Athabasca University in Canada has developed mobile library facilities and learning programmes, including courses for learners of English (http://eslau.ca/mlearning.php) using mobile devices such as cell phones, personal digital assistants (PDAs), smart phones and portable digital media players, which are becoming more widely used and more technologically advanced. As the university website states, these tools are viewed as ideal for learners with little time, who can thus easily connect to their courses and access increasingly sophisticated subject content material from anywhere and at anytime. In the UK, the University of Nottingham has collaborated with Sharp Laboratories of Europe Ltd (SLE) in the Language-Mobile (L-MO) project (http://research.nottingham.ac.uk/newsreviews/newsDisplay.aspx?id=303), the aim being to make language learning fun and effective, by applying current practice in mobile games development to the teaching of vocabulary and grammar on handheld devices. These and other forms of blended language learning have been enhanced by the use of Web 2.0 developments in social software and participatory platforms supporting user-generated content as described by Rüschoff (2009).

Issues for language teachers working in blended programmes

Researchers suggest that language learning and teaching differ from other disciplines in a number of ways. Borg (2006) argues that one reason for this is that the subject matter, i.e. the language, is frequently also the vehicle for instruction. Horwitz *et al.* (1986) suggest that learning languages is not like learning other subjects and that there are more affective concerns, particularly 'language anxiety' and 'communication apprehension'. It is also the case that, because of their very flexibility, blended programmes will result in language teachers working with a wide variety of adult learners with differing needs and expectations. Changes in how and when people study during their lifetime and greater mobility within and between countries mean that there is likely to be a greater diversity in most teaching and learning groups. This is also likely to lead to differing expectations about the role of the learner and teacher and a wide range of reasons for learning a particular language, as mentioned earlier, within a more complex generational, cultural, ethnic and/or behavioural mix in learner groups than previously. Teachers themselves may come from more diverse cultural and linguistic backgrounds, which creates further complexity. A greater focus on choice and an increase in institutional accountability, often enshrined in laws and charters, have also led to increased emphasis on the rights and responsibilities of learners and institutions respectively, which may further impinge on the teacher's role when planning and leading teaching sessions in blended contexts.

All of this leads to the conclusion that teaching languages in a blended context with a diverse group of adults with different expectations and aspirations can be a challenging experience. In addition, teaching practitioners will come to blended provision from a variety of *teaching* backgrounds and therefore with varying levels of expertise in the different blend components or teaching modes. They may be moving to the blended context from a traditional face-to-face setting, from a traditional distance or purely online setting, or from a less complex blend. They may be required to develop materials themselves from scratch, work with materials provided by the institution or adapt an existing scheme of work to a new delivery mode.

Those responsible for the professional development of language teachers will have to work with them in a mutually creative way to establish the best approaches to dealing with the diversity of teaching modes, the pedagogy surrounding this and the support needs of a mixed group of learners in the various component parts of the blend. Views previously held about what and how to teach may have to be challenged and modified. What Kumaravadivelu (2006) terms 'particularity' will have to play a greater part in the teacher's professional response. This means responding flexibly and directly to the demands and issues that arise in the immediate context. As a result, planning itself has to be viewed more flexibly and creatively to allow this freedom. The planning and realisation of teaching in the blended context will have to take account of the physical setting, the teaching mode, the particular group of learners and the individuals within that group, all of which will impact on aims and objectives, use of resources, classroom management, task choice and implementation. Also, teachers may find that in the blended context they are not the primary source of input, as in more traditional forms of delivery, but rather are facilitators or mediators of learning carried out independently by learners. In addition, they may discover that their trusted teaching methods do not always translate easily between delivery modes or between different groups and that new approaches may have to be investigated individually, with their professional peers, mentors and managers, in teacher development sessions and indeed with their learners. Discussion with learners may assume greater importance for those who work in contexts where peer discussion and teacher development opportunities are lacking because there are no other language teachers in the institution, or because they have no institutional affiliation.

Both teachers and teacher developers may also conclude that flexibility and sensitivity play as large a part in the all-round and successful development of adult learners in this context as does language work. Teachers may have to confront the fact that their technological knowledge is not adequate for the delivery mode they are required to use and that this can affect their pedagogic standards while they get to grips with tools. Teacher developers will have to ensure that technical training and pedagogic development go hand-in-hand to support fully integrated teaching in new modes. Teachers may in turn have to support learners in exploiting technology more fully for learning, either because learners are less familiar with the technology in question or because technological changes move so fast that it is difficult to keep pace. In addition, learning is managed in different ways in different institutions and the role and expectations of the individual language teacher will vary according to both the institutional context and the particular blend of instructional technology involved. Teachers are likely to be the 'face' of their institution, the first port of call for any concerns or questions, the prime motivator in learning progress, the developer of independent and autonomous learners, the assessor of formally submitted work, and the source of support who understands and manages the issues when a learner is behind or thinking of giving up. Teachers may have to be familiar with a wide range of resources and delivery modes: synchronous voice conferencing, asynchronous forum activity, self-study materials, a range of online, telephone and traditional assessment formats, and face-to-face teaching. All in all, they may find themselves in a position where they feel they have to be all things to all people, an impossible challenge for any human being. Yet contained within these challenges, successfully supported in teacher development and met with professionalism, is the basis for a highly rewarding teaching experience which leads to progress for learners and a new set of portable skills and expertise for the teacher. This situation reflects Kumaravadivelu's (2006) 'post-method condition', which transcends all methodologies and in which no specific method of teaching is advocated, relying on flexible and creative responses from teachers to their immediate teaching context.

Purpose and content of this book

Language Teaching in Blended Contexts emerges therefore from a clear understanding of the new demands placed on language teachers as a result of the growing need for flexible language learning opportunities driven by economic, social and technological changes and by the impact of the widespread adoption of blended teaching and learning in this subject area. It is written by those who have pioneered within this field, aiming to offer insight, practical examples and advice to teachers. It may also be useful in suggesting areas for discussion and development to those responsible for the professional development of language teaching teams and individual teachers, consolidating good practice, pushing boundaries and offering areas for professional reflection which will be useful within any blend.

Research and scholarship references underpin much of the discussion of practice throughout this book in an attempt to close what has too often been an unnecessary gap between teachers and researchers, as noted by Ellis in his examination of the Second Language Acquisition (SLA)-Language Pedagogy (LP) nexus (Ellis, 2010, p. 182). Action research carried out by practising teachers has helped to close this gap. Edge's concept of 'the thinking teacher [who] is no longer perceived as someone who applies theories but someone who theorises practice' (Edge, 2001, p. 6) is a useful one in terms of bringing teaching and research together. The fact that many researchers in the field are or have been practising teachers or teacher developers is also helpful in bridging this divide. All the authors in *Language Teaching in Blended Contexts* occupy two or more of the roles identified by Ellis (2010, p. 190) as teachers, teacher educators (this book will use the term 'teacher developers'), classroom researchers and/or SLA researchers, which gives them a multiplicity of perspectives and the knowledge of how to make purposeful links between relevant research and practice. The book of course can be easily read without further reference to research works. However, the presence of research references will enable practitioners, should they wish, to refer to sources that may illuminate their practice or satisfy their desire to understand why changes in methodological practice have arisen.

Language Teaching in Blended Contexts is designed to be either read as a whole or consulted on a particular topic as required, as and when the need arises. It is organised into five sections focusing on key issues for language teaching in blended contexts.

Section 1: The learning context

This section begins by exploring the teachers' role in relation to the range of teaching modes, tools and resources that may make up the blend in any particular context, before considering the variety of ways in which these may be combined, illustrated by practical examples. This leads into questions of choice and control over different elements of the 'blend'. The diversity of learners is the second aspect of the learning context covered in this section, including an exploration of the nature of that diversity, and the practical implications for teachers in a blended learning context. Consideration is given to the issues of interpreting diversity, meeting the needs of learners, and the role of teacher provenance in understanding approaches to diversity. The implications for teacher practice in relation to task choice and activity management are then addressed, along with consideration of the use of personal information, physical movement in tasks and the use of target language as the lingua franca of the learning and teaching process. The section refers to theoretical perspectives on a range of concepts associated with the influence of individual experience and situation on all aspects of language learning. The final part of Section 1 examines the concepts of autonomy and motivation in blended teaching environments. It provides an overview of current theory, followed by consideration of how blended learning can support and sustain motivation and foster learner autonomy. It then addresses implications for language teachers and provides some practical examples of learner responses.

Section 2: Assessment

Section 2 deals with both summative and formative aspects of assessment. It explores the role of assessment and its nature in the context of blended teaching and learning, where it often fulfils the dual role of both assessment and teaching tool. The section considers what needs to be assessed and which tools might be appropriate, illustrating how assessments can best be designed to work in situations where teachers and learners may rarely if ever meet face-to-face. Issues of learner preparation, teacher development and quality assurance are also discussed. Where direct contact between teacher and learner is limited or absent, the provision of feedback on assessment becomes a key means by which the teacher can establish a dialogue with the learner, giving written or audio-recorded feedback not only for error remediation but also to facilitate the development of study and learning skills, to help learners extend the scope of their language learning and make progress. Practical guidance is provided on various levels and methods of both written and spoken feedback. Issues arising from the management of learner expectations and quality assurance of assessment feedback are also considered.

Section 3: Synchronous and asynchronous teaching in blended contexts

This section is concerned with the practicalities of teaching using the different synchronous and asynchronous instructional technologies that may form part of a blended teaching context. Section 3 begins with an overview of the issues involved in planning, implementing and evaluating teaching in such contexts. It then looks at these issues in more detail in relation to teaching in specific modes: teaching via the telephone, synchronous online teaching, face-to-face teaching and asynchronous online teaching. In each case the advantages and challenges are examined, together with issues related to choice and sequence of appropriate tasks and activities, teacher roles and learner diversity. The specificity of each environment and its impact on planning and teaching are discussed.

Section 4: Community and indigenous Celtic languages

The issues covered in the sections already outlined are pertinent to the teaching of all languages. However, for community and indigenous languages there are additional issues specific to their teaching and learning which may differ significantly from those that a teacher of other languages has to face. The two chapters in this section provide an overview of community and indigenous Celtic language learning in the UK and Ireland, leading to a discussion of how the teacher may meet the needs of what may be an extremely diverse group of learners in terms of prior language experience, cultural background and specific motivation for language learning. Practical guidance on differentiation, the promotion of learner autonomy and the use of tools and resources to support independent learning of community and indigenous languages is given. These chapters also address issues arising from the fact that community and indigenous language learners may sometimes be taught or supported by native speakers who are not specialist language teachers or whose teaching experience and methodology are drawn from a culture very different from that appropriate to the blended teaching situation in which they find themselves.

Section 5: Teacher development and final reflections

The final section examines the key factors influencing change in the teacher role, including developments in pedagogy, technology and learner demographics. Consideration is given to support for the changing role of the teacher as complex blends and new teaching modes are introduced. It focuses on the implications for teacher development, and provides suggested approaches, both for individuals and for groups. It identifies practical ideas that can be used successfully with part-time and widely dispersed teams using a variety of tools and resources. The book concludes by drawing together some key principles that will enable practitioners to adapt successfully to possible future developments in blended teaching and learning.

Chapter 2: **The Nature of the 'Blend': Interaction of Teaching Modes, Tools and Resources**

Linda Murphy and Margaret Southgate

Introduction

A wide range of teaching modes, tools and resources are available to the teacher and learner of languages in blended contexts: text-based, audio and video, synchronous and asynchronous, physical and electronic, internally produced within the institution for a specific course or externally published. This chapter will provide an overview of the role they might have from the viewpoint of the teacher and teacher developer, as well as the extent and nature of teacher involvement in each. Chapters 7 to 12 will look in greater detail at issues associated with teaching through various synchronous and asynchronous modes.

Garrison and Kanuka (2004) point out that in blended learning the various learning experiences need to be integrated rather than simply mixed together or layered one on top of the other. In every blended learning situation the teacher will need to help learners make connections between these learning experiences, and also between resources, to ensure that learning from one area feeds into activities in another. This chapter will therefore explore and give practical examples of the ways in which a variety of resources and tools can be effectively combined and integrated.

The extent to which the teacher is involved in the design of learning materials or the choice and blend of modes, tools and resources will vary substantially between institutions. In every situation however, the teacher will need to make a variety of informed choices and will need to guide learners, making them aware of the full range of learning opportunities at their disposal. This will help learners to take responsibility for their own learning and make choices of their own. Whatever the teacher's level of input into choice and design, s/he will play a key role in making sense of the blend as a whole for the learners. Moreover, if each mode is to be exploited to its full potential, teacher developers will want to identify support needs for teachers, even for those with extensive experience in conventional modes of delivery.

The teacher's role in different modes and tools

The teacher of languages in a blended context will operate in at least two different modes. Synchronous teaching may take place face-to-face, by telephone or online, and within each mode there may be a range of tools available, such as an interactive whiteboard in a face-to-face classroom or video conferencing in an online environment. There may be asynchronous teacher–learner communication using tools such as email, online message boards or forums; asynchronous communication may of course also take place by post. Some of these interactions will be part of the formal teaching programme while others will be *ad hoc* communications.

Synchronous interaction

One of the main points of contact between teacher and learners will be the occasions when they interact synchronously. Key issues will be addressed in Chapter 7. What follows here is a summary, focusing particularly on the role of the teacher in such interaction. Depending on the course design and the choices made by individual learners, the type and extent of synchronous interaction among learners, and between teacher and learners, will vary considerably. It may consist of face-to-face teaching, telephone or online conferencing in a formal setting, or informal contact between the teacher and individual learners. Learners may also have synchronous contact with one another, either one-to-one or in groups. Communication will usually be spoken, but could also occur as text chat or instant messaging.

Face-to-face

In some cases the teacher may be provided with prescribed lesson-plan outlines for face-to-face sessions, but in many institutions the teacher is expected to design her/his own teaching plan to complement what learners have been studying in other parts of the blend. In some blends, face-to-face teaching may deliver core teaching points that learners will later practise independently. In others it may consist mainly of facilitating practice in what learners have studied independently.

Face-to-face interaction is of particular benefit to language learners for a number of reasons. First, classroom communication can take place not only in speech but also through facial expressions and gestures, which can facilitate learner–learner and teacher–learner communication and allow learners to copy the teacher's lip movements when learning to pronounce new sounds. Second, learners can move around to take part in realistic role-plays or survey-type activities during the session so that they interact with all members of the group present. Group interaction of a social nature can also happen with other learners during breaks or before and after the session and the benefits of this should not be underestimated. Third, in face-to-face meetings there is the possibility of running extended activities in half-day or whole-day sessions, which would be impracticable on the telephone or online. Face-to-face teaching will be addressed in further detail in Chapter 11.

Telephone

Although visual cues are absent, the telephone can still provide a vital communication link, not only for one-to-one conversations between the teacher and learner but also as a platform for more formal teaching of individuals or small groups. Telephone sessions are usually shorter in length than face-to-face sessions. They have the advantage of demanding no special technical skills, and are therefore simpler and generally more accessible for most learners than online alternatives. Chapter 8 will explore issues related to synchronous teaching by telephone.

Online

Synchronous interaction online may make use of a range of conferencing software applications such as FlashMeeting or Elluminate, many of which allow both voice and text communication, and the sharing of whiteboards, web pages and computer applications. Institutions offering blended courses may provide some or all of their language teaching in this way. Chapters 9 and 10 provide further details. Although online systems may have been originally designed for business meetings and the delivery of formal group teaching sessions, they provide a useful means of communication for informal one-to-one support sessions provided by a teacher, as well as for independent learner–learner interaction in self-help study groups.

While synchronous contact with the teacher and other learners is an ideal way for learners to develop interactive speaking skills, there may be some situations where learners are unable to participate in this way. An advantage of online synchronous sessions is that they may be recorded so that those unable to participate in real time may review the session later. Applications such as Second Life, Facebook and various Google Apps may provide further opportunities for synchronous online language learning.

Asynchronous online interaction

Asynchronous online interaction (explored in detail in Chapter 12) can take place via an email conference, a message board or a virtual learning environment. It may be a compulsory and/or assessed element in a learning module or it may be an optional enhancement with which learners can choose to engage or not, depending on their individual preferences and language-learning needs. Asynchronous communication can take a number of forms as outlined below.

Formal learning tasks

Development of writing skills may take place through specific online tasks set by the teacher. These might require a written response posted to a shared email conference or forum, on which other learners may comment. Other tasks may require learners to post material in a blog, comment on others' blogs or contribute to a wiki. Sometimes the feedback given by other learners may be sufficient, but at other times the teacher will provide detailed individual comments on learners' contributions or may give a general response to the whole group at the end of the set task.

Teacher-moderated discussions

Most institutions will also provide a general online forum where learners can post messages to the whole group and read and respond to comments and questions from other learners. Whether this is used for specific L2 practice activities, for resolving issues in L1 or both, it is a valuable tool to develop and support a sense of community within a learner group which, for whatever reason, cannot meet regularly face-to-face. The teacher needs to monitor the exchanges regularly, but when such a discussion area is working well, s/he will need to intervene only rarely to resolve problems.

Independent communications

Learners who have few, if any, opportunities to meet other learners studying the same course can be encouraged to exchange email addresses and develop their language and study skills by communicating with one another, both in L1 and L2. This communication will be entirely unmoderated, but may in some cases constitute a preparation phase ahead of some joint activity at a teacher-moderated session.

The teacher's relationship to teaching and learning resources

The teaching and learning modes outlined above, together with their associated tools which make up the blend, will be complemented by various resources. Learners may use text-based material, audio, video and online resources in a range of environments during formal teaching sessions, independently or informally with other learners, either for new learning or to practise language previously learned. The teacher may be expected to select appropriate resources for use in formal teaching sessions, and provide guidance to learners on how to draw on the many resources that can help to develop language skills and widen cultural awareness.

Text-based resources

Language teachers have at their disposal a wide range of text-based resources either in electronic form or as conventional paper documents. In a blended course, learners will make use of a mixture of electronic and conventional documents of various types, which may include the resources outlined below. Text-based resources for assessment will be considered in a later section.

Core course texts

The extent to which the teacher is involved in authoring or selecting text-based resources will vary, depending on the policy of each individual institution. In some cases a core text that learners study independently, whether on paper or electronic, will provide the main teaching input, thus placing the teacher in the role of a facilitator and supporter of learning, rather than a presenter of new content. In other cases the teacher may deliver the main input based on a core text, and may direct learners to additional resources to consolidate and extend their learning. Where the institution provides or specifies text-based materials, the teacher will want to be entirely familiar with their content and structure in order to provide guidance on how learners can most profitably engage with the material. On the basis of that knowledge, s/he will need to ensure that teacher-facilitated activities are integrated with what the learner is expected to study independently.

Published books and articles in the target language (L2)

Advanced language learners will undoubtedly engage in reading, evaluating and discussing published text-based material in L2. Some of these may be set texts specified by the course designers or assessors, but teachers may also wish to recommend additional published resources, either for self-study to extend more competent learners or as a basis for group discussion. Teachers can develop learners' autonomy by encouraging them to select texts independently to complement what is being taught in the core content. Such learner autonomy lies at the heart of the SOLO approach to course design developed by Bishop and Thorpe (2004), which is based on the premise that learners are more likely to succeed in language learning if they are working on material in which they have a personal interest.

Even from the earliest stages of language learning, beginners will benefit from engaging with authentic texts from which they can draw out key information without necessarily understanding every word, in addition to working with edited 'easy reading' material (see Chapter 14 on the use of authentic material in relation to Celtic languages). Such texts might include timetables, menus, tourist brochures or email messages.

Dictionaries and grammars

Self-study materials may include guidance on the use of dictionaries, but teachers will need to be prepared to provide additional support in this area, particularly in the early stages of language learning. In most cases learners may be left to choose their own dictionary, as long as it is a fairly recent edition. Teachers may also wish to refer learners to online dictionaries, some of which have associated discussion forums on usage such as WordReference (www.wordreference.com), although inexperienced language learners will need guidance to help them discriminate between useful and misleading information on such websites.

There is, however, a compelling argument in favour of requiring all learners in a learning group to obtain a copy of the same grammar reference book or to access the same grammar reference web pages. It could be confusing for learners to rely on a reference work that uses different terminology from that used by the teacher (for example, present perfect rather than perfect tense). The availability of a common reference source is particularly helpful for the teacher when preparing feedback on assessments, since s/he can then refer learners to a relevant page or section of the reference material without the need to explain points in detail.

Study skills guidance
Particularly in the early stages of blended language-learning, learners may need guidance on how to engage with self-study materials, or how to make the best use of reference materials. Institutions offering blended distance teaching may produce handbooks or web pages to which learners can turn for detailed help on a range of study-related issues. Teachers need to be aware of what is available so that they can refer learners to the appropriate resources. If the institution provides only limited or no generic support materials of this kind, teachers will need to bridge the gap by offering additional spoken or written guidance where necessary.

Worksheets
Even if a core text is used, teachers may need to supplement this with other text-based materials to respond to individual needs, facilitate additional learning and practice in reading, writing, listening and speaking skills as well as to clarify and provide practice in particular points of grammar. They may draw on published photocopiable collections of language activity sheets, or may produce worksheets of their own. In blended contexts where classroom time is limited, care will need to be taken to ensure that any worksheet tasks to be completed independently are clearly presented and pitched at an appropriate level.

Other stimulus material
Although some group speaking activities can be conducted entirely orally, it is often useful to have supporting paper or electronic text documents. These might take one of the following forms:
- message, setting a task in preparation for a synchronous teaching session;
- email, outlining the procedure for an online learning task;
- language resources for a synchronous task;
- background information for role-play participants;
- skeleton dialogue (at beginner level);
- forms to be completed during a language-learning activity;
- questions for discussion.

Audio and video resources
On a blended course, if learners are acquiring new language patterns and vocabulary independently, and opportunities for teacher modelling of pronunciation and

spoken interaction are limited, it is essential for learners to use audio resources to support the development of their listening and speaking skills. For many years published language textbooks and course materials have included recordings on cassette tapes or audio CDs. More recently produced language courses may include a DVD-ROM, podcasts or web-based materials containing both audio and video resources with integrated self-study tasks.

To complement these resources, teachers may select or record their own additional audio or video material, either for use during a teaching session or for individuals to listen to or view independently. When making their selection, teachers will want to consider not only the relevance of the topic but also the suitability of the recording in terms of language complexity, speed of delivery, accent and register, extraneous noise, or, in the case of songs, how easily the lyrics can be understood against musical delivery and accompaniment. Some ways in which recordings can be exploited and combined with other resources will be considered below.

Language learners have opportunities to seek out audio and video resources independently on the internet, where most radio and TV channels make L2 material freely available, and where recordings in L2 can also be found on YouTube or iTunesU, for example. Teachers may wish to design learning tasks around some of these resources, or simply recommend them to learners for the extension of language skills and as a source of cultural information.

Other resources

Learning tasks may also be supported by stimuli that are neither text-based nor conventional audio or video resources. For example, pictures may be used to support work on descriptive language; physical objects could provide a starting point for the construction of a narrative; or learners might be prompted to use the language of hypothesising based on having to guess what a series of recorded sounds are.

Implications for assessment and feedback

No discussion of the teacher's relationship to different modes, tools and resources would be complete without considering the area of assessment and feedback on progress. Assessment is a key element of language learning, in which the learner is given opportunities to build on the teacher's feedback in order to progress to a higher level of competence. Chapters 5 and 6 will look in some detail at issues associated with designing, conducting and providing teaching through feedback on assessed performance.

Assessment material design

In some institutions the teacher takes sole responsibility for setting assessment tasks for the course s/he is teaching. In others, a central team will take the design process entirely out of the teacher's hands. In the first instance, the teacher will wish to ensure that the assessment is a fair test at an appropriate level, neither too linguistically or technically challenging nor too easy. In the second, the teacher will need to be entirely familiar with the format and demands of the assessment tasks. S/he will then be able to ensure that learners have opportunities to develop the skills and the range of language required to complete the tasks satisfactorily and to demonstrate what they have learned, while avoiding the limitations of 'teaching to the test'.

Conducting the assessment

Teachers may be required to conduct speaking assessments, either of their own learners or of those from other teachers' groups. This may take the form of a live one-to-one conversation in which the assessor is a participant, or observation and assessment of a live presentation, a conversation or discussion between learners, or of a recording submitted by the learner. Teachers may also be involved in assessing learners' written work, whether individual or collaborative, on paper or electronic.

Providing feedback

A key element of assessment, addressed in Chapter 6, is that of providing teaching through feedback to the learner. Particularly in a blended context where individual contact time is extremely limited, the provision of clear, focused feedback is one of the most important tasks facing the teacher.

Self-assessment materials

Self-study books, CD-ROMs, DVD-ROMs and online quizzes can provide a range of opportunities for learners to test themselves and check their progress against model answers provided in those materials. Although in some cases the teacher may be required to design her/his own online quizzes, in others such self-assessment materials are provided by course designers and textbook writers. The main role of the teacher is to be aware of what is available, and to refer learners back to teaching units and the associated self-assessment materials if further practice is needed in any particular area of language learning.

Ways of combining tools/resources

Having considered the different teaching modes and tools, the range of resources available and the roles required of teachers in blended language teaching contexts, the next question is how best to combine them to create an effective 'blend' that delivers the intended outcomes for a specific learning programme. Whitelock (2004) lists findings from a range of universities that had adopted a blend of face-to-face and online asynchronous learning. These indicate greater learner satisfaction, reduced drop-out and improved performance compared to programmes run entirely online. However, she notes that the question remains as to 'how different media can best be used to produce a successful learning framework' (ibid., p. 6). Littlejohn and Pegler (2007) examine the nature of different blends and propose a planning model for integrating use of a variety of synchronous and asynchronous online tools and face-to-face teaching as well as independent self-guided learning. The key elements in their model are tasks/activities, people and resources, whether planning blended teaching at the level of an entire language programme, a course module, a particular teaching session or at the level of a specific objective within a teaching session (see Figure 2.1 below). Stacey and Gerbic (2008) summarise research on success factors for blended learning and highlight two specific pedagogical considerations:

- any combination should be based on an understanding of the strengths and weaknesses of the tools as well as their appropriateness to the learners involved;
- it is important to have strong integration of face-to-face and online environments.

They see Garrison and Vaughan's (2008) four-phase model as the embodiment of such strong integration. This model takes face-to-face sessions as the starting point and proposes a sequence of tasks before, during, after and in preparation for the next face-to-face session. It uses a variety of technology options, drawing on the strengths of both physical and virtual environments. It is suggested that the central role of the face-to-face mode in the model provides the comfort of a traditional learning environment for learners and teachers. However, in many circumstances, such as in distance or distributed learning, or simply because of the learner's personal context, attendance at a face-to-face session may be problematic. Therefore it may be necessary to adapt this model to base it on any synchronous session, whether face-to-face, telephone or online. Gerbic (2006) in Stacey and Gerbic (2008) finds that some learners did not perceive the online parts of the blend as of equal value to the face-to-face sessions. Her research shows that simply talking about the rationale for online work, or encouraging and reminding learners to participate, was not especially effective in enabling them to make connections between online asynchronous discussions and the classroom. She finds that the more effective approach involved the teacher providing feedback on the quality of the online discussion in the face-to-face class and tasks that prepared and skilled learners for their asynchronous online activities. She concludes that the teacher's attention in class to the online activity legitimised it as part of the course and endorsed its importance for learning. This highlights the importance of the teacher's role in integrating the elements of the blend. Once again, references to 'classroom' here could be substituted by teacher-mediated telephone conference or synchronous online session. In the latter case, the option to record the session means that it can be reviewed later if learners want to check or revise any aspect while they are engaged in the asynchronous activity, and it is also available for those who were unable to attend in person at the time.

Combining resources: examples in practice

Taking Garrison and Vaughan's (2008) model, adapted as suggested above, the following broad combinations can be proposed.

Before a synchronous session individual work can include one or more of the following:

- working through specified course materials (printed and/or online);
- reading specified text-based materials from other sources (e.g. printed material or from websites);
- listening to or watching specified audio or video course materials;
- listening to or watching specified audio or video material from other sources (e.g. internet TV or radio, podcasts);
- engaging in specified online course activities;
- researching a topic (learners select relevant resources themselves);
- finding a picture/a text/a video clip/an anecdote/a song etc. to present to the other learners;
- preparing questions to ask the other learners (e.g. on their chosen topics).

Whatever the resources chosen, there will be a clear purpose and indication of how the work will be used during the synchronous session.

During a synchronous session groupwork can include:

- the opportunity to engage in activities that draw overtly on the resources used before the session (i.e. pooling learner knowledge/experience/opinion in pair/group/plenary activity, including so-called 'jigsaw' tasks where individuals or groups have different information to exchange or pool to complete a task);
- the initiation/preparation of activity to be continued after the synchronous session.

After a synchronous session activities may involve:

- asynchronous discussions based on work done during the synchronous session;
- learner–learner interactions via email or telephone;
- online course activities developing work covered in the synchronous session;
- learner-organised synchronous online discussions based on work covered in the synchronous session.

Preparation for the next synchronous session (individual and/or group) may involve:

- individual or group asynchronous or synchronous preparation for presentation (e.g. summary of online discussion; completed task);
- further work of the types suggested under 'before a synchronous session' above.

Using Littlejohn and Pegler's (2007) planning model, which identifies teaching mode, learner and teacher activities, resource content, online tools and methods for feedback and assessment, a practical example from an online blended teaching course in upper intermediate German (level B2) is presented in Figure 2.1. The

Time	Mode	Teacher activity	Learner activity	Resources (content)	Resources (online tools)	Feedback and assessment
Week 1		Post initial invitation	Post introductory message responding to invitation by introducing themselves		Asynchronous forum	Learners reply/respond to each other
End of week 1	online	Facilitate session	Engage in pair/groupwork to decide on German-speaking destination and debate proposals; consider individual objectives for the module	PowerPoint (PPT) with intended outcomes; visuals to stimulate discussion	Synchronous online conference	Learners provide feedback for each other's proposed destinations
Week 2	offline		Learners finalise their personal goals for the module and email to teacher	Module summary and intended outcomes; course material	Individual work according to preference	Teacher responds to email with acknowledgement and/or suggestions about other resources to draw on
End of week 2	online	Facilitate session	Engage in pair/groupwork on reading strategies; interview each other on reading habits; summarise articles from German press; describe aspects of the German press	PPT with intended outcomes; key vocabulary; sections of a newspaper; current newspaper headlines; websites for online newspapers	Online synchronous conferencing	Learners provide feedback for each other on content of newspapers and preferred reading; teacher provides feedback on language points
Week 3	online	Monitor wiki, encourage participation	Visit website for paper chosen in synchronous session; enter information about it on a group wiki; select an article from the paper and write a summary; post this on the wiki; read information about other papers and articles	Newspaper websites	Group wiki	Learners read and add to information
End of week 3	online	Facilitate session	Engage in pair/groupwork to extract important information; focus on clarity in presenting information; preparation for asynchronous groupwork on cultural heritage of Weimar	Examples of articles summarised in wiki; PPT materials about Weimar and the lives of Goethe and Schiller	Online synchronous conference	Learners respond to each other's summaries and provide feedback on clarity, supported by teacher
Week 4	online	Post message introducing task on forum; set up three threads for group discussion	Work in groups to put together a presentation on an agreed aspect of Weimar/the two poets to be given to the rest of the learners at the next synchronous meeting	Materials from synchronous session; course materials; websites	Asynchronous forum	Learners provide feedback on each other's ideas and agree final presentation as well as who will deliver different parts and any PPT or visuals needed

Figure 2.1: Extract from a blended teaching plan from the Open University course L203 'Motive': Upper Intermediate German

module is taught over four weeks and integrates the use of synchronous conferencing with a number of asynchronous tools. Learning outcomes for the module are that participants will be able to:

- talk about their own use of print media and reading preferences;
- use vocabulary to describe newspapers;
- summarise a newspaper article;
- extend their knowledge of newspapers in Germany, Austria and Switzerland in order to make informed decisions on which papers to read in the future.

Choosing an appropriate 'blend'

Teacher and/or institutional choice

For many language teachers working in blended contexts the reality may be that choices are made mainly by the institution or programme organisers. Decisions about the number and nature of any synchronous sessions, whether face-to-face or online, are generally made at institutional or departmental level. However, teachers may be able to choose between a variety of online tools that develop and build on synchronous teaching (as discussed above) such as blogs, wikis, podcasts, quizzes and discussion forums or chat rooms. As such tools can be used at any time, they are more flexible and may be particularly helpful for those who are unable to take part in synchronous sessions for some reason. Littlejohn and Pegler (2007, p. 96) identify four different components of a blend. They term them:

- the 'space' blend (whether learners meet in a physical or virtual space);
- the 'time' blend (whether learners can meet at the same time; this can be affected by geographical location or life context);
- the 'media' blend (the types of tools and resources available to learners);
- the 'activity' blend.

They point out that the activity component is most likely to be determined by the teacher, but can also be facilitated or led by the learners. Changes in any one of these components have implications for the teacher and the learner. From this analysis, it is evident that learner location and availability may determine the tools and resources that are most appropriate or feasible and shape the activities that the teacher may use. For example, a dispersed group of learners living in different parts of the world and different time zones will find it more practical to use online materials and work together using asynchronous tools such as discussion forums, blogs and wikis. In other words, in this example, the 'space' and 'time' blends determine the 'media' blend and therefore to some extent the 'activity' blend. From an institutional perspective, the choice of tools depends on the target audience for the language programme. From the teacher's perspective, the choice of task and tools depends on the same factors as in any teaching context: the outcomes to be achieved, the needs of the learners in the group and their willingness to take control of their learning (see Chapter 4).

Learner choice

A significant issue in discussing the components of blended teaching and learning is the extent to which the choice of tools, resources and activities rests with the learner. Although the broad pattern may be set in the four-phase model proposed by Garrison and Vaughan (2008), and reflected in the planning model suggested by Littlejohn and Pegler (2007), exemplified in Figure 2.1, there is scope within this framework for learners to make choices. Once again, the four components in a blend, identified by Littlejohn and Pegler (ibid.), come into play. For example, when learners work together between synchronous sessions, the 'space' and 'time' components are relevant to their choice of tools or the 'media' component. They may choose to meet again in real time (for example, by telephone conference, synchronous online meeting or at the local learning centre) to discuss how they plan to tackle a task, and agree how each will contribute towards a presentation. Alternatively, if their work or personal commitments do not allow them all to meet at a particular time, they might opt to discuss the arrangements in an online discussion forum, or by email. In some cases, learners may decide not to participate at all. Once they get into an individual preparation phase they might decide to share their work in progress in the same way or gather contributions via a wiki, which each member of the group can edit. Individuals who feel more comfortable in spoken rather than written mode might add their contribution as an audio file.

There are many possibilities and permutations, but learners can exercise this degree of choice and control only if they are aware of the tools and resources available, if they feel competent and comfortable using them and understand how their use can help them achieve their goals or meet their specific learning needs. This means that teachers also need to be familiar with the affordances of the tools and resources available and need to be prepared to introduce, demonstrate and model their use for language learning in a structured and supported way to begin with, in order to facilitate the 'activity' component of the blend. For example, rather than simply asking learners to post a message on a forum about their favourite leisure pursuit and comment on other people's messages, teachers could explain what can be gained from composing and publishing examples to others even if they are not perfect, and show the kind of response comment that could be posted, such as expressing surprise, asking for more information, expressing agreement and so on. Teachers may find that some learners are wary and see this kind of explanation, like other forms of learning skill development (Murphy, 2007), as a diversion from the main business of language learning. They may feel they have to invest too much time in getting to grips with the tools they need to use (such as forums, blogs or wikis). 'I want to learn French, not IT' may be the complaint. However, the available choices include 'low tech' options and it is important to keep learners' attention focused on the language learning outcomes that can be achieved by integrating different tools in this way.

Alongside this is the question of the extent to which learners can opt out of certain parts of a blended programme because of their circumstances, interests, personal goals and priorities or preferences. If learners are seriously encouraged to take responsibility for their learning, to identify their goals and think about how best to achieve them, then it should not be surprising if they opt out of some parts. At the same time, personal circumstances may also determine some of the choices they make, as a result of the 'space' and 'time' components of the blend. For example, they may not be able to take part in synchronous sessions because of the timing or the location. Chapter 4 examines the importance of learner autonomy and provides examples of the choices learners make in practice.

Reference was made earlier to the possible learner perception that certain 'media' or 'activity' components of the blend, such as asynchronous online discussions led by learners, may be subordinate or of marginal value when compared to synchronous teacher-mediated sessions. The suggested solution was close integration of the different elements of the blend. An alternative used in many institutions has been to make certain elements compulsory and part of the assessment strategy in order to demonstrate successful achievement of specific language learning outcomes. Giving learners grades for contributing to an online discussion is seen as a way of encouraging learners to participate. The grade may be linked to the act of contributing or to the quality of the message posted, i.e. whether it represents meaningful interaction and reflection on someone else's contribution. In this way, it is hoped that learners become more used to contributing and see the value of asynchronous online discussion forums for developing their communication skills. This approach has been contentious. It goes against the notion of choice and efforts to encourage learners to take responsibility for their learning. It may be seen as encouraging a mechanistic and strategic approach where the learner gets 'points' for simply contributing, rather than for the quality of their contributions. An example that attempts to counter this criticism can be seen in the assessment criteria developed for the OU course 'English for academic purposes online'. This course uses a blend of online tools and resources, including assessed asynchronous forums for specific course tasks. Assessment criteria indicate the minimum level and nature of contributions expected, as in Figure 2.2.

Asynchronous forums provide a permanent record of contributions, which can be counted and analysed. The grading of contributions is often carried out by the teacher and this has implications for their role. For much of the time they may be present as a contributor in a forum alongside the learners, responding to postings, encouraging, commenting, questioning and modelling participation strategies, but when a forum activity is assessed they then have to withdraw and switch to assessor mode. This may make their supporting role harder and lead learners to be suspicious or to feel that they cannot respond naturally, but have to monitor their performance all the time. Attempting to 'enforce' participation in this way can therefore

This online preparation task carries 15% of the marks for the assignment. Marks are given for your contribution to the forum dedicated to the preparation for the assignment and for the quality of your comments on at least two of your fellow students' contributions to the forum.

Participation in this forum activity is a valuable part of learning and we expect you to take part in it. Your contributions will be monitored by your tutor who is looking to see not only that you have posted your own thoughts but also that you have engaged in discussion with other students about their ideas.

Marks (15%)	Assessment criteria
7%	Make at least one contribution in response to the online task given in the forum dedicated to the preparation of the assignment in each block. The contribution needs to be relevant to the task and be of appropriate length.
8%	Comment on at least two fellow students' contributions in response to the online task dedicated to the preparation of the assignment. The comment needs to make specific reference to the other students' work and should evaluate it.

Figure 2.2: Sample online asynchronous forum marking criteria.

reduce spontaneity and remove the learner's interest and curiosity in other people's postings which is essential for meaningful contributions. Above all, it removes the ability for both learners and teachers to determine an appropriate 'activity' blend according to learning needs and the particular 'space', 'time' and 'media' blends that apply in their context.

Conclusion

This chapter has outlined the range of modes, tools and resources available to language teachers in blended teaching contexts and discussed the roles that teachers may adopt in relation to these possibilities. It has also considered ways to combine these tools and resources and some of the factors that influence the choices made. In the course of this exploration, some key issues have been identified that are likely to affect teachers. First, this chapter has emphasised the importance for teachers of developing learners' awareness of and ability to choose between a variety of tools, using them to meet their own needs and to work with others in order to achieve personal goals and the intended learning outcomes. Second, it has highlighted the need for teachers to understand that learners may value different parts of the blend because their needs, goals or circumstances differ. It is important that teachers are clear therefore about the extent to which learners can opt out, or whether participation is to be compulsory and assessed and if so why. Third, throughout the discussion it is evident that the circumstances, needs and goals of the learners, together with the degree of autonomy and control they are given, are the vital ingredients in determining the blend, both at the level of the individual learner and of the teaching programme. These issues, particularly in relation to learner diversity and autonomy, will be discussed in detail in the following two chapters.

Chapter 3: Learner Diversity

Helga Adams and Margaret Nicolson

Introduction

Focus on diversity forms part of the socio-cultural approach to learning within a situated context (Lave and Wenger, 1991), where an understanding of social practices and patterns of learner participation becomes crucial. This has assumed greater prominence in research and scholarship literature on language teaching and learning in the last decade. Prior to that, cognitive issues relating to the learner's internal language acquisition tended to prevail (O'Malley *et al.*, 1987; Larsen-Freeman, 1991; McGroarty, 2005). However, as in every sphere of contemporary life, the boundaries between domains of human knowledge are beginning to blur, with the socio-cultural and the cognitive melding more in research and practice (Block, 2003; Zuengler and Miller, 2006). In addition, issues around diversity are generally becoming more complex within educational settings, including in the blended context, so require attention for their impact on teacher practice and understanding.

The need to give greater attention to diversity relies on four key developments. First, legal requirements mean that certain areas of difference, for example disability, have to be formally catered for in all public life. Second, globalisation, although seemingly removing difference and offering a more homogeneous society, has in fact created in individuals the need to differentiate themselves more to assert identity. Third, the rapid pace of social and technological change has meant that generational differences in educational expectations and in behavioural patterns and lifestyles are perhaps more marked now. In lifelong learning and therefore language learning, where a complex array of people from different age groups and social, educational and cultural backgrounds come together to learn, these differences will co-exist more frequently within the same group of learners. Cultural differences may be particularly important in community and indigenous language teaching, as will be outlined in Chapters 13 and 14. Finally, in today's developed societies, individuals, having fulfilled fundamental needs, will seek self-actualisation and peak experiences (Maslow, 1970). In the learning setting, this results in individuals being more ready to assert their specific needs and their expectations of how these should be met. They may be more inclined to challenge what they are offered by institutions or professionals. Indeed, the educational philosophy underpinning the development of the independent learner may even reinforce assertion and expectation.

This chapter will consider understandings of the term 'diversity' and discuss aspects linked to recognising aspects of diversity in the language teaching context. It will also provide practical advice to teachers on how to address diversity issues in all aspects of the blend.

Understanding diversity

Diversity is often understood as linked to visible issues such as disability, race, gender and age. This is perhaps because sight is a dominant sense, so visual markers have tended to lead the way in understanding what makes one person different from another. For example, an understanding of someone's ethnicity is often predicated on skin colour or facial features alone, rather than on the sometimes invisible factors of provenance or cultural background. Disability is not always indicated by the presence of a wheelchair or walking stick, yet such visual clues are often sought to reinforce definitions. In the *social* context diversity describes the co-existence of a rich range and variety of ways of behaving and thinking, based on a multiplicity of cultural, psychological and generational factors to name but a few. In the *educational* setting it involves in addition an understanding of the diverse ways in which people learn, interact in group learning and perceive the role of learner and teacher. In the *language learning context* it captures all these things as well as issues such as diverse levels of communication comfort. The understanding of diversity adopted here, then, is wide ranging, at times fairly subtle and perhaps even difficult to recognise. This will be explored later in the chapter with regard to the blended context.

Positive understanding of learner diversity manifests itself in the acknowledgement and support of individual learning positions and needs by teachers and ultimately other learners. Where such understanding and support are more evident, it is likely that learners will be able to take better control of their learning and start to develop what is commonly termed 'learner agency' (Van Lier, 2008). On the other hand, where diversity is inappropriately handled, this can lead to 'communication apprehension' and 'language anxiety' (Daly, 1991; Horwitz and Young, 1991) where language learners are fearful of participating. In extreme cases this can result in 'language shock' (Holliday *et al.*, 2004) where learners experience a complete block to L2 understanding. 'Critical moments' (Pennycook, 2004) may then ensue. These are understood as incidents that describe 'a point of significance, an instant when things change' (ibid.), causing the learner to falter or become disorientated and then having a negative effect on how they function in the classroom.

Institutions may respond to diverse needs in a variety of ways. First, they may fulfil their obligation to meet legal requirements by reasonable adjustments for those with needs: for example, large print documents for the visually impaired; more time at assessment for those with dyslexia; suitable access to face-to-face sessions for those with a mobility-related disability. Second, institutions may themselves introduce additional measures. Indeed, the introduction of a blended model may in itself be an institutional response to the needs of a wider learner population who require more flexible access because of geographic dispersal, work or caring commitments, disability and the like. An institution may also offer financial support: for example, to help with computer purchase for those without adequate financial means; or to assist with care support for dependants so that learners who are carers can attend teaching sessions. Institutions may also put in place formalised diversity training for their staff.

At the same time, however, specific institutional policy may result in a restrictive understanding of an aspect of diversity, at best preventing the opening of minds more fully on this, at worst creating unwitting stereotypes. For example, in listening exams a policy may be in place that allows lip-speakers to be employed to read transcripts to learners with hearing impairment as a substitute for recorded speech. However, a wide range of hearing impairments exist along with different traditions of deaf education, so a lip-speaker may not be appropriate for someone who has been brought up with sign language. It therefore becomes increasingly important that there is a creative response to understanding the nuances of diversity. In addition, responses need to be dynamic, as diversity factors may evolve when learners experience change in their lives or develop new identities through their language learning and new cultural experiences. McMahill's study, referred to by Norton (1997, p. 426), demonstrates how a language learner can move from one cultural position to another, for example in expressing opinions:

> When speaking Japanese [as L1], it takes a lot of courage to express my convictions or insist upon my beliefs, but in English I can do so with a sense of being equal to the person I am talking to.

That learner should no longer be subject to first impressions as someone lacking confidence in expressing opinions, as this can clearly change. On a practical level the teacher's understanding of learners' development will need to be reflected in subsequent decisions at to what role to give the learner in any task.

From all of this it becomes apparent that Kumaravadivelu's concept of particularity (2006) is key, as mentioned in Chapter 1. This emphasises the need to understand and respond to the unique and context-based factors which are present in any particular teaching and learning situation. These:

> must be sensitive to a particular group of teachers teaching a particular group of students pursuing a particular set of goals, within a particular institutional context embedded in a particular socio-cultural milieu (Kumaravadivelu, 2006, p. 171).

This also indicates that individual and group needs will not remain fixed for all time but may change *within* a single learning episode as well as from one learning episode to another.

Teacher provenance is crucial in approaches to understanding diversity and in diversity training. Yet it can be a complex issue in language teaching. The following factors are at stake and can operate in a different number of combinations:

- Is the teacher an L1, L2 or L3 native speaker?
- Did s/he receive education in an L1, L2 or L3 country?
- Did s/he receive pedagogic training in an L1, L2 or L3 country and when?
- Does s/he teach the L2 in an L1, L2 or L3 country and since when?

The following two examples illustrate this:

- A native speaker of Greek, having obtained a degree in Spanish at a Greek university, did teacher training in Britain and has lived and taught Spanish there for thirty years.
- A British national, and native speaker of English, did a French degree and teacher training in Britain and continues to live and teach French there.

These examples indicate that a complex mix of standpoints may impact on understandings of what diversity is, dependent on differing educational and cultural experiences and differing expectations of learners and teachers. For instance, teachers educated in a culture where the teacher is seen as the fount of all knowledge may need to acknowledge that in certain cases adult learners know more on a topic than they do. This can enhance the learning process, since drawing on learner knowledge pays positive dividends with adults.

Recognising diversity

Some identity markers such as age, gender, appearance, accent, mother tongue origin and speech patterns may be more immediately identified from external visual and audible clues. Others, such as ethnic origin, disability, additional needs, lifestyles, values, aspirations, behaviour norms, sensitivity levels, educational and language learning experience, and confidence levels may be less immediately perceptible. Additional markers of diversity may emerge through language activity: for example, opinions, political leanings, personality, ways of interacting with others and emotional state.

Key here is not simply how *discernible* markers are, but the interpretation assigned to them. Everyone reads markers in different ways. For some the wearing of rings on the third finger of the left hand will lead to the assumption that the person is married or in a civil partnership. For others a ring on the third finger on the right hand will lead to the same assumption. For some neither of these will have any significant meaning at all, being simply the wearing of jewellery.

Three case studies from recent research (Adams and Nicolson, 2010) in the blended context of the OU's language courses indicate how complex the recognition of diversity can be, and even that aspects of diversity can remain hidden:

- Learner A had suffered an illness that resulted in mobility problems. He did everything possible in face-to-face sessions in the blended programme to hide this and was so successful that neither teacher nor fellow learners (bar one) noticed that he nearly fell over in an activity involving movement. This incident deterred him from attending subsequent sessions, since he feared having to undertake movement again and exposing a problem he did not wish to reveal.

- Learner B had issues with use of technology in online teaching sessions. She felt an 'absolute fool' because she could not operate a computer in the way required and dropped out. The lack of technical expertise prevented realisation of her language learning.
- Learner C received all her feedback on her individual language work in L2, which was the teacher's usual practice. The learner was from a more traditional language learning background where feedback was usually in L1. This background also made the learner unwilling to challenge the teacher because of the perceived authority role. As a consequence the learner neither understood the feedback nor benefited from the teacher's suggestions for development.

None of the three learners sought advice or asked for changes to assist their learning. The net effect was that their progress was seriously impeded with one deciding not to continue with the course. The teachers involved were unaware of these specific aspects of diversity affecting these language learners so did not intervene or amend their practice. It seems neither did they follow up with learners why they stopped attending. The decision not to attend any further sessions may have different consequences. If teaching sessions form the main vehicle for input, then the learner's progress might be seriously affected. In teaching sessions with a more facilitative role, learner progress may not be affected in the same way. In both scenarios, however, the teacher's recognition of diversity becomes paramount and needs to be supported by seeking as much information as is reasonably necessary.

It cannot be assumed, of course, that learners A, B and C would have had the same experience in other contexts. Recognition of aspects of diversity must also respect the fact that different contexts result in different dynamics and therefore that individuals may have a different or shifting identity, dependent on the situation in which they find themselves (Hall, 1990). Someone who is highly qualified and confident in another discipline may display extreme *lack* of confidence in the language learning situation. On the other hand, someone without formal educational qualifications may be a confident language learner, having attended language classes for many years. Teachers must remain flexible and not prejudge anyone. The thrusting of identity upon others can be problematic. For example, one languages academic studying a new language at beginners' level did not want his professional status revealed to fellow learners in case their expectations of him were too high. However, the teacher ignored his wish with the consequence that he became aware that it interfered with his learning: others were intimidated by his background and uncomfortable when paired with him in activities.

Meeting diverse needs

Diversity in the language learning context may be more pronounced than in other disciplines. Horwitz and Young, discussing language learning, have suggested that 'probably no other field of study implicates self-concepts and self-expression to the degree that language study does' (Horwitz and Young, 1991, p. 31). Horwitz *et al.* suggest that it is not like studying maths or science and cite communication apprehension (Horwitz *et al.*, 1986, p. 427) as one key area of difference. In language teaching, when attempting to recognise aspects of diversity, teachers need to distinguish between three sets of reactions:

1. Those that are related to the broad language learning context (e.g. fear of speaking the L2 in front of others in *any* formal teaching session in any mode, or the experience of language shock when faced with listening stimuli in such a session, when anxiety overrides their ability to comprehend a barrage of unfamiliar L2 words and phrases);
2. Those that are dependent on a particular issue at that moment in time (e.g. the content or design of a *specific t*ask; the behaviour of another learner at a specific point; or the specific grouping or pairing in which a learner finds him/herself);
3. Those that are dependent on more enduring issues for the individual in all contexts, not just teaching and learning ones (e.g. shyness or fear of speaking in larger groups of people).

Irrespective of the origin of the issue, the effect may be that the learner can no longer function in a meaningful way and will either fail and/or drop out of the course. For some this may reinforce their belief that they are no good at language learning. On the other hand, if diverse needs are catered for, agency will start to emerge naturally as apprehension and anxiety are replaced by success and progress.

In all of this a sense of what is reasonable and possible has to reign. There is no suggestion that teachers can address every aspect of diversity. What is suggested, however, is that the teacher takes a professional decision, in conjunction with the learner, as to what level of priority particular aspects of diversity require.

Diversity and teacher practice

For some aspects of diversity, implications for teacher practice in the blended context may be common to all modes, such as by making clear in advance the aims of the whole session and of individual tasks so that all learners know what to expect and can orient themselves cognitively and psychologically. Other implications for practice may emerge differently according to the specific mode and/or particular individual. In speaking practice in synchronous teaching sessions, for example, an individual's lack of confidence will usually be immediately obvious and will have an effect on levels of integration and success, which the teacher will need to address with the individual learner. On the other hand, in asynchronous interaction, such as online forums and wikis, where responses are not needed in real time, dealing with confidence problems may not be so straightforward. For example, the teacher will want to check whether lack of contribution is a result of the learner taking more reflection time about her/his contribution, whether s/he has perhaps even decided not to contribute for reasons that need to be respected or, alternatively, for negative reasons such as problems with other members of the group, which will need to be tackled by the teacher. Teachers may also have to manage the issue that some learners are fearful of submitting work to asynchronous forums unless it is near-perfect, as the work may be visible for a considerable amount of time.

In assessment feedback on an individual learner's work, the teacher can take account of individual needs as these become known. For example, sensitivities about providing personal information may be attenuated in this mode since only one other person, the teacher, sees this information. On the other hand, in the synchronous class, particularly in face-to-face mode, the immediacy means less thinking time, thus less time to select a response with which the learner is comfortable. In addition, other people's reactions are immediate and noticeable and this can impact negatively. Obviously teachers cannot foresee the myriad of scenarios that might arise and will have to be vigilant regarding the particularity of their own ever-changing context. What follows is an examination of teacher approaches to diversity in five areas of language teaching that are key to successful learner integration and progress in the blended context as in all others in the writers' view.

Task choice and task design

The impact of task choice and design should not be underestimated in terms of learner comfort and success. Task choice and design will normally occur prior to interaction with learners, particularly the creation and/or selection of appropriate self-study materials to provide for learners. For synchronous sessions and asynchronous forum modes there is perhaps more opportunity to involve learners in task choice and design (see Chapter 7). This will help ensure that learners can not only work at their own level but also feel comfortable with the task presented to them. But ultimately the final decision on the best task choice will have to be the teacher's. Also, the amount of learner input and choice may be determined by the institutional framework. If teachers are meeting learners regularly it may be too onerous to ask informally for planning input at each turn.

General advice for all modes
- Try to involve learners in the planning stage where possible.
- Communicate task aims and outcomes clearly.
- Give clear instructions for each task.
- Give clear advice (modified according to mode) on how learners can

develop their own pathway, selecting, amending or omitting tasks according to their needs, previous learning experience, what they feel capable of
doing at a particular stage and what is acceptable in cultural terms.

- Ensure appropriateness of task materials for adult learners. It is better not
  to use materials that have been designed for young learners, even though
  the language input may seem relevant.
- Ensure that task choice and/or design does not risk compromising the
  learner, or have potential for embarrassment or discomfort (e.g. avoid
  tasks that have too strong a focus on personal questions or topics that
  might elicit overly strong opinions).
- Remain alert to whether the design of the task is causing problems (e.g.
  because of the particular peer interaction, movement or presentation skills
  required).
- Discuss learner strategies for dealing with tasks that may be difficult for
  them.
- Do not pressurise learners into participating when there is obvious discomfort or challenge.
- Be prepared to modify or abandon tasks at any stage if they appear to cause
  anxiety.

Advice for self-study materials

Depending on the institutional context, there may be little chance for teachers
to influence the selection of materials given to learners. However, teachers can
counsel learners on how to interact with the material in the way that best suits their
needs. Some language learners, for example, may not need to undertake every task.
However, some learners find selection difficult and have a tendency to want to do
every task offered in the materials. This can, of course, be reassuring in giving an
immediate sense of success, but other factors, such as time, have to be balanced
against this. With support, learners can be encouraged to realise that they can make
choices for themselves and become better agents of their own learning.

Activity management

Language teaching professionals have tended to view active participation, particularly in teaching sessions of any kind, as the best means of achieving language competence. As a result, non-participation has often been viewed as a deficit assigned to
learners. Learner-centred methodology has also, in synchronous sessions, encouraged pairwork and groupwork, where learners are able to work in smaller units,
thought to create security and more practice opportunities. This also means the
control of the activity development is put more substantially into the learners'
hands. Collaborative learning such as this relies on participation of all parties, particularly where formal output is expected. The mode may determine the extent and
the way in which the teacher can intervene should problems or conflict arise.

Advice for all modes:

- Ensure that all learners respect the need for peripheral participation (Lave and Wenger, 1991), where a learner by choice reduces her/his level of participation for her/his own valid reasons: e.g. needing more time to assess what her/his contribution is to be; or needing to listen for comprehension. This may vary from one task or one episode of communication to another.
- Notice and address marginality (Wenger, 2000), where learners find themselves at the edge of an activity or group, resulting in their access to learning being blocked. Unlike peripheral participation this is not a position of choice. It may have arisen because of other people's behaviour, learner anxiety or lack of confidence, a problem with the information required or the way it is to be presented or worked on.
- Notice appropriateness of input and react to stop inappropriate contributions.
- Construct groups and pairings carefully, taking into account what is known about individual learners. Some of this knowledge may have to be gleaned on the spot.
- React quickly to issues that arise in groups and pairings, changing configurations if need be.
- Manage learners with care to ensure fairness for all. Dominant behaviour may need intervention.
- Ensure no contributions are devalued by other learners.

Advice for specific modes:

- In asynchronous and synchronous online forums, remind learners of the computer code of conduct and netiquette.
- In asynchronous forums, remove inappropriate contributions and clarify with the learner why this has happened.
- In face-to-face sessions, make it clear if an utterance is not appropriate and prevent the situation developing further.

Assessment

In blended programmes, management of assessment, and therefore feedback from teachers to learners on their work, may assume greater importance as part of the teaching process than in more traditional provision. In this respect feedback has to be more sensitively handled and more individualised.

Advice for feedback on assessment:

- Acknowledge individual effort and respect learners' work. A poor product in academic terms may still have taken a lot of time and energy.
- Avoid comparisons with other learners' performance on the same task.
- Tailor feedback methods and dialogue to take account of each learner's cultural, educational and generational needs. A more chatty and informal

feedback style may not be appropriate with some learners who prefer a distance of respect between learner and teacher.

- Take account of sensitivity levels. While one learner may take strong criticism on the chin, another may feel devastated by this. Learners who receive feedback at a distance, with no chance for human mediation, are particularly vulnerable to what they read, or hear in recorded feedback. Check that there is no scope for misinterpretation or ambiguity of comment.
- Seek learner views on your feedback content and style.

Language Use

Some schools of methodological thought have expected that L2 should be used for all aspects of teacher–learner interaction (Krashen and Terrell, 1983). Unmitigated L2 use may, however, put unnecessary obstacles in the way of learning (see Learner C, p. 33) and again particularity is advocated here as a way forward. At lower levels of language learning a mix of L1 and L2 may be more suitable, while for higher levels there is greater justification for more L2 use. For individuals accustomed to working in an L2 medium or with strong competence levels, it may pose no problem at any level. For those coming from more traditional learning backgrounds, or who have lower competence and confidence levels, L2 needs to be used selectively. At beginners' level, sole L2 use can evoke a strong emotional response from learners who may feel 'dismayed, excluded, stupid, embarrassed, overwhelmed, nervous, daunted, intimidated, anxious, confused, frustrated, negative, inadequate' (Nicolson and Adams, 2010). Despite this, some learners nonetheless indicate that constant L2 use helps them to learn the language better. They view it as a cod-liver-oil syndrome: '[it] can be intimidating when the foreign language is being used. However, I feel it is the best way to learn a foreign language.' (ibid.)

Advice for all modes:
Make sure that:
- language in task instructions is clear;
- language is appropriate to the learner's level;
- understanding is regularly checked;
- learners check their own understanding.

Advice for self-study materials at lower language levels:
- introduce the L2 instructions gradually;
- introduce L2 instructions along with L1 equivalents to start with.

Advice for teaching sessions (synchronous and asynchronous):
- establish the purpose of the session or forum;
- introduce L2 gradually at lower levels when focusing on language work;
- use more L1 or a mix of L1 and L2 when focusing on study skills, moral support or troubleshooting;

- reassure learners that this is a safe and respectful environment where all learners can express all reasonable views, feelings and needs safely.

Advice for synchronous sessions (all modes):
- use judicious sprinklings of L1;
- reassure learners so they not feel threatened by a lot of L2 input. Explain they may momentarily feel disoriented or not understand but that this is quite normal and acceptable in the language learning process;
- summarise in L1 having first offered the explanation in the L2;
- ask learners to summarise in L1 or L2 as a linguistic exercise in itself;
- offer a slower speed of utterance where necessary, without this becoming disjointed or meaningless in communication terms;
- establish conventions for flagging problems so that learners are not exposed in front of others;
- provide learners with a list of L2 phrases used for classroom management and interaction.

Advice for face-to-face sessions:
- assist understanding by using gesture, mime, drawing and/or facial expressions where appropriate;
- establish appropriate sign language for discreet and sensitive indication of comprehension problems.

Advice for online or telephone sessions:
- communicate in L1 about technical issues;
- allow for thinking time on the part of learners; this may appear longer in this environment without visual clues;
- ensure learners understand and respect silences.

Advice for online sessions:
- take advantage of the variety of tools available to check understanding: e.g. use text chat to clarify individual L2 comprehension issues online so as not to interrupt flow; or ask for emoticons or ticks to be used to indicate all is clear or to support other learner statements;
- use emoticons online to encourage learners and reinforce the mood/humour of L2 speech.

When providing written and recorded feedback on assessment:
- negotiate the amount of L1/L2 used with the learner;
- where institutional guidelines exist regarding L2 use, modify these according to individual needs. Be ready to justify the decision to educational managers;
- irrespective of choice of feedback language, use L2 set pieces for openings and endings or praise and social niceties such as personal messages

regarding the work or progress. This allows learners to become accustomed to L2 use.

Use of personal information

Many beginners' language courses rely on learning outcomes linked to personal information, such as learner's name, age, profession, marital status, family, hobbies and residence. This has historically hinged around the belief that limited knowledge of L2 prevents opening up other areas of discussion. Syllabus and course designers also argue that, at this level, this type of input equips learners for encounters in the L2 country/area while others suggest that providing this information helps group cohesion. Research shows, however, that to personalise these can cause some learners to feel uncomfortable (Adams and Nicolson, 2010). 'Are you married?', 'Do you have children?' 'What is your job?', 'Where do you go on holiday?' may seem unproblematic, but if the learner has just been divorced/widowed/is in a civil partnership/doesn't believe in marriage/can't have children/is unemployed/can't afford to go on holiday, they can become unwanted intrusions. Other sets of questions may be equally difficult for others.

In the synchronous class, answers to these are often given in an open forum where the feeling of comparison, however silent, makes discomfort more acute. Many questions of this kind also rely on certain lifestyle conventions to capture a person's identity: the nuclear family and traditional marital relationships and lifestyles, for example, yet not everyone lives life in this way. By basing language work on these, a certain set of linguistic parameters continue to be promoted, thus limiting learners from extending their lexical and structural base. It may seem obvious to suggest that learners make up information where they do not want to tell the truth. However, research again shows that this is not acceptable in all cases. A learner who was required to discuss his living arrangements in a paired speaking task discovered, as the pair discussion unfolded, that the truth about his sexual orientation was unacceptable to his fellow learner. However, to make up fictitious information about himself he felt he would betray his identity. Consequently, he decided not to attend further teaching sessions. Some may argue, in line with Klippel (1984), that if learners do not want to reveal aspects of their personal identity they should refuse to answer. This in itself requires confidence and can exacerbate anxiety. At higher levels, discussion may involve personal opinions on political, social or moral issues. If views are deeply held or contrast seriously with those held by others, then this equally can lead to contentious conflict within the learner group.

Advice for all modes:
- try to find out what areas of discussion may be problematic for learners where possible;
- share the teaching plan in advance (see Chapter 7);
- examine tasks that involve giving personal information with care and

adapt or abandon if these seem to delve too deeply or encroach on possibly problematic areas;

- give students the choice to make up fictitious identities if this is more acceptable to them than revealing truths about themselves. It can be a beneficial exercise to extend language use in this way;
- offer alternative identities as part of the task. Well-known personalities are often suggested but, again, be sure that the personalities chosen are themselves without contention and are known by the learner assigned the identity. Appropriate historic, literary or sport characters can often be useful in this regard, and they also require learners to develop language beyond what they might normally need;
- choose identities that incorporate aspects of humour or stretch belief and therefore levels of creativity (e.g. appropriate cartoon or fairytale characters) where this is appropriate with the individual or group in question. This can be useful in diminishing inhibitions;
- create imaginative scenarios or creative role-play in which roles are assigned or self-selected. Language development is also richer when a new set of structures and lexis has to be explored. Be aware, however, that some learners resist creative role assignation or find it difficult (Brash and Warnecke, 2009). Negotiation between teacher and learners is important here, and emphasis of the linguistic benefit may help;
- be sensitive to activity development and be ready to step in, modify or abandon if problems arise.

Physical response tasks

Some recent methodological trends have relied on physical response tasks to enhance language teaching and learning in the face-to-face domain (Asher, 1988). Physical responses include any task that involves miming, getting up, moving around, catching or passing of objects. In a face-to-face context they are seen as a good way of enabling students to lose inhibitions about language production by making them focus on other skills. This may need caution when working with adults. They may find movement or co-ordination difficult. They may feel shy in all group situations, or in this particular group, or be uncomfortable with their body or with being the focus of attention.

The advice is:

- where possible check in advance that learners are happy with physical response tasks;
- accept that physical tasks may not be suitable perhaps for a particular group or individual and amend the plan accordingly;
- be watchful during sessions for anyone experiencing problems with

physical response tasks and be ready to step in and modify the approach or abandon the task;

- allocate appropriate roles to learners which are equally important in the task and do not risk learner discomfort.

Conclusion

This chapter has endeavoured to illustrate why it is important to understand and respond to diversity. It has shown that success in language learning cannot simply be attributed to the learners' cognitive development alone but is based on a complex set of interconnecting variables, emerging from diverse needs and understandings, which can impact on how the learner makes choices and therefore makes progress. It has examined how aspects such as institutional approaches and policies, the nature of the blend, teaching approaches and the people involved in teaching and learning create a complex interplay when diverse needs are at stake. Practical advice for the teacher in planning for and dealing with diversity in the context of the different modes of any blend has also been offered.

If the challenge with regard to diversity is met successfully, learners will find themselves in a place where cognitive progress and affective well-being are achieved, while teachers will find themselves in a renewed position of enhanced professional satisfaction. This creates a perfect meeting point with gates opening in all directions, in many ways akin to Bhaba's third space (Rutherford, 1990), which 'encapsulates the idea of a new space, combining old and new, in a successful crucible-type experience, [and] emerging as a third and better entity' (Adams and Nicolson, 2010, p. 105). This does require teachers to push boundaries in their own understanding, response and practice with regard to diversity. It may indeed seem like a search for a teaching and learning utopia. However, without some movement towards the creation of a new type of teaching and learning environment, it may be difficult to meet diverse learner needs in a changing society. In many ways teachers will need to be 'committed to continual critical evaluation in practice' (Blommaert, 2005, p. 238), so they can review approaches to diversity as other aspects of their practice and devise their own professional theories as advocated by Kumaravadivelu (2006). This will allow them to approach the needs of learners within components of the particular blend in a creative way. If teachers can see each of their learners as a unique individual with her/his own identity and needs, then, as Gardner (2008) suggests, they will come to 'respect diversity as a fact of life', an important underpinning in the current educational landscape.

Chapter 4: **Fostering Learner Autonomy and Motivation in Blended Teaching**

Linda Murphy and Stella Hurd

Introduction

Following an exploration of the resources combined in blended programmes and some socio-cultural factors that affect teachers and learners, this chapter turns its attention to autonomy and motivation in a blended setting. It focuses in particular on the teacher's role in creating and maintaining a learning environment that supports the development of autonomy, and why this is important.

The chapter starts by outlining theoretical discussions about autonomy in language learning, its relationship to self-regulation and its relevance for successful learning. Given the link between autonomy and motivation (Dickinson, 1992; Ushioda, 1996) and the importance of autonomy as a key element in maintaining motivation, it goes on to examine briefly the major theories around motivation, and the interaction between autonomy, motivation and learning resources. Examples from research studies are offered to illustrate theory in action. The chapter then explores:

- how specific factors impact on the teaching role, such as the balance of responsibility between learner and teacher;
- the extent of choice and control for the learner;
- what motivates learners and how teachers can find this out;
- what efforts are needed to promote and develop self-motivation and self-regulation strategies in the process of what Little (2003) terms 'autonomisation', whereby learners gradually 'learn how to learn', and in the process become more autonomous through taking control of their learning.

Finally, there is a discussion about the types of blends that might be adopted by learners in accordance with their individual differences, their learning goals, and the possibilities available within their specific educational setting. The authors argue that teacher understanding of autonomy and motivation is crucial when supporting learners, even more so in a blended setting where learners may need guidance in making decisions and choices that are right for them. Researchers have pointed out that in order to provide such support effectively teachers need to engage in conscious, critical reflection (Chamot, 2001) and exercise their own capacity for autonomy through a continual process of inquiry into how their teaching can best promote autonomous learning and support learner motivation. As suggested by Barfield *et al.* (2001), learner and teacher autonomy are interrelated and overlapping concepts that involve both parties in critical reflective enquiry.

Autonomy and language learning: from theory to practice

A number of well-known language researchers including Holec (1981; 2007), Dam (1995; 2003), Little (1991; 2003; 2007), and Benson (2001; 2007a; 2007b; 2007c) have written extensively on autonomy in language learning and have been instrumental in shaping theories, definitions, interpretations and practice. Holec's constructivist view of autonomy as 'the ability to take charge of one's learning' (Holec, 1981, p. 3) is described as a 'foundational definition' (Little, 2007, p. 15) which has 'proved remarkably robust' (Benson, 2007b, p. 22). Little (1991, p. 4) gives his own definition of autonomy as 'the capacity for detachment, critical reflection, decision-making and independent action'. Despite the variety of definitions, Little (2003) suggests that there is broad agreement that autonomous learners:

> understand the purpose of their learning programme, explicitly accept responsibility for their learning, share in the setting of goals, take initiatives in planning and executing learning and evaluate its effectiveness.

In arguing from a Vygotskian perspective, in which learning is theorised as a socially mediated process and autonomy entails 'relatedness', Little adds 'a vital psychological dimension that is often absent in definitions of autonomy' (Benson, 2001, p. 49). His thinking has thus sown the seeds for a growing consensus in the field of applied linguistics that autonomy as a theoretical construct encompasses the dual notion of 'individual-cognitive' and 'social-interactive', and involves 'interdependence,' while at the same time embracing notions of freedom and choice.

Little (2003) cites two general arguments for learner autonomy in practice:

- the connection between reflective engagement with learning and learner effectiveness;
- the link between motivation and autonomy, in that 'autonomous learners have developed the reflective and attitudinal resources to overcome temporary motivational setbacks'.

In terms of language learning specifically, he offers a third argument that socially autonomous learners 'should find it easier than otherwise to master the full range of discourse roles on which effective spontaneous communication depends' (ibid.).

In settings where the teacher is physically absent for a large part of the time, such as self-access and distance learning, or in 'blends' of face-to-face and online learning, more of the responsibility for autonomisation rests with the teaching/learning materials and depends on the commitment of course designers and writers to this goal (Murphy, 2007; 2008). For some learners, the idea of control in the hands of the learner is an alien concept. It is for this reason, as well as to provide clarity, that the materials in language courses or online activities, such as those produced by writers at the OU, are guided and structured. While, in terms of autonomy, this could exemplify 'contradiction in educational terms' (Holec, 1985, p. 189), it is also argued that the skills and strategies inherent in an autonomous approach, such as the ability to organise and reflect on learning, monitor progress, identify gaps and solve problems can be successfully promoted through specially designed activities within course materials (Hurd *et al.*, 2001), as well as through teacher-planned classroom tasks. Teaching for autonomy is thus at the heart of the design and content of the components in blended programmes.

The materials are the cornerstone of any learning environment that involves a degree of self-direction, yet teachers in blended programmes have a mediating role through their contact with learners: via feedback on assessments, during teaching sessions and through online exchanges. The last offers enhanced 'potential for interaction and collaboration between learners and teachers and among groups of learners' (Murphy, 2008, p.86). However, despite the choice and control that the use of computer-mediated communication (CMC) gives to the learner, this does not automatically lead to autonomisation, as Strake (2007, p. 101) citing Benson, warns: 'A great deal depends on the nature of the technology and the use made of it'. Her study of a blended language learning environment reconfirms the teacher as a 'key factor to enhance successful blending', and underlines the importance of 'a positive relationship between self-instruction and the development of autonomy' (Strake, 2007, pp. 101–2). The teacher's role, as Murphy (2008) explains, involves teachers entering into a 'pedagogic dialogue' with learners and encouraging interaction and collaboration as part of the 'explicit conscious processes' (Little, 2001, p. 34) that underpin the pursuit of autonomy. In so doing, they are helping learners build their own 'learner-context interface' (White, 1999) as 'active agents … constructing and assuming control of a personally meaningful and effective interface between themselves, their attributes and needs, and the features of the learning context' (White, C., 2008, p. 7).

The critical role of the teacher in influencing the autonomisation of learners has shifted the focus in the last decade towards the notion of teacher autonomy as inextricably bound up with learner autonomy (Sinclair *et al.*, 2000; Shelley *et al.*, 2006; Murphy, 2007; White, 2007; Lamb and Reinders, 2008; Murphy, 2008), emphasising that, as autonomy implies interdependence, learner autonomy 'is unlikely to be effectively realised without teacher intervention and guidance, and can manifest itself in a number of different ways' (Hurd, 2008b, p. 29). For teachers working in blended learning settings, two key challenges present themselves in this regard:

- learner diversity and its impact on 'readiness' for autonomy (see also Chapter 3);
- expectations of teacher autonomy and the nature and timing of pedagogical intervention.

There may be considerable resistance to autonomy among learners who are more comfortable with an approach that puts the teacher firmly in control. Optimum learner support involves knowledge and understanding, including 'affective as well as cognitive or organisational skills' (Macdonald, 2004, p. 12). But teachers in a blended learning environment may also feel threatened by the 'ways in which their identities are disrupted and challenged' (White, 2007, p. 97) and by the demands of a new learning environment that requires competence in the use of a range of computer applications, entails a shift in the balance of power between learner and teacher, and emphasises collaborative as opposed to individual control (see Chapter 15 for discussion of teacher development in this respect). A blended learning environment provides more/different choices and decisions for learners, so arguably increases the opportunity for learners to exercise their capacity for autonomy. It is also part of a teacher's role to demonstrate a commitment to 'developing a palpable sense of belonging' (ibid., p. 104). In summary, research indicates that:

- autonomy means taking control by reflecting on learning (or teaching) and making decisions, but not necessarily on one's own;
- the teacher's role is to support learners in their decisions and choices as individuals, while at the same time creating a sense of community where decisions can be discussed and shared;
- autonomy is an important factor in maintaining motivation for language learning.

Motivation and language learning

Research carried out over three decades has consistently reinforced motivation as a powerful factor in SLA, closely related to autonomy and, in many instances, the best overall predictor of language learning success (Gardner and Lambert, 1972; Naiman et al., 1978; Ellis, 1985; Oxford and Shearin, 1994; Ushioda, 1996; Dörnyei, 2001). Its link with autonomy is emphasised by Ushioda (1996, p. 2), who states unequivocally that 'autonomous language learners are by definition motivated learners'. The critical role of motivation is illustrated by the way in which it is said to influence or even 'interfere' (Stevick, 1999, p. 50) with learning, as elaborated by Ehrman:

> The affective dimension affects how efficiently learners can use what they have. For example, strong motivation tends to help students marshal their assets and skills, whereas low motivation or intense anxiety interferes with their ability to use their skills and abilities (Ehrman, 1996, p. 138).

Ushioda (2007, p. 22) reinforces this 'dynamic interplay between cognitive and affective engagement' and Arnold and Brown (1999, p. 1) go even further in stating that 'neither the cognitive nor the affective has the last word, and, indeed, neither can be separated from the other'.

Gardner's (1985) socio-educational model of language learning distinguishes between integrative and instrumental motivation, a distinction largely mirrored in

Deci and Ryan's (1985) model of intrinsic (coming from within: for example, the desire to learn arising from love of the target culture) and extrinsic (coming from outside: for example, the need for an externally recognised qualification) motivation. Ehrman *et al.* (2003, p. 320) suggest that 'a learner's total motivation is most frequently a combination of extrinsic and intrinsic motivation' and that it 'depends greatly on the context, people involved and specific circumstances'. Ryan and Deci (2000) argue that motivation is not only sustained by feelings of competence and effectiveness but also by a sense of self-determination and autonomy. This link with other factors reflects the process model of motivation that has emerged more recently (Dörnyei, 2005, p. 66) where motivation is seen as a 'dynamic, ever-changing process' in constant flux as it interrelates with other variables, such as personality, beliefs, attitudes and learning setting, and that these interrelationships are crucial to an understanding of the individual language learner experience.

Motivation is also the factor most frequently cited as critical to successful learning by learners themselves (Hurd, 2000; 2006, White, 1999; 2003). In relation to distance learning, Hurd (2005, p. 9) argues: 'Perceived inadequacy of feedback, frustration at unresolved problems, and lack of opportunities to practise with others and share experiences can have an adverse effect on motivation levels.' Hurd's study of motivation and roles in distance language learning reveal that 'motivation was seen to play a crucial role in success, along with teacher feedback, and personal responsibility for learning' (Hurd, 2006, p. 310). In other words, learners themselves saw how autonomy, or control over their learning, related to their motivation. Two key points emerged from these findings with respect to motivation:

- the importance of good feedback in terms of timing, tone and a staged or 'scaffolded' approach;
- the need for opportunities to develop speaking skills.

A blended learning setting with a variety of communication channels makes it much easier for teachers to respond to learners, although the time factor should not be underestimated. With regard to speaking practice, blended learning offers greatly increased opportunities for communication of all kinds through the various online tools, but can increase the affective demands as learners have to respond to technical as well as linguistic challenges (Shield, 2000; Hampel and Hauck, 2006; De Los Arcos *et al.*, 2009). So while increased opportunities for speaking practice can have a positive effect on motivation levels, in order to make the most of them learners need to develop strategies to cope with emotions that can negatively affect motivation, such as frustration caused by disconnections, and anxiety about language performance, which can be exacerbated in virtual exchanges through the absence of body language and other paralinguistic clues.

The most important strategy for maintaining motivation signalled in Hurd's (2006) study was positive self-talk or self-encouragement (saying positive things to oneself), followed by setting goals. White (2003) also identifies self-encouragement and self-reinforcement (reward on completion of an activity) as useful strategies in her study. However, the most frequently mentioned affective strategy was self-motivation, defined as 'providing an impetus to keep going by reminding oneself of reasons for or advantages of continuing with the course' (White, 2003, p. 117).

In language learning there is constant interaction between motivation, autonomy and learning resources, as learners develop increasing control over their learning, and gain the confidence to exercise a degree of choice over how, when, with whom and using which resources they learn. Bronson (2000, p. 55) makes it clear that 'motivation and self-regulation are highly interrelated, since self-regulated learning can occur only when the ability to control strategic thinking processes is accompanied by the wish to do so', and this is most likely to occur through optimum pedagogic intervention. Littlejohn (2004, p. 3), citing Nicol *et al.* (2003), adds that 'giving students increased autonomy and control of their own environments is likely to increase their motivation and willingness to participate in the learning process'. This point is further reinforced by Little (2003) who argues that making learners aware of relevant skills and strategies for maintaining motivation can help to promote self-regulation and support the process of autonomisation. Teachers can play a big part in enabling learners to become active agents in their learning, by developing a sense of community where learners feel they belong, by helping them to cope with feelings of frustration, isolation and anxiety, and by providing high-quality feedback, including scaffolding activities, both cognitive and motivational (Hurd, 2008b). The key research messages for practitioners are that:

- autonomy and motivation are closely linked: taking responsibility for learning enhances motivation, and vice versa;
- motivation is crucial for successful language learning;
- supportive feedback and opportunities to communicate in the language are vital for motivation;
- teachers can support motivation by encouraging learners to make decisions and to become aware of strategies to maintain motivation.

A closer look at autonomy and motivation in the blended language teaching context

The discussion above outlines key features that characterise the concept of autonomy in language learning and account for its significance. First, learner control: this refers to learners making conscious choices and decisions about aspects of their learning. Second, interdependence and interaction: learners are not working in a vacuum, but interacting with peer learners, teachers and others in the course of their learning. Here the link is made with motivation, which is enhanced through feedback provided during interaction. This feedback may be evidence that another person understands a question posed by the learner, appreciates the ideas they put forward, agrees with their argument, or suggests alternative words or expressions. It does not refer only to evaluation of formal assessments or learning tasks by the teacher. Ryan and Deci (2000) suggest that feedback that prompts learners to make positive self-evaluations can enhance their sense of competence which, as mentioned earlier, sustains motivation. How then can blended teaching contexts support autonomy and motivation? What opportunities can they offer for learners to take control, by exercising choice and making decisions about their learning? As Whitelock (2004, p. 5) asks: 'Do more opportunities arise for students to take control of their learning in blended learning environments?' What opportunities can blended learning contexts offer for interaction that enhances learners' sense of competence?'

The previous chapters in this book have explored the diversity of learners, their varied needs and circumstances and the wide range of elements that may make up the 'blend'. Potential flexibility has been highlighted as a reason for the increased focus on blended learning, because it allows learners to participate in ways that suit their circumstances and needs. To foster learner control, as Whitelock (2004, p. 2) notes, a 'blend' that offers different modes of working can provide flexibility and cater for different learning styles, needs and circumstances. However, definitions of blended learning suggest that it is not simply a collection of different ways of reaching the same goals for learners to choose between, but rather the *integration* of different modes (see also Chapter 2). This means that some of the choices and decisions that learners make may be less obvious than a straight choice between doing things in one mode or another. Blended learning programmes therefore should be explicit about the opportunities for choice and decision-making, and teachers need to support learners in taking control of their learning within the integrated programme as a whole. As Macdonald (2004, p. 24) explains:

> By adopting blended strategies, integrating both synchronous and asynchronous contact, and using a range of media with both groups and individuals in an informed way, we will have the flexibility we need to support individuality and diversity in our students.

Some examples of choices and decisions open to learners are considered below.

Little (2003) suggests that autonomous learners 'share in the setting of goals, take initiatives in planning and executing learning and evaluate its effectiveness'. In blended language learning, as in more traditional programmes, aims and objectives are likely to be pre-defined by a course syllabus. Nevertheless learners are increasingly expected to:

- engage in self-evaluation in order to identify their specific language learning needs, focusing on these within the framework of the overall programme;
- consider their own learning needs, interests and context;
- decide on their personal learning goals.

In blended language learning, the mix of modes may allow learners to choose the order in which they tackle tasks, for example, listening and speaking before reading and writing tasks, depending on individual learning goals or personal circumstances (for example, time available for reading while travelling or the need for a less taxing task at the end of a long day). Participation in asynchronous online activities can be timed to suit the learner's lifestyle, and learners may decide how much and how frequently they contribute. Learner control through choice of content and task is supported and encouraged by clarity from course designers and teachers about the intended outcomes that learners can expect to achieve by engaging in particular activities and tasks. In a blended context, learners have access to a plethora of resources on the internet, which can be harnessed to provide differentiation and cater for individual needs in a way that a traditional classroom setting and course book cannot. Some resources are now adaptive, for example, quizzes, which automatically get more difficult if a learner is doing well and easier if they are struggling. With appropriate help and guidance students can learn to make use of these resources to individualise their studies and enhance their independence.

Blended learning contexts can further support the development of autonomy through the flexibility they offer in relation to assessment. The range of communication channels makes it easier to arrange collaborative assessment integrating synchronous and asynchronous tasks. This kind of assessment provides opportunities for learner control over allocation of tasks and decision-making about the final form of spoken presentation: for example, a recorded or 'live' format, and any other accompanying information. Decision-making becomes a shared and negotiated activity, an example of collaborative rather than individual autonomy. However, some learners may view this process and the compromises that may be necessary as a serious limitation on their individual control, and as a result their motivation may be adversely affected (Ryan and Deci, 2000).

Turning to motivation, blended learning can offer a wide range of opportunities for interaction and feedback through the integration of synchronous and asynchronous online learning with face-to-face learning. Littlejohn (2004, p. 2) notes that 'many teachers are utilising the potential of technology to support and enhance classroom interactions'. For example, a debate begun in a classroom setting can be continued by learners in an asynchronous discussion room or in a synchronous online meeting space where learners can engage in more interaction more frequently and provide comment and feedback on each others' contributions to a far greater extent than can be provided by a teacher alone (see also Chapter 2). In blended learning, opportunities to work collaboratively with other learners are not restricted to classroom meetings either. In collaborative work, autonomy and motivation come together, as White (2007, p. 61) notes:

> The emerging view is that learners can now manage and shape their learning experiences as they collaborate with other learners and teachers, and that it is this collaboration which affords control to learners [...] Learners

> are now able to develop and exercise their control and agency in learning
> through opportunities for negotiation and interaction within the learning
> community.

The ease and speed of online communication also means learners can more easily share experiences, ask questions or seek advice rather than waiting for the next meeting (Heinze and Procter, 2004). It facilitates the use of social strategies for language learning such as 'asking for clarification and verification or asking for correction', 'becoming aware of others' thoughts and feelings' and 'co-operating with peers' (Oxford, 1990, p. 21), and sustains motivation through an increased sense of community as students share enthusiasm for a particular language and culture with like-minded others.

Some blended learning contexts provide online practice exercises to consolidate and extend language practised in a synchronous teaching session (be it face-to-face or virtual), or as preparation for synchronous teaching session activities where the language practised online is put to use in a less structured and more spontaneous way. Whitelock (2004, p. 4) points out that computer systems excel in the provision of large numbers of formative interactive tasks for a learner to work through. The learner decides how many examples s/he wants to complete and how many times to repeat the activities. Moreover Whitelock notes that 'the computer is non-judgmental about such matters' and does not pass on this information to the tutor or the learner's peer group' (although VLEs do allow such information to be collected). Provision of the all-important feedback to the individual learner can be built in on a variety of levels, starting with hints, followed by stronger tips and/or detailed explanations until the learner masters the task and increases their sense of competence.

Research therefore suggests that blended learning can support autonomy and motivation through:

- increased flexibility, variety of communication channels and resources allowing a greater degree of choice to suit individual needs and preferences;
- enhanced opportunities for collaboration which can increase feedback and influence motivation.

Research also suggests, however, that teachers have a significant role to play in guiding learners through the maze of opportunities and supporting them in decision-making.

Teacher support for autonomy and motivation in blended language learning

The possibilities offered by blended learning for supporting the development of autonomy and sustaining motivation, briefly outlined above, make particular demands on the language teacher. As noted earlier, choice without guidance and decision-making without relevant knowledge and skills are not likely to foster autonomy and support motivation. Without a clear picture of what they are expected to do and why, learners cannot make decisions about which tasks to prioritise, the amount of time and effort to devote to them, how to structure their study plan or which materials to consult.

Although information about the aims, objectives and intended learning outcomes may be spelled out for the teaching programme or units within it, the teacher needs to ensure that learners are briefed about the outcomes they can expect to achieve through participation in different tasks in each part of the 'blend'. Learners need a clear picture of the relationship between particular tasks and skills development so they can make decisions about their learning. For example, if learners need to develop their grammatical accuracy and speed up their ability to write spontaneously, they need to be aware of what they could gain from participating in an asynchronous forum, writing entries in their blog, doing online practice activities, doing exercises in their course book, or keeping a private journal. It follows that teachers also need a clear understanding of the affordances of each element of the blend in relation to learner needs, and their role in communicating and clarifying the available choices to learners.

In addition to clarity about potential learning outcomes, the expectation that learners should make choices and decisions, structure work or prioritise tasks within the programme framework also needs to be made explicit. It cannot be assumed that all learners have the awareness and skills to self-assess and self-evaluate to do this. As noted earlier, some may resist taking responsibility themselves. Language teachers need to help learners develop these skills and decide on appropriate plans of action to achieve their personal goals and successfully complete compulsory and assessed elements of the learning programme. Murphy *et al.* (2005) provide learners with a possible structure for this reflective process. In a blended learning context, decisions about how to work towards individual priorities also need to take account of the specific affordances of different parts of the 'blend'.

As suggested in the first part of this chapter, encouraging learners to take control of their learning requires a readiness on the part of the teacher to:
- relinquish control and take on a guiding role;
- accept learners' considered decisions, even when these involve opting out of elements of the blend such as asynchronous forums or face-to-face meetings;
- take a passive role in a specific task;
- use L1 to discuss a particular point where appropriate.

It also implies that teachers should design learning activities that are sufficiently flexible to allow learners to draw on aspects of their personal knowledge and experience as far as possible in the decisions they make.

If motivation is enhanced through interaction and feedback prompting positive self-evaluation, learners may need support to develop their own skills in *giving* feedback to others as well as learning to *use* feedback from others. Teachers will again need to model appropriate responses in synchronous and asynchronous settings, commenting on contributions to discussions or asking further questions, but then gradually reducing their input to allow interaction between learners to increase. In some institutions, learner reluctance to engage with other learners, rather than waiting for teacher 'approval' or comment, has been addressed by assessing contributions, for example, to an online asynchronous discussion. In such circumstances, the frequency and nature of contributions may be closely prescribed, which will adversely affect autonomy and motivation and may lead to less spontaneous and less meaningful interaction.

Teacher awareness of learners' initial motivations for learning a particular language can help in the design of learning activities. A brief survey at the start of the course, as part of getting to know learners, can provide this kind of information. As well as helping teachers add the dimension of relevance to tasks, it also enables them to give guidance on how to make the best use of the different elements in a blended context. The diversity of learner circumstances and life stories means that learners are best placed to maintain their own motivation. The early part of this chapter referred to a variety of motivational strategies that learners may engage in: for example, self-encouragement, self-reinforcement or reminding oneself of long-term goals. Teachers can facilitate self-motivation by raising awareness of such strategies and enabling learners to share experiences of how they keep going when the going gets tough.

However much learners are encouraged to make choices and control their learning, and even if interactive tasks provide plenty of feedback and support positive self-evaluation, efforts will be in vain unless assessment also places value on these activities. Assessment tasks also need to include an element of choice or demand decisions of learners: for example, in the questions they are required to answer or the materials they draw on to complete a task. It should also give credit for demonstration of critical reflection on learning. The 'washback' effect of assessment tests is well known (Alderson and Wall, 1993), and exhortation to make decisions and take responsibility for one's own learning may be ignored if assessment is perceived to be controlling and removes responsibility from learners, thus reducing motivation. 'Constructive alignment' of the curriculum (Biggs, 1999, p. 11) (i.e. ensuring that all aspects of teaching and assessment work towards the same goals) is every bit as imperative in blended learning as in more traditional contexts. Therefore, teachers support autonomy and motivation by:

- clarifying intended learning outcomes and helping learners understand which needs are best met through engagement with particular tools, resources and tasks;
- making explicit any opportunities for learner decision-making;
- providing feedback and modelling feedback strategies for learners to use;
- becoming aware of learners' initial motivation for learning the language and raising awareness of strategies for maintaining motivation;

- ensuring as far as possible that assessment rewards critical reflection and encourages choice and decision-making.

Learner responses to blended language learning

The previous sections examined how blended language learning contexts can enhance autonomy and sustain motivation, and the teacher's role in helping to bring this about. This section looks at how learners may respond to the choices and opportunities available to them in the light of individual differences, learning goals and specific learning contexts, with the help of examples drawn from research carried out with beginner language learners at the OU over a period of eight months. Volunteer learners of French, German and Spanish were asked to complete and return a guided learning experience log month-by-month, in which they noted the highs and lows of study each month, how they overcame difficulties, what kept them going and the support they received from other people (Murphy, forthcoming). These learners had enrolled on a programme with a blend consisting of print and audio self-study materials, synchronous online or face-to-face group tutorial sessions, access to asynchronous and synchronous online conferencing systems for use with peers at any time and support from a personal tutor. The following examples illustrate the choices made by different learners to utilise elements of the blend. They highlight the teacher role in guidance and support for the decision-making process.

Anne (names have been changed) is a forty-four-year-old female learner of French. Her family and work commitments mean she has limited time for study, an issue that she recognised very early in the course, although she indicated that her friends and family supported her and helped her to make some time for study. She was very keen to learn French, and getting a good final grade was important to her. She identified pronunciation and intonation as particularly difficult, affecting her confidence in speaking to others and her understanding of audio material. Having identified these issues, she decided to discuss possible strategies with her tutor. She had no time to engage in asynchronous conferencing or self-help activity with others learners. She was not able to attend group tutorials, so this part of the blend was also ruled out. She therefore decided to focus her attention on audio material, specifically speaking and pronunciation practice exercises, and at the same time reviewed her approach to study. She began to organise her study into short bursts, to capitalise on short time slots available through the day and summarised or simplified key points to fit the time available. She reviewed her progress regularly and was inspired and motivated to continue by recognising an improvement in her skills. The confirmation provided by an improved assessment score and feedback from her tutor further sustained her motivation. Anne had no contact with other learners during the course until the final tutorial session when she managed to join the group for some practice for the final course assessment. In Anne's case, the blend was reduced to a focus on the course materials, particularly the audio extracts and speaking exercises. Her ability to self-evaluate and self-assess enabled her to take strategic decisions about her learning and maintain her motivation, while the logs indicate consultation with her tutor about how to meet her needs drawing on certain elements of the blend, and the importance of feedback from and interaction with her tutor.

The experience of Dawn, a fifty-five-year-old female learner on the same French course, is different in a number of respects. Dawn made a point of attending all the online synchronous tutorial sessions; she also made regular use of the asynchronous conferencing facility and the telephone to keep in touch with other learners, and met with a small self-help group between tutorials. She identified difficulties with grammar points as a key area for attention, and much of her contact with others appeared to focus on resolving queries. For example, she reported that she had been in touch with others not only to discuss verb usage but also used these contacts to practise language points. Dawn's logs indicate that she felt the work took a lot more time than she had expected or planned for:

> I understood that eight hours a week would be enough but it's nowhere near that. I need twice that and can't really spare the time. I am studying at eleven o'clock at night and am shattered at work most of the time.

Dawn also reported feeling that other learners in the group were ahead of her and faster learners, but was determined to continue because: 'I really want to learn French'. She derived considerable support from her contact with others and mentioned the reassurance she gained from finding that others also had difficulties. She recorded that the self-help group was a particular source of inspiration and motivation for her. It seems that Dawn needed guidance from her tutor on a more strategic approach to the way she used the course materials. Although she tended to measure herself against others in the group, their feedback also helped her to realise she was making progress, and she confirmed this for herself by purchasing some additional reading material in French and finding she could now understand a surprising amount.

These two examples could be said to represent opposite ends of a spectrum. Anne took a highly strategic approach, limiting herself to one part of the blend, determined by her circumstances and self-identified learning needs, and in consultation with her tutor. Dawn took advantage of all parts of the blend, but her approach was less strategic, perhaps because she lacked confidence in taking such decisions about her learning, highlighting the teacher role in providing guidance in this respect. She did not show evidence of critical reflection on her learning needs, although she identified certain difficulties, and she did not prioritise specific elements of the blend. As a result, Dawn felt that her study was taking up far too much time and she worried about how to make progress. In both cases, their motivation was maintained by strong initial goals and recognition of the progress they had made. They demonstrate the way in which teacher guidance may enable learners to take control and work with those elements of the blend that best suit their personal context.

Conclusion

This chapter has explored the significance of autonomy and motivation in language learning as well as the links between them, and the additional opportunities for their support and development afforded by blended learning contexts. Learners need to be able to explore and experiment with the blend of resources available to them to help them maintain motivation, develop self-regulation and ultimately be in a position to manage their own learning and achieve their personal goals. In the process, as White (2008, p. 7) argues, they establish and take control of a personally meaningful and effective interface between their needs and attributes, and the features of the blended learning context. Teachers have a crucial role to play in guiding this process and helping learners to become aware of the decisions they can and should be making.

Section 2:
Assessment

Chapter 5:   **The Role and Nature of Assessment in Blended Contexts**

Annette Duensing and Felicity Harper

Introduction

This chapter considers the role and nature of assessment in the blended context to enable teachers to construct assessment tasks for this learning environment and help learners prepare successfully. As in other teaching and learning situations, assessing in blended teaching programmes requires a grasp of the concepts involved in assessment design and administration. The use of new methods, teaching modes and tools may also require adjustments in assessment tasks, as these cannot necessarily be mapped from the traditional classroom or distance learning environment on to the blended one. Indeed, a new assessment strategy may be necessary.

This chapter first touches on some general assessment theory and on concepts helpful to those responsible for assessment strategy design. These will also be useful for teachers involved in discussions about assessment or whose focus is to prepare learners for assessment. In the blended context, where learners are often expected to have more control over their learning, preparation for assessment will be key, since learners will have to focus their learning and evaluate their progress in light of the assessment strategy, among other factors.

Within the blended context, the role of assessment as a learning/teaching tool is also fundamental. Assessment feedback becomes a place for dialogue and a basis for the learner's further study, as will be discussed in Chapter 6. In any context, for this to work effectively there needs to be a clear link between learning outcomes, teaching and assessment.

In the blended context, if new tools are considered appropriate for certain tasks within the teaching, this choice of tool and task should be reflected in the assessment strategy. The chapter therefore concludes by exploring in greater depth the use of different assessment tools in blended learning.

Key questions

In approaching assessment design there are a number of key questions that the practitioner working in blended provision might usefully consider:

- What is the role of a particular piece of assessment?
- What referencing and marking system is to be used?

- Where does the assessment fit in the overall assessment strategy?
- When and how is it to be carried out?
- How will the assessment be made valid and reliable?
- What does the assessment aim to measure?
- Who is assessing and who is being assessed?
- What is the best choice of mode for the assessment?
- How can learners be helped to prepare?
- How is quality assurance to be carried out?

The role of assessment

Assessment serves a variety of purposes. Final assessment is a benchmark of achievement for teachers, learners and future employers. Interim assessment, i.e. assessment that happens during the course, helps teachers determine how best to continue supporting learners and enables learners to see what progress they have made. Well-designed assessment is aligned with the course of which it is a part, assessing what has been taught and consolidating progress by allowing learners to apply their learning to a new context, bringing together individual areas of study such as vocabulary, grammar points and skills. In the blended context, how assessment tasks fit in with learning outcomes and levels of achievement needs to be made explicit. Relevant information needs to be made available to learners either on paper or on shared websites to ensure they can make the links between aspects of the course and map their own progress on to this.

A key role for the teacher will also be to help learners perceive assessment as central to learning by showing how preparation, execution of the tasks and the resulting feedback can contribute to language and study skill development. Preparation, for example, involves the learner in strategic engagement with the learning materials, diagnosis of strengths and weaknesses and possibly collaboration with other learners, all of which can be considered crucial in the blended context, where enabling learners to negotiate their own autonomous path through the materials according to their needs is essential (see Chapter 4). The ensuing mark and feedback are important in making explicit the connections between the learner's personal progress, the overall design of the teaching and the learning outcomes. Learner achievements can be mapped on to detailed assessment criteria and learning outcomes.

Referencing systems

Referencing systems describe the outcome of an assessment. A norm-referenced system compares candidates to each other, seeking to achieve a 'normal' distribution of marks. Marks may be adjusted to maintain a regular distribution and show that standards are being maintained over time. While a norm-referenced test is a useful indicator in a competitive situation, it does not allow for fluctuation in ability between cohorts of candidates.

Part of overall mark	Content	100–85 Very good	84–70 Good	69–55 Satisfactory	54–40 Adequate	39–0 Poor
25%	Selection of relevant materials and ideas and appropriate use for task completion	Very good choice of materials and ideas. Entirely appropriate use of materials and ideas	Good choice of materials and ideas. Mostly appropriate use of materials and ideas	Satisfactory choice of materials and ideas. Usually appropriate use of materials and ideas	Adequate choice of materials and ideas. Not always appropriate use of materials and ideas	Choice of materials and ideas does not match the task. Materials and ideas are not used appropriately to complete the task
25%	Structure and synthesis of materials and ideas appropriate to the task	Response is entirely coherent and has a very clear structure throughout. Materials and ideas have been drawn together very skillfully	Response is mostly coherent and has a clear structure throughout. Materials and ideas have been drawn together skillfully	Response is usually coherent and clearly structured in the main. Materials and ideas have been drawn together satisfactorily	Response is not always coherent and does not always have a clear structure. Some attempts at drawing together materials and ideas	Response is not sufficiently coherent nor clearly structured. Little or no drawing together of materials and ideas
Part of overall mark	Language	100–85 Very good	84–70 Good	69–55 Satisfactory	54–40 Adequate	39–0 Poor
25%	Accuracy and range of vocabulary and linguistic structures	Very good accuracy of vocabulary and linguistic structures; good range and variety of vocabulary, complex linguistic structure appropriate to the task	Good accuracy of vocabulary and linguistic structures; very good range and variety of vocabulary, complex linguistic structure appropriate	In the main, accuracy of vocabulary and linguistic structures satisfactory; satisfactory range and variety of vocabulary, linguistic structures appropriate to the task	Accuracy of vocabulary and linguistic structures adequate; adequate range and variety of vocabulary and linguistic structures appropriate to the task	Accuracy of vocabulary and linguistic structures not adequate at this level; range and variety of vocabulary and linguistic structures insufficient to the task
25%	Pronunciation, fluency and intonation	Very good pronunciation, very fluent delivery, intonation very appropriate and accurate throughout	Good pronunciation, fluent delivery, intonation appropriate and accurate throughout	Pronunciation satisfactory, delivery mostly fluent and intonation mostly appropriate and mostly accurate	Pronunciation with errors that at times impede communication, delivery not flowing well, intonation at times inappropriate and inaccurate	Inadequate pronunciation, delivery and intonation not appropriate at this level

Figure 5.1: Marking criteria for speaking tasks at second-year-university level used by the OU.

Nowadays, language assessments mostly use a criterion-referenced system that assesses the candidate against the requirements of the task. An example is provided in Figure 5.1. This measures the candidate performance against different aspects being tested, here 'Content' and 'Language', which are then further divided. Criterion descriptors lay out the different levels candidates might reach. To align teaching and assessment, any criterion-referenced system must reflect the defined learning outcomes of the course and vice versa. Criterion-referencing is therefore a more accurate basis for the self-evaluation learners may have to carry out in blended contexts, since they can clearly see what standard they have achieved and what they are able to do. A norm-referenced assessment may not include descriptors against which the learner can judge her/his performance, or may use descriptors whose absolute value changes year on year, depending on how capable the cohort is overall. This makes it difficult for learners to assess objectively what they are able to do in the language. In blended contexts, which may seek to encourage mutual support outwith teacher-led sessions and include assessed group tasks, criterion-referenced assessment encourages learners to co-operate, since they are not competing against each other.

The final level achieved can be described in a number of ways. Most commonly, an overall mark or grade is assigned. This can be made up of scores for particular tasks or aspects of the test. Alternatively, a descriptive profile may be provided of what a candidate can do, either written by the teacher or referring to pre-written descriptors, as for example in the UK Languages Ladder (Figure 5.2). These descriptors have a summative and a formative purpose, because they function as a level indicator as well as a checklist for learners to identify further learning needs. They can be useful in closing the vital feedback loop in blended courses to help learners make the connections between their own achievement and the standards of the course. As already mentioned, in the blended context learners may have to engage with this reflection autonomously and there is a danger they may progress less well if they cannot make this connection. Assessment criteria and related information can be provided on a shared website together with the assessment tasks, and activities can be set for the learners to engage systematically with criteria to see how they can target their study to achieve particular standards. Here feedback that makes clear links to the descriptors, checklists with 'can-do' statements and self-reflection tasks can provide gradual steps towards making such a connection (see Chapter 6).

Reading		
Breakthrough	Grade 1	I can recognise and read out a few familiar words and phrases.
	Grade 2	I can understand familiar written phrases.
	Grade 3	I can understand the main point(s) from a short written text in clear printed script.

Figure 5.2: Asset languages, descriptor of learner's reading attainment at Breakthrough Level.

The nature of assessment

A course assessment strategy lays down how the standards of performance are assessed, that is, which marking system and what tasks are used, how many assessments there are and at what stages in the course. In some blended programmes, the strategy may stipulate more frequent ongoing assessment to offer regular checks of learners' progress in independent study and provide learners with feedback.

A general distinction is often made between summative and formative assessment. The purpose of summative assessment is usually to test achievement at the end of a unit of study, with the outcome counting towards the award for that course. Formative or diagnostic assessment may test the same unit of work but be used to diagnose what has been successfully learned and what needs further revision. Marks or grades here, if awarded, are unlikely to count towards the overall course qualification. Many pieces of assessment, however, may in fact serve both purposes.

Formative assessments need not be teacher-mediated only. In a blended programme, learners may post pieces of work on a forum for comment by other learners as well as the teacher. In some cases these might serve as preparatory work for later summative assessments. In contexts that involve a lot of independent study the teacher will need to provide clear feedback and 'feed-forward', that is, advice that focuses on how to progress. This advice can also be a springboard for a dialogue between teacher and learner, covering how the learner can address immediate study needs, preparation for future assessments and clarification of specific language issues (see Chapter 6).

Particular parts of the assessment strategy may be given different weightings, reflecting their relative importance in the learning outcomes or their timing in the course. An early assessment may have a low weighting to give the learner a chance to become familiar with assessment methods, for example. The formality of the assessment context can also vary. Informal assessments may consist of teacher observations carried out unobtrusively. Sometimes a portfolio of tasks may be put together by the learner retrospectively. Blended courses involving the use of a range of teaching modes and tools give learners a variety of ways to gather evidence of their language skills: for example, in their portfolio learners may include forum postings or recordings of online discussions carried out during their course. Formal assessments tend to be defined more clearly in scope, content and timing. They are assessed tasks or exams carried out under formal conditions, invigilated carefully with restricted reference materials and strict time limits.

Assessment may be ongoing/continuous, final or a mixture of both. Ongoing or continuous assessment consists of a number of smaller formal or informal tasks throughout a course, the outcomes of which are added together. A final assessment is usually a more formal extensive task, project or examination at the end of a course covering all the content and having a higher weighting than the individual components of the ongoing or continuous assessment.

Assessment opportunities are also defined by who sets, administers and marks an assessment. Assessments can be designed and set by an examination body, the institution itself, a subject or course leader or the teacher. While in some teaching settings one teacher may undertake all or most of a group's teaching, in blended contexts different elements of teaching and assessment may be shared between the self-study materials and the teacher or teachers. As a result, teachers need to have a clear understanding of the following so that they can facilitate learner understanding:

- the evidence to be presented by candidates, i.e. what tasks must be completed and when;
- the overall standards needed for final marks or levels, i.e. how different assessment tasks combine to give an overall score;
- the elements to be considered in different categories of marking;
- the pass mark;
- the highest mark possible;
- different divisions: e.g. merit, distinction;
- whether particular weightings are given to different tasks or criteria.

With this knowledge, teachers can help learners on blended programmes to make strategic decisions about how they prioritise their study.

Designing assessment fit for purpose

Validity and reliability

It is important in the blended context to have a clear understanding of reliability and validity so that these concepts are not ignored when transferring assessment from more traditional teaching environments. Validity is concerned with whether a test measures what it is supposed to measure. Does it:

- assess what has been taught?
- assess what it claims to assess?
- assess the content at the right level for this stage of the course?
- assess skills and content appropriate to learners' needs?
- use assessment tools appropriate to the task and reflective of those used in the teaching mode?

Where blended teaching makes use of online tools, assessment should also do so to constructively align it with the teaching (Biggs, 1999) and to make it authentic (Torrance, 1995). Ideally, the blend used in assessment should reflect the blend used in teaching and learning. Teachers involved in designing the assessment strategy for a blended course will also want to consider how this affects the level of skill that learners can be expected to achieve. For instance, while interactive speaking can be practised and assessed to a high level in a classroom-based course, it may be inappropriate to expect the same level in a blended context, where learners may spend more time working on their own or interacting via written forums. If learners perceive the assessment to be invalid because they are tested on aspects they have not covered, or are asked to engage in tasks using unfamiliar or inappropriate modes and tools, this may lead to demotivation regarding both the assessment and the learners' overall attitude to language learning.

Motivation has been described as an interaction between the perceived probability of success and the value of obtaining the goal (Eccles *et al.*, 1983; Wigfield and Eccles, 1992; Wigfield, 1994). Teachers need to explain why a particular skill is relevant and important for the learner, and to demonstrate how it contributes to the learner's ultimate goal in her/his language study. In blended programmes, teachers also need to ensure that learners understand why certain tasks are carried out in certain modes. Well-designed assessment will match task to mode and in many instances reflect common practice in the outside world. For example, where interaction is tested online, learners can be helped to appreciate that communication regularly takes place online in certain day-to-day contexts, and that language courses will reflect this. Using email, web forms or telephone for assessment may reflect the fact that, for example, booking hotel rooms, car hire or appointments in advance is more likely to use one of these forms of communication rather than a face-to-face conversation, as favoured by more traditional forms of assessment.

While validity is concerned with getting the right assessment, reliability is concerned with getting the assessment right (Reece and Walker, 2007, p. 331). A reliable assessment will be a consistent measure irrespective of when, where and by whom it is applied. A test assessing similar learners, in different places, at different times and marked by different examiners should produce similar results.

Assessing performance or knowledge of the language system

A distinction is often made between system-referenced and performance-referenced assessment tasks. The former test the learners' knowledge of the linguistic system (for example, grammar or vocabulary through gap-fill or matching exercises), while the latter focus on actual use of the language (for example, in writing an email). Performance is typically tested in the four language skills: the receptive skills of listening and reading, and the productive skills of speaking and writing. These can be assessed individually or in an integrated manner. In individual skill assessment, learners might listen to an audio clip and carry out comprehension checks by answering questions or evaluating true/false statements. In an integrated skills assessment, learners use the content of the stimulus to produce more language (for example, writing an email to pass on some of the information gleaned from what they have heard or read). The term 'authentic assessment' is sometimes used to describe tasks that closely mirror real-world usage. If languages are taught with a particular target audience in mind (for example, business people), tasks can be set to test the skills needed in context (for example, simulation of an online business meeting).

Some tasks require learners to transfer skills and knowledge acquired in one teaching mode or context to another. Writing a blog entry, for example, requires learners to choose the correct tense from those studied across a unit of work. The more transfer required, the harder it can be for learners to perceive a connection between what they have studied and the content of the test. In blended programmes it is particularly important for teachers to ensure that these links are made explicit in the task requirements: for example, by stating that learners must use the appropriate tense, verb forms, vocabulary; or by referring learners to specific sections of material, work in another mode or a preparatory 'can-do' checklist. Tasks can be scaffolded or divided into stages to help learners build up to a final integrated task. Preparation may also involve the posting of drafts or practice tasks to obtain peer feedback.

The requirement to apply what has been learned can be motivating for learners, as it indicates whether they can use the language in a quasi real-life situation. Subsequent feedback, especially for learners working more independently in a blended context, must comment on the integration and the learners' ability to transfer. When assessing integrated tasks, it can be difficult for the teacher to see where problems lie and provide appropriately targeted feedback. A learner may produce a poor written task, for example, because of inadequate writing skills or poor comprehension of the input material. To aid error analysis and feedback, it is helpful to structure tasks so that each step of the process is recorded, even if marks are not separately awarded.

Who assesses, who is assessed?

Traditionally, assessments were set, administered and marked by teachers and assessors. In all teaching contexts, changes in teaching approaches (for example, learner pairwork and groupwork, self-study and online working) require new approaches to assessment, taking account of the learner's more active role.

Peer assessment

The online component of a blended programme offers a variety of opportunities for learners to post examples of their written work and record spoken or written discussions. In peer assessment other learners are involved in allotting all or part of the mark for a task. This requires clear and fair parameters giving guidance on the aspects to be assessed and the approach to be taken. These could be provided in advance or decided jointly by the group. To avoid the potentially anxiety-provoking nature of peer assessment, teachers may ask candidates to select for themselves a particular aspect for consideration. Often it is easier and fairer for fellow learners to address non-linguistic issues such as level of contribution to a discussion rather than to expect them to judge standards of language produced. Peer assessment can be restricted to formative feedback, even to the good qualities of a particular performance. Conversely, the recipient of the comments might ask for a focus on areas that s/he feels may need improvement. Chapter 6 will consider how learners can benefit from peer assessment.

Self-assessment

Learners need to be encouraged to self-assess and evaluate their strengths and weaknesses so that in combination with teacher feedback they can target their learning appropriately. Self-assessment opportunities can be built into learning materials or assessment briefs and can promote the internalisation of assessment criteria. Fostering this internal quality control could be considered the ultimate goal of feedback (Sadler, 1989) and is strongly associated with increased learner autonomy.

There are different kinds of self-assessment. Receptive language skills, grammar and vocabulary can be checked with gap-fill, multiple-choice, true/false statements, for example, on paper or online, and learners can use these informally (for example, at the end of a self-study unit). An answer key with generic feedback and explanations can be provided, and may direct learners to reference or teaching materials. Some learners may like to repeat tasks at a later stage to monitor progress. Productive language skills are difficult to self-assess fully, but learners can be trained to check their work (for example, by being given generic or task-related checklists) (see Figure 5.3). Informal reflection to help with internalisation can be carried out with self-assessment checklists referring back to whole chunks of work (for example, using 'can do' statements or a learning log, or by comparing stated learning outcomes given at the start of a unit of learning with capabilities at the end of it).

¡Comprueba!

When you have written your message, ask yourself:
- **Have I covered all the points asked for in the instructions?**

Check your message carefully, paying particular attention to:
- **appropriate forms of the verbs ser, tener, estar, estudiar and hablar**
- **gender and noun agreements**
- **vocabulary**
- **spelling**

Figure 5.3: Self-assessment checklist provided as part of an OU assessment task

Co-operative and collaborative assessment

Co-operative and collaborative assessment is not new, but in blended contexts the ways in which learners work together with or without teacher input are likely to be more varied. These may include face-to-face, telephone or online communication tools, such as forums, blogs, wikis and online audio-graphic or audiovisual meeting rooms. Where co-operative and collaborative learning is part of the blend, assessment can also be group-based. In co-operative assessment learners carry out a task together, but individual performances are assessed separately (for example, learners might be asked to discuss a picture, as in the Cambridge First Certificate in English as a Foreign Language. In collaborative assessment, learners work together planning and contributing to an assessment task with a joint outcome (for example, designing a tourist guide, for which a common mark may be awarded).

In both cases, teachers and learners need to understand how the work as a whole and each individual's contribution are assessed. Some learners enjoy working in teams and feel reassured by the contribution or encouragement of others, while others find this more daunting, particularly if previous educational experiences have not included this. Co-ordination and teamwork can also be problematic, especially when nobody is prepared to assume overall responsibility (Murphy *et al.*, 2009). Other potential difficulties may involve disparities in the quality or quantity of individual contributions, personality clashes, or a reluctance on the part of some learners to criticise or be criticised by their peers.

Some of these issues can be pre-empted by careful assessment design. Testing of transferable skills such as teamwork and discussion skills can be built into the task. Learners can be asked to collaborate on task preparation but produce individual pieces of work. Learners need to know how to acknowledge contributions from others appropriately (for example, if referring to comments from a forum or blog). In blended teaching, collaborative and co-operative assessment should arise naturally out of a context where learners have been working together using similar tools for similar tasks.

It can be challenging to design an assessment that encourages collaboration but does not depend on full contributions from everyone or does not unfairly penalise a learner for the failings of others. Teachers will want to explain to learners how they can benefit from collaborative assessment and to provide a clear framework in advance for addressing learners' questions such as:

- Is there a free structure, or will an outline be provided?
- Is everyone contributing to the whole document, or are sections to be shared out?
- How many sections must each person contribute?
- Are learners expected to edit work from others or only comment on it?
- What is the minimum number of comments each learner should make?
- How is it ensured that each learner receives at least some comments from others?
- Is the learner group expected to self-manage, or will the teacher moderate their interaction?
- How is the use of the target language checked: by authors only, by peers or general feedback from the teacher?
- Is an overall mark given and/or is each contributor marked on their contribution?

Final feedback on the assessment activity can be given generically and/or individually as appropriate. There might be generic feedback on the overall product and individual feedback on learners' own contributions. In blended programmes where there may be fewer opportunities for *ad hoc* individual feedback, any decision to provide generic feedback only would need to be taken carefully.

Using appropriate tools for assessment in blended contexts

Allen (2009) suggests that traditional forms of assessment, such as essays, presentations and learner-centred discussions, will appear inauthentic if they are merely transferred rather than adapted to the online environment. He cautions that the use of tools should reflect how learners use them in everyday life. Since, however, the language classroom has traditionally been a place of 'otherness', where learners engage in role-plays and simulations to develop linguistic competence so they can function in a range of situations in the future, learners are accustomed to some inauthenticity in the present as preparation for potential realities. What is crucial is that tasks are set that suit the tools, mirror how people interact with them in real-world usage, and that the methods used for assessment align with teaching modes and how learners are used to working.

Assessing speaking in blended learning

The assessment of speaking will reflect not only elements of the blend but also the appropriateness of certain tasks to certain modes and tools. The assessment strategy for speaking may in fact need to include a variety of modes. Real-time audio and/or video conferencing via Skype (www.skype.com) or Elluminate (www.elluminate.com), for example, allows for interactive speaking assessments. These can be conducted in pairs or groups, with or without teacher participation. It may be that some learners have little experience of real-life spoken communication using online technologies or telephone group conferencing, so even for those who have used these tools during their studies their familiarity with the conventions, levels of confidence and belief in their authenticity may be low. Learners need to be assured that due regard is paid to the difference between this and face-to-face communication: for example, difficulties in interpreting learners' silence without visual clues may require the assessor to allow longer for learners to answer. Teachers may also need to provide written guidance to supplement experience of the tool during the course: for example, outlining online conventions such as using the 'raise hand' icon before speaking. However, it can be argued that this is no different from asserting protocols for face-to-face meetings.

Task design and assessment criteria will need to be adapted to take account of the fact that learners being assessed online are able to consult preparatory work and reference materials during the test. While technology may be a barrier for some, because of concerns about its possible malfunction or lack of confidence in its use, the relative anonymity of online communications can help others feel less anxious in interactive tasks (De Los Arcos *et al.*, 2009).

Learners can also be assessed on their speaking performance in recorded presentations, either using audio-based tools alone or supporting a presentation with visuals such as PowerPoint. Another possibility might be to use computer-generated spoken questions, to which learners record their responses. The audio tool Learnosity (www.learnosity.com) allows learners to use mobile or landline telephones or Skype to access such questions and to record their answers. It has been successfully trialled for tests in the Irish language in six schools in Northern Ireland and the Republic of Ireland (Keogh and Ní Mhurchú, 2009; Cooney, 2010) and for French at the OU (Cooney, 2010). The teacher, the learner and peers can all be given access to recordings. Comparing their evaluation of their own performance with the views of others can help learners to gauge their performance realistically against the assessment criteria and set themselves achievable goals.

Assessing writing in blended contexts

As in other contexts, learners on blended courses may be asked to write an individual assessment task, or to formally collaborate or co-operate on a task. In both scenarios an appropriate tool has to be chosen. Choice may be governed by what tool is appropriate for the particular piece of writing in question, whether learners are producing an individual piece of work informed by peer comments, whether two or more learners are collaborating on a project or whether the aim is to produce a joint text by a number of contributors.

Sending documents by email attachment is a useful tool for learners to gather peer feedback on a document, as others can insert comments and return the document directly to the author for reflection. This approach can also work for collaborative writing between two people, who might gather comments from peers as well as each other. More discussion can be had if the document is posted in a shared area where contributors update versions of the document as they react to comments from others, but the document can become unwieldy if comments are kept visible. Other tools facilitate this process. Blogs allow learners to publish a portfolio including images, and readers can add comments. If learners are producing a piece of work on the same topic, forums allow them to share documents and discuss items in various threads. Constructing an assessed text between more than two people, however, is best done using a wiki (see Chapter 12). With a normal word-processed document, it can be difficult to keep track of and acknowledge contributions from individuals. A wiki includes an editing facility and a history (see Figure 5.4), so the stages through which a document has passed can be seen. Some wikis also include the facility to comment.

In any of these formats, contributions can be assessed. Equally, learners can be asked to explain in a reflective piece how they used the feedback. This can encourage them to engage actively with feedback and learn from it. When working with asynchronous tools learners do not need to be present at the same time, but enough

The table below displays all changes that have been made to the current page.

You can view old versions or see what changed in a particular version. If you want to compare any two versions, select the relevant checkboxes and click 'Compare selected'.

Date	Time	Actions	Changed by	Compare
17 May 2010	08:21	View (changes 17 May 2010 08:21)	Ruth Grenville	Select 17 May 2010 08:21 ☐
14 May 2010	15:08	View Revert (changes 14 May 2010 15:08)	Umar Ahmed	Select 14 May 2010 15:08 ☐
	15:05	View Revert (changes 14 May 2010 15:05)	Anna Johnson	Select 14 May 2010 15:05 ☐
	14:38	View Revert (changes 14 May 2010 14:38)	Dena Attar	Select 14 May 2010 14:38 ☐
	13:45	View Revert	Simon Rosenthal	Select 14 May 2010 13:45 ☐

Figure 5.4: Example of a wiki editing history page.

time should be allowed for them to contribute sufficiently. Synchronous online tools that allow document sharing can also be used to compose a written product jointly, so that discussions can be more immediate and spontaneous. Such discussions can be written or spoken, for example, via Office Communicator (www.office.microsoft.com/en-us/communicator) or Elluminate (www.elluminate.com), and they can be recorded and assessed, if appropriate.

Although teachers and peers may have easy access to all the steps taken by learners in collaborative assessment, it is important not to over-assess. If learners feel that every online interaction is going to be critically evaluated, this can militate against the benefits of collaboration and make learners self-conscious and anxious.

Assessing receptive skills in blended contexts

As in any context, receptive skills may be assessed individually or as part of integrated skills assessment tasks. In the latter, learners may produce ideas or language based on comprehension of spoken or written input and may be credited with understanding this in their output in writing or speaking.

In blended courses, online quizzes can be produced to reflect a range of question types commonly used in paper-based assessment, including matching sentence halves, true/false, multiple choice, reordering of paragraphs and gap-fill, all of which can be marked by computer and to which instant feedback can be provided. Depending on the software used, automated feedback can be written at a range of levels to:

- indicate right/wrong;
- provide the correct answer;
- refer the learner to the relevant section of the input material;
- provide the target language answer as spoken/written in the input material;

- direct the learner to relevant study support.

Such quizzes can also form part of an integrated skills assessment, having the benefit of making available to the teacher a record of what the learner can understand.

Facilitating the assessment process in blended learning

In many traditional teaching settings, teachers continuously make judgements about how well learners have understood teaching content and can perform various tasks. Before a formal assessment, they can ensure that appropriate material and skills are covered to address specific weaknesses. In addition, learners will have frequent opportunities to discuss how best to prepare and follow up any issues from the assessment feedback. In blended contexts, where direct contact between teacher and learner may be reduced, the teacher needs to ensure that the assessment process facilitates a dialogue and provides the learner with the tools necessary for adequate preparation and successful learning from the feedback (see Chapter 6). Effective use of the time leading up to the assessment will enable the learner to approach the assessment with the necessary skills and knowledge.

Learner preparation for assessment

To prepare effectively, learners need to know exactly what they are expected to do, and the teacher will have a role in communicating this clearly. An assessment brief will typically include some or all of the following:

- the assessment title;
- the purpose of the assessment;
- learning outcomes;
- dates and other details for submission;
- materials required and/or permitted;
- time and/or word limits;
- marking criteria;
- details of the assessment task itself;
- details of resources to support preparation;
- for collaborative tasks, clear guidance on the various stages and roles of participants.

In addition to general guidance, learners need direction about where to focus their individual efforts. Some courses include review sections in their materials, while, in others, the teacher or learner may need to plan appropriate tasks. A teacher-moderated task might be a forum activity in which learners contribute postings. The teacher can give general feedback and a list of resources or course references from which individual learners select what applies to them. Forums or blogs can be used for peer support. Self- or computer-mediated quizzes can be supplemented with resource references that learners follow up according to individual need. An audit of skills required to complete the assessment (Murphy, 2007) can help learners to reflect on their previous learning and personal strengths and weaknesses, and to draw up an action plan based on one or two priorities specific to the assessment task ahead. All these activities are a form of scaffolding (Ridley, 1997) towards independence in addressing their own learning needs.

Research suggests that the lack of instant *ad hoc* feedback from teachers is one of the greatest causes of anxiety among learners in blended distance contexts, causing frustration and demotivation (Hurd and Fernández-Toro, 2009). This can be particularly so in the time leading up to an assessment. Online communication tools can be of help by facilitating regular contact between teachers and learners and peer support from other learners.

Quality assurance in blended teaching

In blended programmes, teachers may often work in greater physical isolation from each other than in traditional settings, particularly where distance or open learning is at stake. Online tools, however, facilitate co-operation, collaboration and sharing of good practice, and these tools can be harnessed in the quality assurance process. In any teaching context, the institution or awarding body will need to approve the processes in place. Scores may be recorded on an online system, allowing easy generation of statistical information. Reliability can be checked through a comparison of test scores from year to year, between groups, between markers and even between institutions. In many cases, a teacher's assessment decisions will be verified by colleagues, marking team leaders, external examiners or by an internal or external examination board. This can involve second marking of all or a sample of assessments. Within an institution, colleagues may agree or average a final grade. Where an examination board or external examiners are involved, moderation may result in all the marks being adjusted. In blended programmes, the various modes in use for teaching can also facilitate teacher participation in discussions and ensure distribution of relevant information, so that teachers can develop their future practice accordingly.

As well as ensuring the standard of marking, attention needs to be paid to the quality of feedback. A second marker can offer constructive advice on the style and content of the teacher's feedback to help her/him to identify areas for reflection and development. Again, teachers can use the same online collaborative tools in the blend to share experiences and evaluate and develop their performance as assessors.

A further and invaluable source of information to the teacher is feedback from the learner (see Chapter 7). Institutions may ask learners to complete satisfaction questionnaires or teachers may survey their learners themselves. Teachers can thus investigate learner responses to the assessment strategy, preparation and feedback. Research has shown that there may be a stark contrast between a teacher's perceptions and the reality of how her/his feedback is received (Maclellen, 2001). Learners' comments may equally uncover problems with the constructive alignment (Biggs,

1999) between a teacher's intentions and learners' perceptions, or between teaching and learning, and assessment design. This information can be used by teachers to adapt their practice appropriately.

Conclusion

This chapter has outlined the concepts underlying assessment and explored how assessment can be tailored to the blended contexts. It has considered how new technologies in the blend can be used to offer opportunities for contact between the teacher and the learner and among learners themselves. It has shown how various tools can be used for alternative forms of assessment, such as collaborative tasks and peer or self-assessment. It has touched on the importance of feedback in developing a dialogue between learner and teacher. The next chapter explores in depth how teachers can provide effective feedback on assessment and use this as a teaching tool, aiding learner progress and development of study skills.

Chapter 6:   Teaching Through Assessment

María-Rosa Amoraga-Piqueras, Anna Comas-Quinn and Margaret Southgate

Introduction

This chapter will address in detail the way in which assessment can be exploited as a teaching and learning tool. It includes a discussion of what constitutes good teaching when providing assessment feedback to language learners, and the role of such feedback in establishing a teacher–learner dialogue. The chapter offers practical advice on how teachers can best provide feedback on writing and speaking tasks and also addresses the challenges of giving feedback in new forms of assessment, such as computer-marked tasks as well as peer and collaborative assessment.

The role of assessment feedback in blended contexts

Research has shown that good-quality feedback is the most powerful factor in improving learning (Hattie, 1987; Black and Wiliam, 1998), so, whether assessment is formative or summative, it should include feedback on the learner's performance. More importantly, in blends where opportunities for face-to-face contact between teachers and learners are limited, feedback on work submitted can be a key component in the teacher–learner dialogue as well as being an essential part of the teaching and learning process.

Feedback should include a comparison between the learner's performance and the reference level, and an indication of how the learner can bridge the gap between the two. Ramaprasad (1983, p. 3) defines feedback as 'information about the gap between the actual level and the reference level of a system parameter which is used to alter the gap in some way'. The comments must aim 'to help the student to reconstruct her/his knowledge, understanding or skills such that it is closer to what is desired' (Walker, 2009, p. 68). Vygotsky's 'zone of proximal development' (ZPD) is a useful concept in illustrating that learners can close the gap and achieve a better performance through working with the teacher or with more knowledgeable peers (Vygotsky, 1978, p. 86) than on their own.

Feedback useful to learners will provide guidance that pushes them further in their understanding, but will not stretch them beyond what they are capable of grasping at the time. Some learners do not make use of feedback because of difficulties understanding it, so teachers need to acknowledge that learners will have to 'construct actively their own understanding of feedback messages from tutors' in order to internalise them (Nicol and Macfarlane-Dick, 2004, p. 3). It is easier for learners to do this and the feedback becomes more usable (Hyland, 2001; Walker, 2009) when feedback includes an explanation rather than simply indicating or correcting problems.

Feedback must not confine itself to content and retrospective corrections of learners' work, but should be part of a continuing dialogue (Nicolson, 2010) to help them improve their performance. It should include an element of 'feed-forward' or guidance on how to reduce future gaps in their knowledge, understanding or skills (Walker, 2009). For example, Hyland (2001) suggests that language learners particularly value grammar explanations as they can use this information to avoid mistakes in future work. Good-quality feedback and feed-forward will inform learners' reflective observation and abstract conceptualisation as outlined in Kolb's (1984) experiential learning cycle, an adaptation of which, relating to assessment tasks, is shown in Figure 6.1 (adapted from Baxter et al., 2009, p. 14).

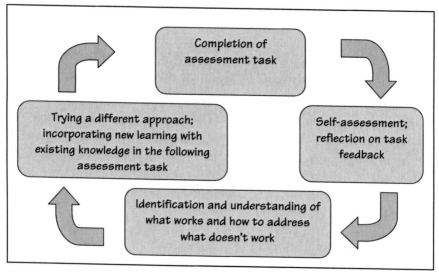

Figure 6.1: Feedback and feed-forward mapped onto Kolb's experiential learning cycle (Baxter et al., 2009, p. 14).

Research has shown that for feedback to be of good quality and usable it has to: be detailed, frequent enough and timely; concentrate on the learners' performance; be appropriate to the task and the learners' understanding of it; and be attended to and acted upon by the learner (Gibbs and Simpson, 2004–5). In addition, it should encourage positive motivational beliefs and self-esteem, teacher and peer dialogue, and should facilitate reflection in learning (Nicol and Macfarlane-Dick, 2004).

Affective factors such as motivation, anxiety and identity have been shown to have a powerful influence on the effectiveness of language learning (Hurd, 2008a; Dörnyei and Ushioda, 2009), so teachers need to recognise the key role that positive feedback plays in supporting and encouraging language learners (Hyland, 2001; Walker, 2009). Feedback that covers skills, particularly language learning skills, as well as content can also play an important part in the development of learners' autonomy (Nicol and Macfarlane-Dick, 2004; Murphy, 2007; Dyke, 2008).

When feedback is accompanied by a numerically marked or graded assessment of the learner's work the two have to be consistent, even though they are trying to achieve different things. Marks and grades reflect how the learner's performance compares against objective criteria, while feedback is personalised to support learning and progress for each individual learner. Marks and grades without feedback or feedback that is not consistent with the mark/grade given can have a negative impact on the learner's self-confidence and sense of competence (Gibbs and Simpson, 2004–5).

Establishing a teacher–learner dialogue

This section will address the practicalities of facilitating a productive dialogue between teacher and learner(s), in both written and spoken modes, both with individual learners and with the learner group as a whole.

First steps

The initial steps in establishing dialogue between teacher and learner need to be taken at the start of the course. If the course is to be conducted mainly or entirely online or by telephone, with few opportunities for face-to-face meetings, the teacher will wish to send an introductory message or perhaps speak to each learner individually by telephone or online to begin the process. Although in some blended contexts there may be initial group meetings where the teacher can give general guidance to the group, it would be inappropriate for each learner to discuss their individual concerns with the teacher there. Teachers may find it helpful to give or send a form to learners at the start of a course inviting them to express their aims and any worries they have.

Any information that the learner provides about their aims in studying a language, and their concerns about completing the course, will need to be taken into consideration when providing assessment feedback. The teacher's approach to providing feedback will depend on awareness of each learner's circumstances. If the teacher knows that a particular learner has limited study time and aims to do just what is necessary to pass the course, feedback may have to focus more on the key learning points only, so that the learner concentrates their efforts, whereas feedback to a time-rich learner who needs a little help with more basic points may include guidance on extension learning beyond the confines of the course materials (Nicolson, 2010).

The tone of teacher feedback

The tone of the teacher's feedback will be significant in allowing learners to feel comfortable about continuing the dialogue and asking for further clarification if they feel unsure. In the case of weaker learners a balance has to be found between the need to give positive encouragement and the need to provide an honest assessment of their strengths and weaknesses. To avoid discouraging or demoralising a learner, feedback could be couched in terms such as:

- You succeeded in ….;
- You may wish to consider … / Have you considered …?
- You may find it helpful to have another look at /listen again to …;
- It might have been better/clearer to …;
- Perhaps you could have expressed [X] like this …

Learner development

Teachers of languages in blends that rely heavily on assessment feedback as a teaching mechanism will need to devote attention to developing each learner's ability to learn through assessment and the associated feedback. Some learners, for example, may regard assessments purely as a means of obtaining grades and passing the course, taking little notice of comments and corrections.

Some institutions provide guidance for learners on planning an assessment task. The OU, for example, has provided for learners the model shown in Figure 6.2 (The Open University, 2007, p. 13). For the purposes of this chapter, the first and last stages, 'your strategy' and 'getting it back', are of particular significance, although teachers may find that they need to provide guidance to inexperienced learners on each of the seven stages.

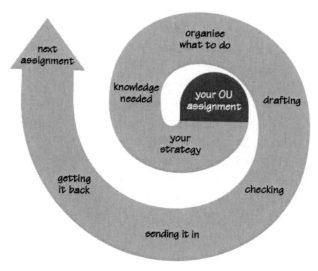

Figure 6.2: The seven stages of planning an assignment.

All but the most experienced language learners will need specific guidance on how to engage in an assessment-related dialogue as they work through the stages of completing the assigned task. Learners may need to be made aware of the value of letting the teacher know about any specific difficulties experienced during the process. One tool of help to learners in focusing their thoughts is a self-assessment document that they can complete and submit with the task to be marked. The example shown in Figure 6.3, Part 1, is based on a form originally also available in both L1 and L2 at the OU (Murphy, 2007), which allows the learner to share her/his personal priorities, strengths and weaknesses, and equips the teacher to provide targeted feedback.

Learning from assignments

Please fill in Part 1 and send it with your assignment.
Fill in Part 2 when it is returned with your assignment.

Part 1 - Self-assessment

1. The skills which I have chosen to work on for this assignment (my priorities):

2. Things I think I have done well in the assignment, and why:

3. Things which I think I had difficulty with in the assignment, and why:

4. Other comments/questions:

Part 2 - Reflection

1. Summary of my tutor's comments on this assignment:

    Good points:

    Things to work on:

2. Skills I am now going to try and improve on:

3. I intend to improve in these areas by doing the following:

You will find it helpful to refer to this sheet as you work towards your next assignment.

Figure 6.3: 'Learning from assignments' sheet.

Equally important is the need for learners to devote time to working carefully through the teacher's feedback and revisiting any parts of the course to which the teacher refers them for remedial or extension work. Teachers may find it useful to provide written guidance outlining what learners might do when a marked assessment is returned. OU research into use of feedback by learners on beginners' language courses found that those who used feedback strategically, integrating it into the learning process, were more confident and more likely to maintain long-term motivation. Those who took little account of it or did not use it strategically were less confident and motivated (Furnborough and Truman, 2009). The reflection section of the sheet shown in Figure 6.3, Part 2, therefore encourages learners to reflect, in the light of the teacher's feedback, on:

- what worked well;
- what might have worked better;
- what the learner intends to focus on for the future.

It may be useful to encourage learners to understand learning through assessment feedback as a process that continues throughout their language learning, with each piece of work produced building on previous learning. They may need to be shown that the cycle in Figure 6.2 does not end with 'getting it back', but points forward to future assessments. Progression will be supported if the teacher provides guidance on how the learner can move forward, developing the study skills essential for the independent learner and the language skills that form the building blocks for future progress. Teachers whose general feedback includes a summary of the learner's progress since the last piece of assessed work and who commend learners for putting into practice what was recommended in earlier feedback (or point out failings in this regard) will help to develop and foster this sense of progression.

Managing expectations

Expectations can differ in a variety of ways. Learners, teachers and quality assurers may each have different views on what can be expected as far as feedback on assessment is concerned (Nicolson and Gallastegi, 2006). Some institutions may determine as a matter of policy whether teachers are expected to correct and explain every error, or whether some element of self-correction is expected of the learners. Other institutions may leave the teacher and learner to negotiate the level of correction suitable for the individual learner. Where there is to be an element of self-correction, learners need to be made aware of what is expected of them. Furthermore, each individual learner will have different expectations. Differences in learning styles and in priorities will lead to a variety of attitudes and responses to assessment feedback (Furnborough and Truman, 2009). Teachers will therefore need to be sensitive to such expectations and respect each individual's position.

Learners can justifiably expect to receive feedback on their assessment promptly. If feedback is slow to arrive, learners may move on to work associated with the next assessment rather than seriously considering the feedback on the last one. If a learner is required to submit a draft for comment in preparation for a later assessment, s/he will recognise that acting on feedback is essential, but it is less obvious when there is no explicit link between one assessment and the next. Teachers need to show that ideally they expect learners to use every assessment to feed into the next, even if only at the level of developing the ability to assimilate and apply new language patterns. A simple way of further promoting a sense of dialogue is for the teacher, at the end of the feedback, to invite contact for further clarification if necessary.

In managing expectations, teachers also need to specify the preferred mode of communication for the ongoing dialogue about assessment feedback. In some blends, the teacher may specify a physical or online location where s/he can be contacted at designated times, either by appointment or at a drop-in session. In others, s/he may invite learners to telephone or email, specifying times when calls can be taken, or indicating the usual response time for email queries.

While progressing towards autonomy (see Chapter 4), learners may also approach teachers for extra support. It is therefore advisable from the outset to be clear about boundaries, and to make learners aware of what support is or is not available. A teacher who devotes some time initially to managing learners' expectations and guiding them towards taking responsibility for their own learning will be less likely to be overburdened by learners' demands for detailed help at a later stage.

Spoken feedback

Specific issues relating to the provision of feedback on spoken assignments will be addressed below. It is also useful for teachers to consider the value of spoken feedback on *written* work. All such feedback may be provided as a separate audio file, an embedded recording in an electronic document or by using an application such as Jing (see 'Using embedded audio comments', p. 88).

A written document may be the most suitable medium for providing detailed feedback, as the learner can easily refer to this when completing later pieces of work. However, no matter how careful the teacher is in choosing an appropriate tone, there remains a danger that the learner may misinterpret written feedback as personal criticism. Recorded spoken feedback is therefore valuable in providing encouragement. The 2008 'Sounds Good' project at Leeds Metropolitan University shows that hearing the reassuring, encouraging tone of a teacher's voice enriched the learner experience and added a personal dimension to the teacher–learner dialogue. Spoken comments allowed the teacher to express nuances that were difficult to convey through written comments (Rotheram, 2009). For example, the relative importance of issues raised could be made clearer (Dixon, 2009), while explanations could be phrased in ways not normally adopted in written feedback.

Group feedback

Group feedback can take several forms. If the blend offers a synchronous session after the return of an assessment, general feedback to the group may be offered there, focusing on common problems or issues arising from the assessment. Learners could raise questions about the last assessment (which other learners may be able to answer) or tell the group what they learned from it. To reduce the time learners spend silently listening, the teacher may include some general remedial tasks in the programme for the session, or invite learners to discuss solutions to common problems in small groups.

Those teaching languages in blends that rely on distance teaching may choose to prepare a feedback summary sheet or an audio recording of common repeated errors and problems and make it available to all learners to complement specific feedback on individual work. It can be a source of encouragement to struggling learners to find that they are not alone in experiencing certain difficulties.

Amount and nature of feedback

Language courses have clearly identified learning outcomes: for example, the subject-specific knowledge that a learner is expected to acquire and understand by the end of the course, and the skills to be developed. Research shows that feedback which contains comments related to skills development has the most effect on learners' work (Walker, 2007, p. 3).

Level and depth of feedback

Ramaprasad's definition of feedback (1983, p. 3) points to the notion that usable feedback consists of four possible components, which are referred to here as 'levels':

- Level 1 informs the learner about her/his competence in a topic based on her/his performance in an assessment task (the actual level of the system parameter).
- Level 2 comments on the desired knowledge, understanding or skill (the reference level of the system parameter).
- Level 3 compares the learner's knowledge, understanding or skill with the desired knowledge, understanding or skill. This level of feedback provides the learner with information about the gap between the actual level and the reference level.
- Level 4: offers advice on how to reduce or close the gap (feed-forward comments).

Brown and Glover (2006, pp. 83–4) classify comments by depth. Their classification takes into consideration comments referring to content and skills development as well as motivating comments. Figure 6.4 illustrates the depth of comment in relation to the levels of usable feedback in a table, based on work by Walker (2007) which combines both these classifications.

Level of usable feedback (Ramaprasad, 1983, p. 3)	Depth of comment in relation to skills and motivation (Brown and Glover, 2006, p. 83)	Content and skills development comments	Motivating comments
Level 1 states learner's level of competence	Depth 1	Indication of error	Indication of successful work
Levels 1 and 2 indicate gap/ good work but learner has to deduce how to bridge gap and what was good about the work	Depth 2	Correction of error	Amplified praise for successful work
Levels 1, 2, 3, 4 inform learner of her/his actual level in comparison with the reference level, indicate that there is a gap and explain how to close it. They also indicate and explain what is good about the work	Depth 3	Correction and explanation of error	Explanation of why work was successful

Figure 6.4: Levels of usable feedback and depth of comment.

From Figure 6.4 it can be deduced that the most useful feedback comments are those in the depth 3 category. They give learners a clear indication of their level of language skill competence in comparison with the desired level, they indicate and correct errors and praise good work but, more importantly, they afford the learner the necessary explanations that can enable them to bridge the gap between their present performance and the desired level. In addition, they guide the learner to the appropriate sources of information for reference and study, thus encouraging future learning. At the same time, it may be argued that, with regard to comments on errors, depth 3 is more appropriate for weaker learners while depth 1 may be sufficient for more competent learners, if the latter are able to reflect on the inaccuracies of their work and make use of reference books to correct them. However, most learners will need support in learning how to take responsibility for self-correction and further development, and even the most successful learner will benefit from motivating feedback given at depth 3, which draws her/his attention to areas of linguistic competence and progress made in skills development.

Remedial marking of linguistic inaccuracies

In their learning process, most learners will display linguistic inaccuracies. These are classified by Powell as slips, mistakes and errors (Powell, 2001). Slips of the tongue can be detected and corrected by the learner. Mistakes can be corrected by the learner if they are pointed out to her/him. Errors indicate that learning has not been internalised and therefore cannot be self-corrected until further relevant learning has taken place. When offering such remedial marking, teachers should consider which important errors their comments should focus on. Teachers have to decide whether to correct all errors, correct a selection or just indicate the nature of the error (for example, agreement, verb tense) or allow learners to correct their work (see Figure 6.5). The three choices given, by no means exhaustive, require different levels of competence in the learner's ability to work independently. The depth of error correction comments will depend on the extent to which the learner still needs to internalise the linguistic structures being assessed.

Depth of comment 1	**Indication of problem:** **Learner's work**: El Banco de España es en la Avenida Madrid. Es un edificio moderna. *Grammatical inaccuracies are highlighted. No explanation given.*
Depth of comment 2	**Correction of problem:** **Learner's work**: El Banco de España es *está* en la Avenida Madrid. Es un edificio moderna *moderno*. *Grammatical inaccuracies are highlighted, crossed out and corrected. No explanation given.*
Depth of comment 3	**Explanation of correction:** **Learner's work**: El Banco de España es *está* en la Avenida Madrid. Es un edificio moderna *moderno*. **Teacher's comment:** ESTAR is used to explain where a building or monument is located. Noun and adjective also have to agree in gender and number: edificio (masculine singular) moderno (masculine singular) *Grammatical inaccuracies are highlighted, crossed out and corrected. Grammatical rules are explained.*

Figure 6.5: The three depths of feedback comment in remedial marking.

Guidance on content

In some language assessments, the learner's achievement is affected by shortcomings with regard to the content. Feedback comments at depth 1, for example, might simply point out that all required elements were included, or that some content elements were missing. At depth 2 the teacher could invite learners to consider whether they have looked carefully at the question and understood what they were required to do. S/he might specify what the learner had or had not included, or whether s/he used the linguistic structures and vocabulary necessary to convey the information clearly. Guidance at depth 3 would give reasons why the inclusion or omission of certain elements was important. Although the learner may have included all the necessary content in their assessment, one further consideration is that inaccuracies in the use of language may make it difficult to comprehend. In this case the feedback will also contain remedial comments on the linguistic inaccuracies.

Generic skills development

Traditionally feedback tends to focus on the content and language aspects of the assessment and perhaps pays less attention to the development of language learning skills. Comments relating to skills are useful in bridging the gap because skills are used repetitively in assessments whereas content is specific to each task (Walker, 2007). In language courses, learners are often not only assessed on linguistic competence but also on academic skills such as organisation and task completion, structure and development of ideas.

Some learners' performance may be affected by underdeveloped study skills such as in note-taking, summarising or paraphrasing. For others, performance may be compromised through misunderstanding of the question or poor organisation of the material. Unless these issues are addressed, it is probable that the same errors will recur. Good, balanced feedback will comment on such deficiencies and enable the learner to progress from her/his present performance towards the desired level of competence. At beginner level, effective feedback will also address the development of specific skills, such as use of the dictionary and accurate learning of vocabulary. In blended contexts using distance learning, assessment feedback may provide the main opportunity for the teaching of these skills.

Advice for further development

When offering feedback to learners who are struggling, the highlighting of every single error can have a demoralising effect on motivation. In such cases it is advisable to concentrate on a few aspects of their work that are in need of development, if possible offering a combination of comments addressing content and skills. At the other end of the spectrum, teachers will encounter learners' work that contains very few or no errors. In such cases remedial marking is not required, but learners will benefit from extension marking. An example at beginner level might be:

> You are able to write simple sentences very accurately. Try to make your writing a little more varied now by using a wider range of verbs, including a few adjectives and introducing some subordinate clauses, for example.

Teaching through assessment will encourage learners to become more sophisticated in their use of language, addressing use of register, variety of lexis, idiomatic usage and style (Nicolson, 2010).

Balanced feedback

As mentioned earlier, since feedback, whether formative or summative, can have a positive or negative effect on a learner's self-esteem and motivation (Nicol and Macfarlane-Dick, 2004), the tone has to be appropriate, respectful, encouraging and appreciative of the learner's efforts. The feedback will both provide corrective advice and identify areas for potential improvement. The positive effect of feedback can be maximised if the teacher creates an environment that invites the learner to take an active part in the assessment process, as in this way s/he is more likely to understand comments and their relevance for future improvement. Effective, balanced feedback will:

- offer gap-bridging comments;
- provide comments that are clear to the learner;
- refer clearly to the marking criteria;
- give the learner specific points of reference for further revision;
- include motivating comments;
- praise the learner for what has been done well;
- offer explicit guidance on areas that need further improvement;
- explain corrections and achievement;
- prioritise areas for improvement;
- use a non-directive tone;
- engage the learner in her/his learning;
- focus on both content and skills.

Providing feedback on written tasks

In blended contexts relying on distance learning, the teacher–learner dialogue may be, for learners unable to participate in synchronous teaching sessions, the principal, if not the only formal source of feedback on progression, particularly in speaking and writing (Nicolson, 2010). This section will consider the provision of clear, understandable feedback on written language tasks using annotations of various kinds, including written or spoken inserted comments and summaries. Word processing software enables teachers to provide script annotations in a variety of ways, for example highlighting in different colours, inserting text comments in colour, inserting comments or using footnotes. Whichever system is used, the teacher should be mindful of the difference between proof reading and useful correction or indication of errors.

Written feedback on the script

Using symbols

In the body of a written assessment itself, it is advisable to be cautious about the amount of feedback inserted, particularly in the case of a weaker learner who could be demoralised by a large number of amendments and annotations. Positive feedback using symbols such as ticks and one-word comments on the script can be a useful source of encouragement. These can be as valuable to the learner as indications of errors. Where such short commendations are used, the teacher will need to make clear whether they relate to content, to language accuracy or both. Some teachers may prefer to reserve the use of ticks for the indication of successful communication of the required elements in a piece of writing, or to use different colours to distinguish between commendations for communication of ideas and for accuracy.

Symbols or abbreviations can also be used to highlight specific grammatical errors but a list of symbols and their meaning will need to be provided for learners with the first marked assessment. The following short list of abbreviations was devised for use with learners of German at beginner level, and can be adapted to meet the specific requirements of other languages, or presented in L2 for more advanced learners:

adj	adjective ending
c	case
f	feminine
g	gender
m	masculine
nt	neuter
v	verb form
wo	word order

If self-correction is being encouraged, then many errors will need no more than a symbol to indicate the nature of the error. Underlining protocols may also be introduced (Nicolson, 2010) to distinguish between different types of error. The teacher will, however, need to judge what is achievable by the student. S/he may choose to include a corrected version or 'answer key' at the end, may invite the learner to make contact to discuss any outstanding issues after self-correction, or have a two-stage process where the self-correction is resubmitted to the teacher. The teacher needs to be confident that the learner will, after further contact if necessary, understand what was incorrect and how it should be changed, bearing in mind that the learner who is able to act on the feedback offered by a teacher is at a more advanced developmental level than one unable to do so. According to Aljaafreh and Lantolf (1994, p. 468), interactive teacher–learner communication is a crucial element in the feedback process in which 'the expert tries to discover the ZPD of the novice in order to determine if help is required and, if it is, jointly to work out the appropriate level at which to provide it.'

Using footnotes
Whether the script is to be marked on paper or electronically, the use of highlighting combined with footnotes or endnotes is a neat way of providing detailed comments without making major changes to the learner's original work. An example is shown in Figure 6.6.

Using inserted comments
The use of the 'insert comment' facility on electronic documents is also helpful for the annotation of scripts, although it needs to be used sparingly if the links between the highlighted words and the comment are to remain clear, particularly if the

Lieber¹ Louise,

Meine² Hobbys sind: kochen, reisen, lessen, stricken, und schwimmen³ und die⁴ Sprachen lernen. Ich spreche Russisch, Englisch und ein bissen⁵ Deutch⁵.

---

¹ adj (f): *Liebe Louise*
² The usual German letter-writing convention (which is also followed in emails, as in the reading Texts 2-4 for this assignment) is to end the greeting with a comma, and to begin the first sentence of the message with a small letter:
        Liebe Louise,
          meine Hobbys sind ...
³ Although these words come from verbs, they are used as nouns here, so they need to begin with capital letters. Note the spelling of *Lesen.*
⁴ *die* isn't needed here. You are referring to languages in general, not to 'the languages'.
⁵ sp.

Figure 6.6: Example of highlighting and footnotes on a marked script.

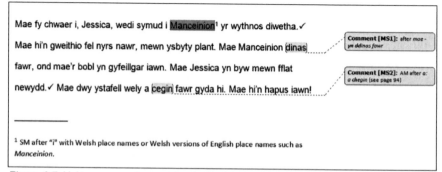

Figure 6.7: Using comments combined with footnotes.

learner is going to print the document. In Figure 6.7 inserted comments have been used for short annotations, and a footnote used where a lengthier explanation was required. At higher levels, teachers may want to consider using 'insert comment' for content issues and footnotes for language issues.

Using embedded audio comments

Teachers who wish to overcome the potentially impersonal nature of providing only written comments on a script may choose to embed audio comments into an electronic assessment document. The 'help' facility of most word-processing packages will include detailed guidance on how to achieve this. A further enhancement is provided by software such as Jing (www.techsmith.com/jing) which allows teachers to record themselves commenting on a section of text as they point to the screen. This mimics how a teacher in a face-to-face setting might talk through errors in a written task with a learner, albeit as a monologue rather than a dialogue. Jing can be used in conjunction with written script annotations to ensure clarity and provide a quick reference for the learner.

Providing a separate general summary

When assessing a piece of written work, the teacher's feedback will relate to a range of criteria, such as the content and structure of the piece, the extent to which successful and clear communication has been achieved, the standard of accuracy in the use of vocabulary and linguistic structures, the appropriate choice of language and the range of expressions used by the learner. Rather than covering the learner's script with comments relating to all of these, it is advisable for the teacher to prepare a separate summary of strengths and areas for further development, structured according to the marking criteria headings specified for that particular assessment task, so that the learner can easily see where marks have been gained and lost, and where her/his strengths and weaknesses lie. The general summary document would be the appropriate place to list the key aspects a learner needs to concentrate on, with references to course or study skills materials where necessary.

Providing feedback on speaking tasks

Although the general points relating to balanced feedback are applicable to feedback on speaking tasks, there are a number of different factors for consideration. In blended contexts relying on open or distance learning, opportunities for direct assessment and feedback on a learner's linguistic competency in the spoken use of the language are often reduced as a result of infrequent synchronous sessions or because attendance at such sessions is not a prerequisite for the successful completion of the course. In such cases, the teacher's spoken comments in assessment feedback will be one way of developing a sense of proximity between teacher and learner.

Audio recordings made by learners

Language learners on blended courses, again particularly in open and distance programmes, may be required to complete spoken assessment tasks to send to the teacher, usually as an audio file or on a CD. As with written tasks, the learner's work will be assessed according to the marking criteria for that individual task. Fell (2009) indicates points to consider when giving audio feedback: optimum time length, style of feedback, tone of voice, register of the language and engagement with feedback. Her recommendations are applicable to feedback for language learners. The teacher will have to decide whether to give feedback in L1 or L2, and, when using L2, the complexity of the structures as well as the speed of speech. This will depend on the competence of the learner and the course level. Another point to consider is the content of the feedback. Comments relating to linguistic structures may be better presented in written form, whereas comments that address intonation, pronunciation and fluency are best dealt with in audio feedback.

Teacher's spoken feedback

Bearing in mind the point about 'optimum time length' (some institutions, for example the OU, limit it to three minutes) teachers are advised to structure their comments and to concentrate on pronunciation and intonation. The following steps may serve as guidance for recording spoken feedback for beginners' courses. The amount of feedback given in L1 will depend on the level of linguistic competence of the learner:

- welcome learner in L2, using a friendly tone of voice;
- mention and praise what the learner did well;
- mention pronunciation errors in categories (e.g. vowels, consonants, nasal sounds);
- record correct form, leaving a gap between utterances to allow repetition from student;
- comment on intonation;
- select a few points to concentrate on (not more than three for struggling learners);
- direct the learner to relevant sources for further practice;
- indicate how advice given can potentially improve her/his performance in speaking L2. The learner will be more likely to act upon the advice given;
- farewell (in L2) and end recording.

More proficient learners, irrespective of level, will benefit from knowing what makes them proficient and will appreciate extension comments.

Teacher's written feedback

Errors in the use of language are best dealt with in written form. Comments must refer to the marking criteria and should be well structured. In accordance with the guidelines for balanced feedback above, the most effective comments will explain the correction and/or praise the learner's competence. To aid the learner, systematic errors can be summarised: for example, her/his attention can be drawn to revising the intonation pattern for questions and greetings. Learners can also be reminded that (as is the case with Spanish) the written accent indicates where the stress falls on a word. Teachers need to reflect on how to present and offer advice on language learning skills and study skills.

Feedback in new forms of assessment

Use of new technologies

Most computer-marked assessment packages offer the option of building in an element of feedback (see Moodle quizzes at www.moodle.org or the Learning Object Creator at www.llas.ac.uk/loc) as well as sometimes including a measurement of progress, storing results so that teachers are able to monitor learners' performance and identify areas of difficulty for individual students. Computer-marked assessment can address some of the conditions that Gibbs and Simpson (2004–5) established as supporting assessment for learning, such as providing short assessments at frequent intervals rather than one major final assessment. However, it requires a considerable investment of time upfront to design questions and write the feedback to help learners reconstruct and further their knowledge.

The advantages of feedback via computer-marked assessment are that it can be frequent, immediate and tailored to the stage the learner is at in the process, and can be designed to direct the learner to further questions or activities, or other sources of support (The Open University, 2009). However, automated feedback is not totally individualised and may not fully address each learner's specific knowledge gaps, so its authenticity and validity are sometimes questioned. Despite these barriers and the need to allow time and resources to build up the necessary technical skills among authors and teachers, computer-marked assessment provides a forward-looking, cost-effective solution in the long term to the limitations on teacher–learner contact in blended distance contexts.

Collaborative assessment

Collaborative online tools, such as forums and wikis, have made it more feasible to use collaborative assessment methods in blended contexts, particularly in distance education. As seen in Chapter 5, how to assess the joint outcome and distinguish individual contributions from the work of the group are two of the challenges of this kind of assessment. Whether assessment is formative or summative might also affect the feedback provided. General issues that affect most students can be addressed to the whole group, whereas some feedback may need to be provided individually to respect privacy. Feedback can be given on the product and on learner reflection on the process or can concentrate on the content and the language. Since the technology and the process might be new to many learners, feedback needs to provide support with systems as well as with the task and the language. Peer assessment feedback can be very valuable and appropriate in collaborative assessment.

Peer assessment

Chapter 5 outlined several forms of peer assessment, which can serve as a valuable additional teaching tool. Immediate feedback from peers, even if not as detailed and accurate as a teacher's feedback, might have a greater impact on learning than excellent feedback provided by a teacher some time after the work has been completed. Some guidance should be provided by teachers on what constitutes constructive, sensitive feedback. It is important that teachers work through the assessment criteria with learners and ensure that these have been fully understood before learners attempt to provide feedback to their peers. Peer assessment in language learning can help learners and peer assessors in several ways by:

- actively involving all group members in the assessment process;
- identifying elements that can be effortlessly corrected by learners themselves;
- uncovering problems that require further attention so that learners can

revisit incorrect notions and reconstruct them with the help of the teacher or the learning materials;

- helping peer assessors consolidate and clarify their knowledge through the process of providing feedback for their peers;
- allowing learners to benefit from seeing alternative approaches to the task;
- requiring learners to engage with the assessment criteria (Macdonald, 2001).

The peer assessment process can also help learners to develop the ability to self-assess, which is crucial in many blended contexts. In this respect, 'the real value [of peer assessment] may lie in learners internalising the standards expected so that they can supervise themselves and improve the quality of their own assignments prior to submitting them' (Gibbs and Simpson, 2004–5, p. 17). This aspect of peer assessment rewards the peer assessor with increased awareness and understanding of the marking criteria and expected knowledge, as well as providing learners with an additional source of feedback.

Conclusion

This chapter has provided some practical guidance on achieving an appropriate level and balance in teaching through assessment feedback, and on selecting a suitable mode of delivery. It has demonstrated the key role such feedback plays in establishing and maintaining an ongoing dialogue between learner and teacher in blended learning contexts, particularly where there may be limited opportunities for direct contact.

If teachers themselves adopt a cyclical approach (Kolb, 1984) similar to that recommended for learners in Figure 6.1, their own reflective practice will help them to develop reflective practice and autonomy in the learners they are supporting, and to respond appropriately to their diverse needs.

It is acknowledged that as new technologies and new forms of assessment are developed, the nature and mode of feedback will also continue to develop in new ways. The teacher who is a reflective practitioner will remain alert to such possibilities and will constantly seek to develop an approach that makes the best use of the available tools.

Section 3:
Synchronous and Asynchronous Teaching in Blended Contexts

presenting
facilitating

Chapter 7: Teaching in Synchronous and Asynchronous Modes

Margaret Nicolson, Margaret Southgate and Linda Murphy

Introduction

Teaching sessions in synchronous and asynchronous modes may assume different purposes depending on the type of blend in operation. In some, the teacher will present new material that the learner then works on independently after the session. In others, particularly in open and distance blended programmes such as at the OU, the teacher will support and facilitate practice of learning undertaken independently before the session. This does not preclude the teacher having to present new input when the need arises, but this will not be the primary focus.

Teaching sessions may also vary in frequency depending on the blend. Where they are the main source of input they are likely to occur more often. Where self-study and learning via assessment feedback (see Chapter 6) is more important in the blend, sessions may be less frequent. The length of sessions will also vary depending on the teaching mode. Online synchronous and telephone sessions are likely to be shorter, for example, than face-to-face sessions.

The focus of the session may also differ depending on the blend or teaching mode in question. In open and distance blended programmes, synchronous sessions may focus mainly on spoken interaction, as this may be difficult to cover in self-study. In blends where the session is the main source of teaching input, all skills may have to be covered. In any blend, asynchronous sessions are likely to lend themselves to the practice of grammar, writing or simply the exchange of study information. In some blends, teachers will also use their teaching sessions to support learners, either in groups or one-to-one, in their choice of resources and provide guidance on language learning skills as well as general study skills.

There are obvious implications for teachers. Those working in programmes that require them to present new material will want to ensure they do this sufficiently clearly, so that learners can work successfully on their own in self-study between sessions. In open learning contexts, where learners may be expected to select their own resources for self-study (for example, from a resource centre), teachers will want to ensure learners have an understanding of their needs. Teachers will also want to develop a strategy to help learners overcome challenges between sessions.

In contexts where teachers are facilitators of learning rather than presenters of new material, they will need to review and preview the learning points offered via self-study materials, bringing these to life for learners, designing tasks to suit the teaching mode, the group and individuals in question, resolving problems and supporting study and learning skill development for learners who may be working in isolation for much of the time.

In acknowledging the existence of these different factors, this chapter will provide an overview of the key elements common to planning, delivering and reflecting on teaching sessions in blended contexts.

Planning for different modes of teaching

If the planning process is distilled into a series of questions for teachers, the following emerge as key:

- What am I going to do?
- Why am I doing it?
- How am I going to do it?
- Why am I doing it that way?
- What contingencies have I got if it doesn't work?
- How do I involve learners in my planning?
- How do I assess if my planning worked?

The answers to these questions will be reliant on key factors that teachers will want to take into account when preparing a session. The mind-map in Figure 7.1 starts to plot these. Deliberately, no chronological order is given for planning as individual teachers will have different starting points and the areas may intertwine regularly through the planning process. For each part of the 'blend', the key areas in Figure 7.1

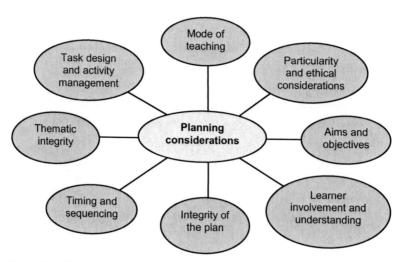

Figure 7.1: Key planning areas when preparing to teach.

need to be considered. In the following paragraphs they are explored in turn, and inter-relationships are highlighted.

Mode of teaching

Where the teaching mode is part of a blend predetermined by the institution, then choice and responsibility (see Chapter 2) will be less in the hands of teacher and learners and they will have to work within the institutional pattern set for them. Where teachers and learners do have choice and responsibility, the decision about which mode and tools to use is likely to depend on the aims and objectives of the teaching and the intended learning outcomes. Chapters 8–12 will highlight the advantages and affordances of specific modes and tools.

Particularity and ethical considerations

All aspects of the plan will need to be underpinned by an understanding of the particular needs of the group and ideally of the linguistic and skill needs of the individuals within it. It should also take account of ethical considerations such as ensuring that no task is threatening to learners, may make anyone uncomfortable, has the potential to develop in a direction that would be unwelcome or provoke any sort of hostility or problems for cultural or personal reasons. It should also take into account issues related to disability which arise in the specific mode concerned. Parts of the blend may be more accessible to some learners than to others and, where choice is possible, this can be taken into account in deciding which mode to use.

Aims and objectives

Decisions will need to be made as to what the aims and objectives of the overall plan and of the individual tasks within it are to be. A number of areas need to be taken into account. These are not mutually exclusive, but for the sake of clarity are outlined separately here.

Linguistic

This will focus on what language points are to be presented or practised to fit with course requirements and learner need. These may be:
- lexical, aiming to build up use of a set of vocabulary;
- grammatical, focusing on the use of a structure;
- functional, covering broader forms of interaction such as seeking information or arguing a case;
- phonological, practising intonation and sounds.

Most often, the four linguistic areas will overlap. If time is at a premium the most important points to be covered in the teaching session are those integral to the course, its learning outcomes and its assessment, or possibly those causing most challenges as identified by the teacher and/or learner.

Example: Learners have been introduced to the imperfect tense, either through self-study materials or in a teacher-led presentation. They also need to extend their vocabulary relating to daily routine and leisure activities. The teaching session tasks therefore concentrate on exploring what daily routines or leisure activities people used to undertake in the past, with comparison to the present where appropriate.

If sessions are supporting the practice of a certain skill such as speaking, the language points, particularly grammatical input, will be best contextualised within speaking tasks, rather than reviewing them in isolation.

Example: Learners have been working on the conditional tense in self-study materials and the synchronous teaching session needs to give them speaking skill practice in this. The teacher plans tasks around the function of speculating about what would happen, with a link to a relevant lexical area. In the teaching session learners are invited to say what they or others would do in a number of situations, such as winning the lottery.

At a more advanced level the above example might include a discussion of what learners would do if they were the prime minister/director of a theatre/head of town planning.

Skill-based

The practice of specific language skills may also determine planning. If learners are used to working on reading and writing in self-study materials then the focus in sessions may have to be on speaking and reactive listening. Where synchronous contact time is limited, it is advisable to avoid asking learners to undertake individual reading and writing tasks which they could do in their own time. However, it may be beneficial for learners to practise integrated study skills, such as note-taking, summarising or skim reading by embedding these within a speaking task.

Example: In the teaching session learners are to work on activities that link speaking practice with reading and note-taking. They are split into groups of three or four. Each participant is given five minutes to read a piece of written information and make notes on the key points. Each member of the group then summarises her/his information orally, and the others take notes. This leads on to a group discussion of what has been presented.

At different levels, the subject-matter in the above example might be a range of possible menus for an event, venues for a day out or environmental projects to be adopted by a city council. It is useful to follow up such a task with a discussion of the approaches adopted by learners and how the study skills can be enhanced.

Thematic

In some instances, all aspects of a specific topic have to be covered so learners become adept at discussing it from all angles, particularly at some assessment points. In such a case the topic itself takes precedence over specific linguistic or functional points. Ensuring that learners can deal with all aspects of the topic is the key objective of the plan and the sequence of tasks within it.

Example: The topic of travel or holidays has been fully explored either in synchronous presentations or in self-study materials, covering aspects of transport, eating out, cost, facilities, best places to go and ideal holidays. Learners are asked to engage in activities appropriate to this topic, using a variety of tenses, comparative and superlative adjectives, prepositions, numbers and the like appropriate to their level and the course requirements.

. . . .

Interactional/social

At times in the session, interactional or social aims will take precedence over linguistic aims. There are varying reasons for this. Members of the group may need time to get to know each other and work comfortably together or to warm up towards more complex language tasks, or they may need downtime from intense language practice.

In all synchronous teaching sessions, the teacher may wish to give the learners space before the session or in a mid-session break to interact with each other. In early language learning this may be in L1, but at more advanced stages this could be in L2. This provides a valuable opportunity for learners to encourage one another, exchange views and share study skills advice or simply to have a break from effort. This tends to happen almost spontaneously in face-to-face situations, but may need to be presented and facilitated by the teacher in a more structured way if learners are meeting in a synchronous online environment or by telephone conference.

In an asynchronous environment it can be useful to provide a separate asynchronous conference in which learners exchange messages not directly related to structured tasks in the course. Sometimes calling these 'virtual cafés' or 'chat rooms' clearly demarcates the purpose.

Learner involvement and understanding

At all planning stages it is best if learners are free to be involved, to state need and also that they understand the 'rules of the game' as played within the language learning context as well as in the particular teaching mode. Advance warning of aims and objectives and of the *modus operandi* in the teaching session is crucial. The learner response may be proactive or reactive: learners may offer input not only at the planning stage but also have a right to raise challenges to existing plans and suggest changes. Asking learners in advance about their needs, telling them what interaction protocols will apply and what is expected from them during the teaching session, and inviting their involvement and comment at the planning stage may be helpful in pre-empting issues, as teachers will be less likely to include anything that will cause unnecessary discomfort for any learner at the session itself.

Integrity of the plan

The integrity of the plan for a teaching session, that is, the way it holds together and gives the learner a sense of direction, is fundamentally important. This is true whether the session is concerned with new input or with language practice of material already studied, whether it takes place in one mode (for example, face-to-face, telephone or synchronous online) or combines different tools and modes of teaching (for example, synchronous and asynchronous online). The plan should not appear as a string of unconnected tasks, otherwise learners will not experience a sense of progression nor be able to integrate new language into their existing knowledge.

The plan for an individual session may adopt a traditional *beginning-middle-end model* where tasks gradually build linguistically, becoming more difficult and more open-ended as the session progresses in a crescendo model. On the other hand a *rolling model* may be preferred. Here the gradient is not linear but accrues laterally: for example, through extended role-play via the development of scenarios which build in layers. In this model it is hard to predetermine the linguistic points to be covered exactly, since the imaginative nature of the task may take learners in many linguistic directions as they explore the scenario in their own way. A *workstation* or *carousel model* is also possible in face-to-face and synchronous online sessions, where learners move around a real or virtual room from one task to another. In this situation the overall aim (for example, revision or study skill discussion) provides the broad integrity for the plan, and integrated sequencing may not be so crucial. The rolling model and workstation model will be discussed in Chapter 11.

Plans for sessions combining more than one mode may look somewhat different again (see also Chapter 2). For example, the plan may start with tasks for a synchronous online session in the beginning-middle-end model or the rolling model. It may then include tasks developing from that work in other skills such as writing, which learners are to work on in a second phase in asynchronous forums. Tasks in a follow-up synchronous session may then provide the opportunity for reflection, discussion of progress and study skills, and a more open-ended discussion to round off the work.

Timing and sequencing

The integrity of the plan will be dependent on good timing and sequencing. This will in part be driven by the particular mode adopted for the teaching session. In face-to-face mode, where sessions may last 2–3 hours, there is the chance to have longer activities without compromising variety, while in telephone or synchronous online sessions of one-hour duration it will be sensible to plan a series of shorter tasks.

In an asynchronous environment, timing parameters will differ. Teachers will have to decide how much time contributors need to work through a task and when to 'close' activities after a certain number of days or weeks, so that contributors have the opportunity to participate when they can but the task does not drag on. Pacing of tasks is just as important in asynchronous online sessions as in synchronous sessions.

Sequencing of tasks is also important for the plan's integrity. Learners need to understand why one task follows another to get a sense of orientation from the order. Sequencing also has to make logical sense. For example, brainstorming relevant vocabulary should come before a discussion task. The overall sense of the build-up of the full sequence (from closed to open-ended linguistic output, for example) must also be clear to learners so they can chart their own development and notice their growing confidence and progress.

Thematic integrity

A broad thematic approach can help learners make better sense of the direction of the teaching session and is particularly helpful when trying to contextualise specific yet disparate language points. The following suggestions for thematic approaches are not mutually exclusive and in any model or plan there may be different thematic combinations.

The content theme

This takes a certain topic, such as the learner's home area (at beginner level) or climate change (at advanced level), and builds all tasks around it. The adoption of a topic focus is helpful in signalling to learners that the choice of certain linguistic functions, structures and vocabulary has a link to a specific content theme. For example, transactional contexts such as shopping will involve structures around polite and formal greetings, asking for things, clarifying cost and facilities, description, numbers, quantities, while contexts involving discussion of complex or disputed concepts, such as climate change, may involve hypothesising, questioning and stating points of view supported by reasons or evidence.

The language function theme

This takes a certain function, such as describing things at beginners' level or hypothesising for more advanced levels, and allows for practice of this in different tasks and contexts. For example, at advanced levels learners may move from simple speculation about what is happening between characters in a picture to perhaps more complex hypothesising about what will happen at the next general election.

The grammatical theme

This takes a grammar point and weaves the teaching session around it. For example, past tenses may form the core theme of a session. Tasks may range from learners saying what they did yesterday to more imaginative tasks such as Alibi, where, for a mock investigation, learners have to invent details of what they were doing at the time of a fictitious incident.

Task design and activity management

At the planning stage, decisions need to be made about how tasks will be constructed, conducted and managed. This will be dependent on the mode and context and again will vary according to factors to be outlined in the following chapters. The teacher will need to consider the following questions:

- Should the task be learner-centred or teacher-centred? What balance of the two should there be overall? What control will the learner have over the choice of topic or extent of their engagement in the task? How can the teacher influence engagement? In asynchronous or synchronous online modes, for example, learners may opt out or not engage for technical or other reasons, and it may be difficult for the teacher to influence this or know the exact reason at the time.
- Where pairings and groupings are envisaged, how should these be constructed? Mixed randomly or according to competence, confidence, other social or interactional needs, or a mix of all of these?
- What use of resources is relevant to the particular teaching mode and the context in question?
- How can the teaching environment be used to best effect? What protocols need to operate within it? Online synchronous sessions may rely, for example, on turn-taking and not support spontaneous interruption or polite disagreement in the way face-to-face sessions or telephone may.
- How are roles within tasks to be assigned? According to level of competence, confidence or need for linguistic practice? How is linguistic input and output to be differentiated, taking into account individual competence, confidence and social issues alongside group needs? It may not always be possible to make such plans in advance where the teaching group population changes from session to session, but it is possible to have contingency strategies to hand nonetheless, by planning a variety of roles with differentiated linguistic input and output possibilities, which can be drawn on as necessary.

The teaching session

References to 'sessions' in the following paragraphs should be understood to refer to structured asynchronous online tasks as well as to any type of synchronous teaching session (online, telephone or face-to-face). The main focus of each teaching session will depend on the nature of the blend. As mentioned earlier, in some cases the teacher will be presenting mostly new language which learners will make active use of later, perhaps in another part of the blend. Other contexts may require the teacher to concentrate on facilitating rather than presenting, providing opportunities for learners to practise interacting with language they have already worked on in self-study. However, it is not always possible to draw clear divisions, and the teacher will need to be prepared to exercise flexibility on the spot in response to the needs of the participants within the framework of the session plan.

Explaining the rationale for the session

At the outset it should be made clear to learners exactly what is expected of them in the session. The teacher will explain not only how the synchronous learning session or asynchronous task will be run but also why it has been designed in that particular way. S/he will highlight the learning outcomes to help learners focus on the purpose of the session as a whole and also explain the rationale for each task as the session progresses. Links in tasks or in the overall plan to other modes or tools in the blend can also be usefully explained. As in all teaching contexts, learners need to be aware that they can ask for clarification, if necessary, about what they are required to do, about procedure and about the language required in order to complete the task. In a blended learning context, where language learners are often encouraged to assume a greater responsibility for their learning than in some conventional classroom-based courses, learners can also be expected to exercise a degree of autonomy not only at the planning stage as mentioned above but also during a session and with regard to the tasks offered by the teacher. Learners can also be invited to comment on the plans at the session, if they have not already done so, or on the way in which tasks are to be conducted, and to propose adaptations which will meet their language-learning needs more appropriately. As emphasised in the earlier part of this chapter, learners will engage in activities with greater commitment where they have had an opportunity to contribute to their planning and implementation, and when they have a clear sense of purpose.

Flexibility in following the session plan

Teachers will have a plan for moving through the various stages of the session (for example, opening/warm up, main activities and conclusion/feedback) with approximate timings for each section and the tasks within it. Whatever model has been prepared, however, the teacher must be willing to make adjustments within the overall framework as unexpected needs or questions arise. It may transpire that an asynchronous task has been misunderstood by a number of learners, or that learners are unfamiliar with a language structure required for a synchronous speaking task, so that further clarification or amendment is required. An asynchronous activity that requires input from several different groups may not work if participation is low, and the teacher may need to be flexible in substituting an alternative. Creative learners may suggest new ways of conducting or extending an activity. The responsive and flexible teacher will be able to handle such adjustments and provide room for elements of creativity without allowing the session to be blown entirely off course. S/he will need to evaluate each issue as it occurs, decide whether it is best addressed in the present session or in a later one, possibly in a different mode of communication, and decide whether it is appropriate to respond in L1 or in L2.

Management of groups and individuals

One of the key areas of interest for the teacher when facilitating a learning session is the management of the group and individuals within it. In a blended learning context, where there may be infrequent contact in person between teacher and learners, it is particularly important for the teacher to be alert to the needs and sensitivities of individuals within the group. S/he will need to take such needs and sensitivities into consideration, and be aware of group dynamics when setting up pairs or small groups, although options may be limited where the number of participants is low. The teacher may need to intervene or make adjustments during a session if individuals are found to be dominating an activity or being marginalised. Identifying such issues may pose greater problems when interaction is not face-to-face. Issues specific to each particular mode will be addressed in the following chapters, and confidence-building is covered later in this section.

However carefully a session has been designed to cater for the needs of a diverse group and however sensitive a teacher may be to individual responses during a session, it may be that some learners will still choose to opt out altogether, or to participate in some but not all parts of the blend.

Active participation

Where participation is required of learners in order to pass the course, the teacher may need to make a judgement as to whether an individual's level of participation is sufficient to meet the criteria. Those who do not meet the required level may need additional individual intervention and support from their teacher or from a generic study adviser. In some blended contexts, however, such as in open and distance learning, teaching sessions may be provided as an optional enhancement to the core self-study materials, offering interactive practice in synchronous speaking or asynchronous writing. In such cases, therefore, the teacher will ultimately have to respect each individual learner's decision, even though s/he may strongly recommend active participation and encourage learners to engage in interaction with others.

In a synchronous context a learner may attend the session but listen rather than be an active participant in discussions. In asynchronous tasks, some may choose to be a silent reader rather than contribute to a thread. The teacher will want to examine whether the learner's positioning results from a proactive choice, in which case active learning is still taking place, or from some difficulty of a linguistic or social nature which needs to be addressed. Here, there is a distinction to be made between peripherality (Lave and Wenger, 1991) as a positive choice, where the learner

peripherals/ marginating

feels comfortable as a listener/reader rather than a speaker/writer, and marginality as a negative position, where the learner may experience feelings of inadequacy and exclusion. Unless active participation is a requirement of the course, the teacher will need to respect the learner's decision in the former case, and consider how best to provide individualised support to a marginal learner in the latter case. Learners who are identified as at risk of becoming marginalised because they have problems with their study deadlines or certain task types could be encouraged to say 'I haven't done this yet' or 'I am not good at this sort of activity'. This, as Pellegrino Aveni suggests, prepares others for the interaction 'in order to lower their expectations of the learner's performance, thus reducing the risk of condemnation for inadequate performance' (Pellegrino Aveni, 2005, p. 136). Resolving issues of marginalisation to do with group mix and dynamics will in many ways rely on the teacher's ability to foster a supportive environment where dominant or inappropriate behaviour towards other learners is not acceptable.

Differentiation

There are many ways of achieving differentiated teaching. In teaching sessions generally, whether in plenary or in smaller groupings, varying the level of questioning and hence the expected level of answers can help to involve all learners at their appropriate language level. In teaching modes that permit the creation of pairs or groups, accelerating or decelerating the pace of activity or modifying steps within it will help differentiation and allow learners to achieve their personal best while ensuring this does not compromise their integration into the group as a whole. To this end it is also important to keep pairings and groupings flexible and permit movement between them. Teachers can also differentiate by roles within pair or group activities. For example, at beginners' level a confident speaker might be given the role of a shopkeeper or hotel receptionist, asking the questions, while a less confident learner takes the role of customer or hotel guest, responding in shorter phrases. In a debate between more advanced learners, a confident, able learner can be given the role of facilitator or chairperson while others in the group contribute ideas to the debate in the way that suits their confidence and competence levels.

It is important to take account of preferred learning style here, too, and to adjust tasks and activities accordingly. Some learners may prefer visual learning (for example, through pictures or handouts), while others prefer auditory learning, although it is acknowledged that individual learner styles may vary from episode to episode and task to task. In the blended context it can also be helpful to learners if teachers point out how the different modes themselves can accommodate different learning styles and preferences, as this may influence learner decisions about their own participation and learning.

Confidence building

A key purpose of teacher-mediated synchronous and asynchronous sessions will be to build learner confidence. The teacher will have planned some structured activities to allow participants to become familiar with the basic building blocks of the language to be practised in the session, which could have a lexical, grammatical or functional focus, or possibly a blend of more than one of these. Beginning with a low-risk, structured task will encourage less-confident learners to make their voice heard or to write a contribution on the group message board. The teacher will need to pace the activities in a way that draws the learners steadily from low-risk to higher-risk utterances, from structured interchanges to spontaneous conversation or text chat. Where, as is often the case, a group consists of learners operating at different levels, with a diversity of backgrounds and prior knowledge of L2, the teacher must be aware of issues that could affect an individual's confidence. Questions the teacher might consider are:

- If the teaching mode permits the creation of sub-groups, would the learner benefit from being paired with someone at a similar competence or confidence level?
- Would it be beneficial for the less confident or competent learner to be paired with a sympathetic, more confident or competent learner?
- Have I reassured the group that some people within it are operating above the required level for this course so that false assumptions about level are not made?
- Is the less confident/competent learner ready to be moved on to a more challenging activity?
- Am I making good use of open-ended activities which allow the learners to interact at their own individual level?
- Have I suitably considered various aspects of differentiation which might meet the needs of all the learners?

Teacher and learner participation levels

In some contexts where new material is presented during a teaching session, the teacher may be a significant participant. The learners may play a more passive part at times, although they may be involved in working out rules together, in questioning or in follow-up practice activities, for example.

Where the teacher's role is that of a facilitator rather than the presenter of new learning, although s/he may introduce the task and provide error correction and feedback at the conclusion of the activity, during the activity itself s/he will step back and observe. Her/his intervention will be limited to providing guidance and support only where needed, although it may sometimes be appropriate for the teacher to become an active participant to work with an individual student or group who may be experiencing challenges of some kind.

During a teaching session, whether synchronous or asynchronous, the teacher will also wish to monitor each learner's level of activity to ensure that no individual is allowed to dominate or to become marginalised, as mentioned earlier, and to take appropriate action either publicly with the group as a whole, or privately with the individual(s) concerned, depending on the circumstances. It therefore follows that a successful session will generally have included a relatively high and balanced level of learner–learner interaction, with every learner who wishes to participate having done so, and a much lower level of teacher–learner interaction.

After teaching

After a teaching session, the language teacher will want to evaluate what happened, decide what to follow up immediately and consider any implications for future planning. As earlier in this chapter, 'session' here refers to structured asynchronous online tasks as well as to any kind of synchronous teaching session (online, telephone or face-to-face) or a combination of these modes.

Evaluation

At the end of a teaching session, it is important to allow some time for reflection, difficult though that may be for busy teachers. Much has been written about the way that reflection on experience can help professionals in any walk of life to learn from their experience and so develop and improve future practice, based on the work of Schön (1983), for example Kolb (1984), Boud *et al.* (1985) and Boud and Walker (1993). Some teachers may find the notion of 'reflection' rather vague, or difficult to get to grips with, but it is a matter of asking oneself questions about a teaching experience. For the teacher of languages in blended contexts, key questions to think about include:

- How did the session go overall? How did I feel afterwards and why?
- Were the intended learning outcomes achieved? How do I know?
- What worked well or less well? What are the possible reasons?
- Who participated or didn't take part? How active were individuals during the session?
- What do the learners think about the session and particular tasks?
- What next? How does this experience relate to other parts of the blend?

These questions are now considered separately, though in reality they may be closely linked.

How did the session go overall? How did I feel afterwards and why?
Teachers experience a wide range of emotions after a teaching session, ranging from elation to despair. Sometimes these feelings may get in the way and it is necessary to recognise and accept them in order to be able to examine what happened during the teaching session in a more analytical manner. This is particularly relevant where teachers are working in a less familiar mode with tools they are less confident about.

Were the intended learning outcomes achieved? How do I know?

Aims, objectives and intended learning outcomes are a key component of planning for the teaching session (see Figure 7.1, p. 96, and the accompanying discussion). All the other aspects of planning are really subordinate to or in support of this key component, so it is only right to ask oneself afterwards if the intended outcomes were actually achieved, and in particular what evidence there is for the judgement. Blended teaching contexts may offer a wider variety of opportunities for gathering such evidence. In traditional face-to-face teaching and in synchronous online sessions, much of the evidence may come from observing or listening to how learners perform during tasks as they interact with each other or with the teacher. In face-to-face or telephone contexts, the teacher engaging in post-session reflection has to rely on memory, but asynchronous and synchronous online sessions can provide a written or audio record of performance which the teacher can use to check post-session impressions. Learner feedback may provide a different perspective, as discussed below, which needs to be considered.

What worked well or less well? What are the possible reasons?

Having considered the extent to which the learning outcomes were achieved, it is time to turn attention to the individual components of the session and the outcome of other decisions made at the planning stage. If tasks go as intended and learners are fully engaged, it may often be attributable to the decisions related to group management, pacing, structure of tasks and their complexity and the opportunities that learners have to make choices about how they participate as discussed above. If activities do not work out as intended, often it may be as a result of the instructions or explanation or the complexity of the task. Clarity of instructions is vital in all teaching contexts, but particularly in telephone, online synchronous and asynchronous modes where teachers cannot immediately see consternation or incomprehension. Here teachers need to prepare explanations and ways of checking understanding that do not rely on simply asking 'do you understand what to do?' to which the answer may be 'yes', regardless, because nobody wants to admit otherwise. Open questions, which do not invite a yes/no answer, are more likely to give a clearer idea of comprehension.

Complexity may refer to the language points, the subject matter, the structure of the task and instructions or the technical moves required to participate. Researchers such as Robinson (2001) have examined the relationship between task and linguistic difficulty and the impact on learner accuracy and fluency. Samuda (2005) is also concerned about the different layers of complexity in task design requiring linguistic, thematic and strategic decisions on the part of the learner. If complexity levels are high in two or more areas, tasks may not work as intended. For example, intermediate learners of Spanish in an online synchronous session were asked to pick a person from a picture gallery of famous South Americans without telling others who they had picked, then describe the person and say something about their life while the rest of the group guessed who it was. To get information about the character concerned they had to navigate to a different screen and read some notes. This task proved too difficult for many participants because they knew little about the famous people, did not have enough language skills to talk about the lives of a very diverse set of characters and in some cases could not find the extra information. The task was too complex in the areas of subject matter, language and technical manipulation. Teachers working in blended environments need to bear in mind the overall complexity of tasks in relation to the intended outcomes and what the mode is best suited to.

Who participated or didn't take part? How active were individuals during the session?
The answers to these questions depend on monitoring undertaken by the teacher during the session. In synchronous online, telephone or face-to-face sessions, this can be done by simply placing a tick against a list of participants' names as they speak. A slightly more sophisticated approach could be to note the type of interaction they engage in: for example, initiating discussion, asking questions, answering questions, one-word answers or longer utterances. Online asynchronous sessions rely on written contributions from participants, or learners may be invited to post podcasts or short audio recordings instead of writing, making monitoring of the extent and nature of participation a lot easier. After the session, reviewing the results of this monitoring will determine what individual follow-up is needed and how it is implemented (see below). It may also lead to changes in group management (for example, if pairings or groupings appear to inhibit members).

What do the learners think about the session and particular tasks?
At the beginning of this chapter the importance of involving learners in the planning of teaching sessions was stressed. A key part of that involvement is inviting them to provide feedback on the session afterwards. Apart from checking whether they felt that they had achieved the intended learning outcomes, learners can be asked to give feedback on a range of aspects depending on the particular focus of the session or the concerns of the teacher. For example, the teacher may want to check the L2/L1 mix, the complexity of tasks, the mix of task types, the mix of modes, groupings, content and enjoyment. At the same time it is important to allow learners the opportunity to give feedback on any issues *they* want to raise. The way in which feedback is gathered can vary depending on the mode of teaching, but significant issues are whether or not it is gathered anonymously, privately or publicly and in L1 or L2. Anonymity may encourage more honest comments but make it harder for the teacher to respond to individual need. Public discussions or expressions of opinion can be intimidating or can lead to those with strong opinions overriding the rest or the feeling that dissent from the majority view is not possible. In online synchronous

or asynchronous sessions, anonymity can be difficult to arrange as contributions can be tracked. Seeking feedback by email or electronic surveys may be an answer, but may not get a response.

The use of L1 or L2 may depend on the level of the learners, but honest feedback depends on the ability of learners to express their views comfortably. They may not have acquired the metalanguage necessary to do this in the L2. Teachers will probably have to use a mix of approaches: for example, brief discussions, short email questionnaires or an invitation to write a key word in the text chat from each participant to sum up how they feel. A mixed approach is likely to provide the most useful information as using the same method every time may lead to mechanical responses. If an open, non-judgemental, comfortable working climate has been created, learners will be happy to provide honest and thoughtful feedback.

What next? How does this experience relate to other parts of the blend?
After thinking through these questions, decisions can be made about immediate action to follow up the teaching session and how the outcome of the evaluation will feed into future plans. Issues for immediate action may include following up non-participants. As discussed earlier, they may have considered the options and decided to opt out of that particular session, preferring to take a peripheral position. However, they may have opted out because they lack confidence, are concerned that they have fallen behind, are not sure what to do, cannot get to the venue or have experienced some kind of technical problem. Some may have conflicting commitments. Teachers may be able to resolve questions, dispel doubts or provide reassurance or additional support. Maintaining contact with learners and keeping them in touch with what is happening helps them to feel part of the group even if they choose not to participate. Teachers in blended contexts may have more avenues for doing this, for example by:

- posting on a message board a summary of a synchronous session and materials used;
- providing learners with a link to a recording of the session which they can access when they want to;
- encouraging those who do not take part in structured teaching sessions to keep in touch with the group and share information (such as film screenings, interesting websites, impressions of places visited or TV programmes viewed);
- archiving asynchronous discussions and tasks so that they can be referred to later as and when learners need them.

Of course all these actions mean that participants can review or revisit the teaching sessions too.

After the immediate follow-up, attention turns to planning for future sessions. Perhaps tasks can be simplified or would be better suited to a different mode next time? New ideas for linking this session to other tasks in a different mode may emerge. Reflection on the questions above together with feedback from learners will suggest new courses of action to be tried out in future sessions and fresh responses to the planning issues outlined at the start of this chapter. And so the cycle begins again …

Conclusion

This chapter has examined how blended teaching contexts affect the teacher role and has provided a general outline of key elements in the planning, implementation and evaluation of structured teaching sessions in such blended teaching contexts. Many of the elements will be familiar from traditional classroom teaching, but need to be reviewed in blended teaching. The following chapters in this section will examine the issues highlighted here with regard to the specific teaching modes that may make up the blend: namely synchronous telephone, online, and face-to-face modes, and online asynchronous teaching. They will also include practical examples of tasks that work well in these modes, and explore how and why this is so. They will consider what each mode can offer within an overall blend and the kinds of language skill development best supported in each case.

Chapter 8: **Teaching by Telephone**

Bärbel Brash and Margaret Nicolson

Introduction

Telephone teaching has assumed an important role in blended contexts. In many ways it led the technological revolution which allowed blended teaching and learning in all four language skills to flourish, well before the advent of synchronous online facilities. This chapter will provide an overview of telephone teaching, examining different types of telephone provision, the planning and management of telephone teaching sessions, current and future developments in the field and the place of telephone tuition in the blended mix.

As well as its role in one-to-one tuition and in learner support, telephone conferencing had originally allowed providers, particularly in part-time, distance and open teaching contexts, to offer access to the teacher and/or an element of synchronous tuition without requiring learners and teachers to travel distances to face-to-face sessions. This was particularly important in offering practice in and validating the inclusion of speaking skills in blended environments. Telford College in Edinburgh used the telephone to support Gaelic teaching (see also Chapter 1) in the 1980s and 1990s while the OU began to use telephone conferencing in language teaching in 1995, although telephone teaching in other subjects was well underway there before that.

Early research demonstrated that learners learned as much, if not more, in telephone teaching sessions as in face-to-face situations (Rao and Hicks, 1972) and that telephone teaching was popular and rated highly by learners (Davies, 1976). More recently, Gaskell and Mills (2004) show that support via telephone can aid learner induction, retention and performance as well as help learner integration into the institution. Horton-Salway *et al.* (2008) show that patterns of learner uptake and participation are in fact similar in telephone teaching to face-to-face group teaching.

For some learners the mode provides security and safety precisely because identity in this environment is not based on visual or physical appearance. From informal learner feedback during OU teaching by telephone conferencing, it is also clear that some learners prefer telephone to synchronous online tuition because more supporting language cues, such as laughter, encouragement or agreement from other participants are immediately audible. Telephone teaching, however, brings its own challenges, such as ensuring that those with hearing difficulties have the appropriate equipment, that those using mobile phones can maintain a good connection and sound quality, and that the lack of visual cues does not lead to misunderstandings in communication. In international programmes, there is also the question of timetabling calls across time zones.

As part of the e-learning movement, mobile learning has been scrutinised in recent research (Zhao, 2005) with a focus on the use of PDAs, mobile or cell phones and other handheld mobile devices. Some researchers claim that mobile phones are becoming so crucial to our way of communicating with others that they can be viewed as an extension of the user and part of her/his identity (Pettit and Kukulska-Hulme, 2007). They will therefore undoubtedly figure more importantly in the future development of telephone teaching.

Types of telephone teaching

There are three clear types of provision: one-to-one calls, group calls, and group-to-group calls — a group being anything from three people upwards.

One-to-one calls

Educational providers and teachers find one-to-one telephone contact useful in blended teaching programmes for a variety of reasons, such as:

- making contact between the teacher and learner on distance or open learning programmes where attendance at the institution is not an element of the blend;
- providing teaching or academic and study/learning skill support to individuals, either because the programme offers this or because they have an additional need entitling them to this support;
- reaching learners who have access only to the telephone as a teaching mode for reasons of disability, technological restrictions such as no broadband connection, no computer or no information and communication technology (ICT) knowledge, or because they are in a secure institution and unable or not permitted to access online or face-to-face components of the blend;
- assessing an individual learner formally in speaking and listening skills.

Group calls

Telephone group conferencing can be used within blended teaching programmes to:

- offer synchronous language tuition as part of a mix of delivery modes. The nature of the input may differ according to the mode and mix of modes within the blend. Some programmes will deliver entirely new input during telephone sessions, which learners then follow up in self-study afterwards. In programmes where new teaching is carried out exclusively via self-study materials, then the purpose of such telephone sessions may be to support the practice of skills such as speaking or to review material already worked on by learners in their own time;

- provide group teaching sessions to learners who cannot access other forms of teaching offered in the blend (such as face-to-face or online) for reasons of dispersed geography, travel, disability, caring and/or work commitments, or online access difficulties;
- allow learners to participate in a session focusing on a specific skill area or on a language point because of an identified need for remediation;
- facilitate learner self-help or study groups, enhancing the learning process for them and strengthening group identity when learners cannot meet physically;
- assess learners formally.

Group-to-group calls

These are generally used for less formalised contact, for example to allow a group of native speakers to interact with a group of learners. This allows for the development of situated intercultural competence, beyond the formalised demands of the classroom context as shown by Wienroeder-Skinner and Maass (1997).

Planning

Providers and practical considerations

When planning what sort of telephone provision is best, the teacher will need to take into account the number of participants and the main objectives of the session. The following section outlines some possible options for work with individual, small or larger groups of learners. A call with an individual can be done from a mobile, landline or computer telephone. A call among three participants can be facilitated via BT three-way, provided the telephone set has the requisite buttons. This type of call does not require pre-booking. However, the service may increase the cost of the monthly landline rental and attract higher call charges.

BT MeetMe, another contract service from BT, can connect up to forty participants anywhere in the world into a conference call without pre-booking. Additional web tools can be added to the contract, which allow shared web workspace during the telephone session. Other providers, such as CallVox, offer audio conferencing without contracts or pre-booking but at a higher call charge. Community Network provides audio conferencing with contracts and pre-booking and will provide an operator-enabled connection. Other providers may allocate pin numbers to allow computerised access. Skype and MSN provide free services for some connections and chat facilities via the internet, but charge for audio conferencing use. For such facilities users must have an internet phone compatible with their computer set-up. Some institutions, such as the OU, use their own in-house conferencing facility. Some providers, such as Community Network, allow the main group to be split, or bridged into smaller groups, to enable pairwork or groupwork during the teaching session — a useful asset to vary group mix and enhance activity development.

When arranging a telephone session it is important to adhere to data protection conventions and to observe the need for confidentiality about details such as participants' telephone numbers. Similarly, when discussing sensitive personal data such as learning needs or disabilities via telephone, the teacher needs to ensure to the best of her/his ability that no other person, for example, an operator or a colleague, can overhear the conversation. Teachers also need to be aware of health and safety concerns surrounding use of the telephone for longer periods, so that seating and equipment are appropriate. Some employers provide microphone headsets to avoid repetitive strain problems.

Planning the teaching session

In contrast to face-to-face or online sessions, where teachers may not know which learners will take part on the day, the technical requirements for group telephone sessions usually mean that participant lists have to be planned in advance. Decisions then need to be made about what length of call is suitable. The number of participants can be a determining factor, as are the objectives of the call. Where language teaching input or language practice is the focus, then the language level and the specific needs of the group and individuals within it have to be considered. The fact that working with another language in a teaching and learning situation on the telephone can be an intense one also comes into play. A high level of concentration is required (Hewer et al., 1997, p. 7) as a result of the continuous focus needed to follow the interaction without any supporting visual cues. This gives fewer opportunities for lapses in concentration or informal 'downtime' and the session length will have to take account of this. Figure 8.1 gives some advice on optimal length and number of participants.

	Advised length of session (minutes)	Optimal no. of participants
Beginners (group)	45–60	6 + teacher
Intermediate (group)	60–75	6–8 + teacher
Advanced (group)	60–75	6–8 + teacher
One-to-one	20–30	1 + teacher

Figure 8.1: Optimal length of telephone teaching sessions

Planning a successful telephone teaching session, whether for an individual or a group, relies, as do other teaching modes, on clarifying protocols specific to the environment and sharing the agenda and objectives in advance, via letter or as email attachment, to allow learners to prepare for the session. Part of that preparation will involve drawing learners' attention to the need to participate in the conference in a comfortable, quiet, well-lit place, with space to lay out the agenda and papers, minimal background noise and good phone reception, where possible. Provided sound quality is good, a speaker phone, if available, is preferable to a hand-held one.

Telephone teaching is perhaps reliant on more systematic planning in some aspects than other teaching modes, as there are fewer avenues for deviation once the task materials have been sent out to learners. Visual or written resources cannot be brought in at the last moment in contrast to online or face-to-face modes, and supplementary material, which may not be needed, would have to be sent in advance with the risk of learners querying its necessity if not used, or feeling overloaded. This will undoubtedly change as the use of mobile technology during telephone teaching develops.

As in all modes, the teacher will need to strike the right balance between language skills work, study skills development and revision, and the need to plan for different learning styles in a mode where much relies on the spoken word and strong listening skills. Group-to-group telephone sessions, which can be used as a way to create collaborative exchange between a group of native speakers and a group of language learners, need to be planned even more meticulously as a quick succession of language tasks, and it is even more crucial here to organise who speaks when and to whom in order to maximise speaking time for every participant.

Planning a telephone session for one learner will require many of these considerations to be taken into account but may also include individual issues such as the discussion of specific learning barriers or specific academic needs. In a one-to-one situation, the learner may feel more exposed and nervous, and teachers need to assess sensitively how this may affect concentration and work levels.

As telephone sessions require continuous focus, teachers need to consider what thematic links are provided to ensure participants know where they are heading (see Chapter 7). A suitable task base for the teaching mode is discussed below. The teacher may also want to ensure that problematic identity issues are covered ahead of time. In a telephone session it can be beneficial that participants do not have access to visual identity markers (Nicolson and Adams, 2010, p. 6) such as age, appearance, mannerisms, additional needs and the like, since this prevents the construction of stereotypical views of others, which can be liberating both personally and as a language learner. However, learners may also struggle with the absence of visual cues in terms of communication and validation of what they say.

A sample plan (Nicolson, 1997) designed specifically to practise speaking skills is given in Figure 8.2 to illustrate how a telephone session may evolve.

The telephone teaching session

Without visual cues, it may not be easy to gauge when participants want to speak. It is therefore important for teachers to set a careful framework of openness and fairness regarding contributions. It is certainly helpful to acknowledge at the start that participants may feel nervous or uneasy if they have no prior experience of this

Overall aim To encourage discussion in comparing past and present, contextualising lexical and grammar practice within communicative tasks.	Theme 'Now and then' Level: Intermediate
Objectives ○ to boost confidence; ○ to accustom learners to speaking in L2 in telephone context.	**Joining task (2–3 min.*): Informal conversation** As learners join the call, teacher engages them in informal conversation, e.g. 'How are you? Where are you?' Alternatively, a guessing game such as 'What/Who am I?' can be set in train. This can stop and start at a moment's notice as others join the call and can be finished later if necessary. It can also link to the theme of the tutorial 'Now and then' by focusing on a past product/radio or TV programme, etc.
Objectives Functional: ○ stating the case as it was and is; ○ stating preferences and beliefs. Lexical/grammatical: ○ use of adverbs of time, tenses (imperfect and present), comparatives.	**Task 1 (6–8 min.): 'Just 30 seconds' monologues** Teacher gives learners a broad topic in advance of the session, e.g. 'Comparing now and then' and asks them to revise imperfect and present tenses and vocabulary as appropriate. At the session, learners are invited to speak spontaneously for 30 seconds on a specific area, such as shopping now and then, school now and then, leisure now and then. The amount of preparation required should be relevant to the context and learner group.
Objectives Functional: ○ asking and stating what the case is. Lexical/grammatical: ○ practise use of question forms and statements with imperfect/ perfect/present tense.	**Task 2 (8–10 min.): Comparing pictures 'now' and 'then'** Visual materials are sent in advance, one group sent a 'now' picture, the other group a 'then' picture. Groups compare their pictures, asking each other what has disappeared, been added, etc. Where available, bridging (i.e. splitting into two groups) could be used for the first section of this task, with each group discussing their own picture, or preparing the questions to ask the other group.
Objectives Functional: ○ making statements of belief/ possibility/preference; ○ making comparisons; ○ justifying and asking for justification; ○ agreeing/disagreeing. Lexical/grammatical: ○ expressions of beliefs, possibilities and preferences with appropriate tenses.	**Task 3 (10–12 min.): Cued debate 'Now and then'** A role-play in which learners give their thoughts and comparisons about 'now and then', e.g. about how a place or a way of life has changed in a town, because of a new road/ building/law etc. with supporting statements for their reasoning. Supporting instructions are sent in advance (e.g. learners could be asked to revise phrases to do with beliefs/hypotheses/ preferences). Learners can be asked to assume roles, such as architect, councillor, developer or resident of an area. Again, bridging could be used for two smaller debates or for preparatory work, with learner levels mixed or not, depending on roles and needs.
Objectives Functional: ○ stating beliefs/hypotheses; agreeing/disagreeing; ○ justifying and asking for justification; ○ comparing; ○ summarising. Lexical/grammatical: ○ practice of imperfect/present tenses and comparatives in contextualised, communicative setting.	**Task 4 (10–12 min.): Open debate on 'Now and then'** Teacher initiates an open debate on 'now and then'. Learners are invited to state their own opinions on past and present life. Round-up: Learners summarise key points that have arisen during the debate.
	End of tutorial task, if time (2–3 min.) Teacher offers a quick fun task (e.g. complete 'What/Who am I?' if this was not done at the start of the call).

* the duration of tasks are suggested as a guideline only

Figure 8.2: Example of a telephone group teaching session plan

teaching environment and that the absence of visual cues may be daunting. This may assist in sensitising participants to the teaching mode and to other learners' feelings. On a practical level it can be useful for participants to state their name every time they contribute until voice recognition is achieved. However, it is also crucial that silence is respected in telephone teaching, as the natural reaction can be to fill the space with sound and words. In the same way as Van Lier (2008) points out that participation does not always result in progress, so it can be posited that silence does not always mean learning is not happening. Where silence is the result of obvious marginalisation (Lave and Wenger, 1991), this needs to be more proactively managed by the teacher speaking to the learner after the session to discuss issues and solutions.

Whereas in a face-to-face situation a learner might assess via body language whether hesitation is a 'positive' or 'negative' response to their contribution, in a telephone session a hesitation or silence may seem threatening. Teachers can encourage learners to translate hesitation or silence into speech by giving them set phrases or by explaining their own hesitation, saying, for example: 'This is an interesting idea, and I need a moment to think about it.' This signifies to the learner that the teacher is giving the contribution some thought, and that hesitation or silence is not to be equated with negative evaluation. Similarly, teachers can make encouraging sounds, in L1 or L2 as appropriate, such as 'mmm ...', 'yes ...' etc., which serve both social and functional means. They can also ensure that communication has been successful by checking learners' understanding frequently. Clear communication can also be helped by speaking slowly and enunciating well.

In any teaching session, balances have to be struck in many respects. While the six areas of potential tension outlined below are of relevance to all teaching modes, they have particular importance in the telephone teaching context.

Close management of agenda and time versus flexibility

As mentioned earlier, there may be a higher degree of tight agenda-setting in this mode because of the shorter allocation of time, the intensity of the experience and the parameters surrounding use of the technology and use of resources. However, changes still need to be possible. It is, for example, not uncommon for learners to cancel participation in a telephone session call at the last minute. This may then make certain tasks impossible or require new grouping arrangements for tasks. Pacing and structuring are essential for the success of any tutorial, and it is sensible to estimate how long every task will take, yet to be prepared for them taking more or less time than planned. Some useful tips include:

- build flexibility into plans and remain flexible during the session;
- have additional tasks available that do not rely on material resources;
- have alternative ways of doing tasks available in case of changes in participant numbers;

- ask learners to choose from the agenda if time is running out and defer remaining points to the next telephone session or allow them to use exercises as follow-up work themselves.

Turn-taking versus spontaneity and interruption

In telephone work, at the start of the session, teachers and learners need to discuss and agree on particular conventions so that turn-taking, including polite interruption or disagreement or breaking a silence, can be managed in the best way. Participants should know whether everyone is allowed to contribute or break a silence at any time or only at specific times and this may vary according to the task. It can be helpful for the teacher to keep a record of participants' contributions. S/he can then decide whether politely to curtail some contributions, if one individual is dominating the call, or to invite more participation from learners who are not contributing much. Ideally, in blends where speaking practice is the focus of the telephone component, teachers would encourage participants to pass the 'speaking baton' to others in the group directly, rather than via the teacher as 'chairperson'. Some useful tips include:

- encourage learners to address each other directly, not always via the teacher;
- encourage learners at higher language levels to chair parts of the session where speaking practice is the focus;
- start the telephone session with a teacher-led task and increase learner-led tasks until a comfortable balance and level of control for learners are achieved.

Silence versus participation

In conferencing contexts, such as telephone teaching, silences can stand out more, as Brash and Warnecke (2009, p. 104) point out, and 'may be perceived as more threatening'. They suggest that teachers should not allow silences to become too long. However, they also balance this with the thought that silences can provide new opportunities for learners since '[situations] in which it is unclear who will speak next afford more opportunities for all to contribute ...' Some useful tips include:

- encourage learners to appreciate silences as potential thinking and learning time and not as unsettling moments;
- encourage learners to respect the silence of individuals who want to attend but not participate fully at any stage.

Accuracy versus communication

In a telephone teaching situation it can take longer for the teacher to become aware of confidence issues. An overly strong focus on error correction may exacerbate this, with learners becoming too focused on grammatical accuracy rather than meaning, and so losing confidence to contribute further. However, if the focus is too much

on communication then learners may have difficulty understanding other participants, or mistakes left uncorrected risk being repeated by others. As in all modes, it
is helpful to clarify the protocols for error correction in the telephone setting. Some
useful tips include:

- plan for a variety of learning objectives so that error-focus does not
  dominate;
- ensure learners are aware of how errors will be dealt with;
- prioritise the correction of errors with a serious impact on the learning
  points to avoid them being repeated.

Differentiation versus integration

The management of some types of differentiation in telephone teaching relies to
a large extent on technical possibilities for varying the groupings. Where it is possible to split the group during the call, this is a useful way to divide learners into
competence or confidence levels and provide them with a series of tasks of varying
complexity. It also allows them to set their own pace and results in different group
achievements. However, in any single telephone teaching session, it is obviously paramount to balance integration within the whole group with differentiation strategies that may remove learners from the whole. It is also important to make sure that
an individual's progression is not impeded by the group mix in which s/he finds
himself, and the teacher will want to check what groupings work for each student.
Some useful tips include:

- check out technical options for splitting the group;
- make sure individuals are happy with how the group is split.

Prepared and low-risk activities versus spontaneous and high-risk ones

Prepared contributions may be more crucial in telephone teaching because they
enable learners to build confidence in what can be a challenging mode initially. Frequent use of the telephone may be normal to them for social conversations but not as
a teaching mode. Prepared contributions may ease learners into use of L2. However,
in blended programmes where telephone teaching sessions are the source of new
input, this may not be possible, as learners will not have the knowledge to prepare in
this way. In blends where learners work on self-study materials in advance and are
able to prepare, there can be a danger that some learners meticulously over-prepare
every agenda item and simply read this work out during the teaching session. The
telephone setting can encourage this behaviour because the reading of notes is not
visible to others, although it is often audible through a distinct intonation or delivery style. Teachers may need to interrupt to ask questions or to extend the prepared
work into a more spontaneous, if higher risk, area afterwards, by inviting more discussion. Alternatively, the teacher could pre-empt this at planning stage by asking
learners to think about their favourite book, for example, but not telling them in

advance how the information is going to be used. It is important for learners to learn how to deal with the unexpected and move to spontaneous and higher-risk language tasks as soon as possible. Some useful tips include:

- in speaking practice situations, give learners general rather than detailed guidelines on what to prepare in advance;
- help learners with strategies to deal with the unexpected during activities.

The different stages of a telephone session

The stages of the telephone session can be broadly broken down as follows to ensure each fulfils its intended purpose in the development of the whole session.

Opening stage

- Do a sound check to ensure participants can hear and be heard and start to recognise each other's voices. This makes learners comfortable and creates the feeling of a learning community in the mode. The teacher can also use this stage to explain the framework, learning outcomes and protocols on the telephone such as turn-taking, and also ease participants into L2.
- Suitable tasks may include low-risk and short tasks: for example, ice-breakers (such as 'Bingo'); informal chat (introduce yourself; interviewing each other; talking about holidays etc.); guessing games (such as 'Who am I?'); general knowledge quizzes as well as prepared activities (such as reporting on an internet search; preparing a role for a role-play); listing things that make them happy; telling a story (which can be either true or false); or sharing a picture (which is sent in advance).
- Teachers can also integrate study skills work such as listening skills into this stage, which could then be used as a thread through a session to help learners evaluate how best to listen for gist, for detail or for targeted information.

Middle stage

- Encourage participants to progress from prepared to spontaneous language, and to speak in L2 as much as possible. Differentiate language tasks and help individual progress based on their language knowledge, confidence and experience. Check grammar and pronunciation, and give feedback on problematic areas.
- Suitable tasks may include debates, discussions, information gap tasks, role-plays, storytelling or picture descriptions (where teachers may decide to give vocabulary beforehand). Plan a quick succession of short tasks on a topic such as 'food and drink', and then build up to a longer interactive task such as planning a picnic together. Revise grammar points, such as tenses, and embed these in new speaking tasks. Build in guessing games (such as 'What happens next?'). Encourage paired tasks and mini-presentations on topics embedded in the course material. Have some questions ready to

break a silence or change direction should this be necessary. Summarising and reviewing progress can be a useful way of recapping and moving the session forward at this stage.

Final stage

- Ascertain that learners have achieved the learning outcomes. Allow them to relax; take final questions; end on a positive note.
- Suitable tasks may include a short summary of what has been achieved, discussion of the next session, quick quiz, question and answers etc.
- Encourage learners to carry on the discussion on their own via telephone, either on a one-to-one basis or as a mini self-help group, or perhaps in an asynchronous forum if this is part of the blend.

Issues arising after the telephone session

After the session, teachers may want to:

- invite feedback on the telephone session from the group and suggestions for the next telephone tutorial;
- assess what has and has not worked well based on evidence. Were there technical issues or problems with hearing? Were the objectives achieved? Were the tasks of a suitable length and level of difficulty for the mode? Did learners progress well? How well did the tasks differentiate between different levels of ability? Was the pace appropriate?
- follow up discussion by email, telephone or letter to individuals or to the whole group;
- develop an action plan for future tutorials with individuals who were not able to follow the session well enough;
- consider contacting learners separately by telephone to smooth out misunderstandings that may have arisen and check that they were comfortable discussing grammar or linguistic problems;
- provide a short synopsis of the telephone session to the group, incorporating error correction or referring back to course materials for further clarification of linguistic points;
- consider if the appropriate level of L2 for the course, the teaching mode and the individual learner was used, whether there was enough or too much guidance for the tasks;
- consider whether there was too much or too little correction of error, whether feedback was appropriate for the teaching mode, and if learners took notice of corrections;
- consider if learners were confident with the protocols for this mode. Were all suitably involved, and was there sensitivity to individual needs? Was there too much or too little silence? Was there too much teacher-talk time? Were learner questions fully answered at the end?

Some conferencing providers can record telephone sessions, and teachers may want to explore this so they can review the telephone session at a later stage. This does, however, require prior permission from all participants.

Future developments

Chinnery (2006) expounds the benefits and challenges of mobile-assisted language learning. Benefits include price, availability and mobility, but the challenges are small screen size, audiovisual quality, virtual keyboarding and one-finger data entry, limited power, limited non-verbal communication and message length, lack of cultural context and potentially limited social interaction. Kiernan and Aizawa (2004) point out that mobile phones are moving away from verbal to visual forms of communication. In this regard, the technical advances, particularly in the resolution of display screens on mobile phones, may yet overcome issues linked to the absence of visual cues currently experienced by learners in telephone teaching.

Much of the latest research focus surrounding mobile phones in language teaching is on discrete language points. Brown (2001) describes one of the first projects using mobile phones for language learning. This included vocabulary practice, quizzes, word and phrase translations and access to teachers talking 'live', all of which was deemed effective and of great potential. Stockwell (2007) reports on the potential of an intelligent mobile-based vocabulary tutor. Thorton and Houser (2002; 2003; 2005) carried out projects using mobile phones to provide English vocabulary lessons by SMS to Japanese university learners and report very good results. Demouy and Kukulska-Hulme (2010) trialled the use of mobile phones for interactive dialogues and report on its benefits and challenges. Todd and Tepsuriwong (2008) researched a more communicative paradigm, an action reading maze game, and underline its benefits.

The OU has also taken a more holistic approach and developed content for iTunes U (www.apple.com/education/itunes-u) including languages, where learners can download materials without charge. Since the launch of this facility in 2008 there have been more than 20 million downloads, of which a total of 20% are in languages (Henderson, 2010).

It can be expected that, with further technological sophistication, there will be both developments for the mode in its own right and the combination of telephone with other modes. Gaskell and Mills (2004) predict further use of text messaging for sharing organisational information, such as reminders about teaching sessions or assessments and for administrative support. Mobile phones may also increase global access to language learning. There are already some free and commercial language learning programmes available for mobile phones, such as BBC World Service, which offers English lessons via text messaging in some countries, such as Bangladesh. Norbrook and Scott (2003) claim that portability and immediacy, rather than location, are the essential motivating factors in mobile language learning. With increased availability and affordability of mobile telephones there is likely to be a higher demand for and uptake of such programmes. Portability of the mobile phone and the language learning resources it affords will also allow learners to work in small bursts as and when time is available. Linking-up facilities such as Bluetooth and GPS-enabled mobile phones may further invite co-operation between learners, while increasing sophistication may mean mobile phones offering conferencing with a visual channel and portable keyboard.

Further use of web browser capacities and Wireless Application Protocol (WAP) will develop more language activities such as moblogging, a combination of mobile and weblogging. The OU is also trying to optimise mobile access to online course materials through Moodle (http://docs.moodle.org/en/Moodle_for_Mobiles). These innovations will further develop 'flexible and individual distance teaching with the learner group as social and academic support for learning' (Rekkedal and Dye, 2007). The design and use of educational language games and simulations for mobiles will also undoubtedly be developed.

The combination of telephone with other technologies — for example, automatic speech recognition such as Write-By-Phone (Donahue, 2005b) or Telephone Learner (Donahue, 2005a) — is already being exploited for language learning. Here, an automated telephone language learning system provides listening and speaking tasks, which can help reduce language teachers' workload in that learners' interactions are evaluated automatically on the Web. However, a debate may be had about the fact that such tools remove the teacher and the human contact from language learning.

Developments should be viewed with two caveats. First, blended learning as a whole is a complex infrastructure requiring specific support for learners. While telephone teaching in itself may be a relatively simple mechanism, its place within such an infrastructure becomes more complex. There is a need to explain to learners what particular role the telephone plays and how it dovetails with other elements of the blend. Second, much of the use of mobile phones for learning over the last years has been driven by the desire to use the technology rather than address learner needs. Salaberry (2001) argues against 'technology-driven pedagogy' and Beatty (2003, p. 72) warns 'that teachers need to be concerned about investing time and money in unproven technology'. Kukulska-Hulme and Traxler (2007, p. 190) conclude that individuals have to use mobile technologies in a personalised way to ensure that 'learning designs are ... more likely to be exciting, innovative and challenging'.

Conclusion

The telephone may have recently become the less fashionable option for language teaching sessions when sophisticated online technological options are on offer. In fact, in some cases, it may simply have become the fallback option when technical problems arise online. However, this chapter has highlighted its invaluable place in blended learning. Its familiarity, relative ease of use in what can be a technological jungle, and its cost-effective nature make it a more accessible and less challenging tool for many teachers and learners. It offers immediacy and flexibility of contact and can cover a myriad of support and tuition needs. While it can require intense focus because of the voice-only contact, in language teaching this has proved to result in noticeable cognitive gains (Stevens and Hewer, 1998). As new telephone technology develops it can be anticipated that it will continue to be a relevant teaching tool.

In contemplating the future of telephone teaching in blended contexts, three pertinent sets of questions emerge. First, will the telephone emerge within the blended learning jigsaw as an element of equal value to others, or will it continue to live in the shadow of online synchronous conferencing and face-to-face tuition? In this respect will providers of blended learning courses offer a 'holistic' package to learners, taking learner choices and learning preferences seriously enough to develop all teaching elements, including telephone conferencing, in their own right? If so, what kind of ongoing training support will they offer to teachers and learners? Second, will telephone conferencing continue to be more affordable and technologically less challenging than online conferencing? How will ICT-related geographical, financial, technological and educational challenges affect the development of telephone teaching, and how will this mode be used to overcome some of these obstacles? Third, will telephone conferencing benefit from technological advances to provide, for example, voice recognition for individual or group speaking assessments or voice-recognised transcripts of recorded teaching sessions, for the benefit of learners? Or will technological developments involve a merging of telephone and synchronous online conferencing? Only time will tell.

Chapter 9:   **Planning and Preparing for Synchronous Online Teaching**

Sylvia Warnecke and Loykie Lominé

Introduction

Synchronous communication facilitated by online technology is having a significant impact on how people connect, work, learn and collaborate. Technologies that 'support the dynamic exchange of information and experiences' (Agostini *et al.*, 2000, p. 381) allow people to be constantly 'connected to place, task and others' (Adams *et al.*, 2010). What started with instant messaging, a form of real-time direct text-based communication between two or more people in the 1960s, long before the dawn of widespread internet use, has today become a domain where users communicate in multi-modal applications either via computers or mobile devices. Van't Hooft (2008, p. 31) suggests that such communication 'enabl[es] us to have rich experiences as we access, aggregate, create, customise and share digital information in a variety of media formats, anywhere and anytime'. This technological development therefore supports increasingly complex forms of interaction between users.

Synchronous conferencing in the language teaching and learning context

The use of synchronous communication tools in education varies and can affect how teaching and learning take place. The list of web conferencing providers has become very long with a growing number of applications, such as Dimdim or 1videoConference, made available on an open source basis, or FlashMeeting, which is freely available for educational use. Other web conferencing applications are commercial products including Elluminate, Genesys Meeting Center or iLinc. Users can attend so-called 'webinars', conduct meetings, undergo training, or learn and practise speaking a language. Apart from making use of these audiographic conferencing tools, teaching languages is also carried out in virtual worlds such as ActiveWorlds and Second Life. Using instant messaging in teaching languages is covered here, but teaching in virtual worlds is beyond the scope of this chapter.

The proliferation of online tools available for teaching has prompted discussion about the differing skills base of learners and teachers and therefore variations in their use of these tools. White's suggested distinction between 'digital visitors' and 'digital residents' highlights the divide between internet users who consider 'the web as a "place to live" as opposed to a collection of useful tools' (White, D., 2008).

In language learning and teaching, the adoption of synchronous online communication tools has revolutionised course design and delivery. It has led many educational institutions to combine aspects of self-study with face-to-face, online synchronous and asynchronous teaching: for example, the Goethe-Institut has introduced a variety of blended language courses that now link learners of German both within individual countries and internationally. Yet, despite the fact that many educationalists enthusiastically embrace the new technology for teaching languages via audiographic synchronous sessions, others are more cautious. Duensing *et al.* (2006, p. 35) stress the need to establish whether this mode of delivery can provide the quality of social interaction that is essential for the language learning process and that is possible in face-to-face contexts. They go on to point out that effective synchronous online communication ought to allow language learners to 'engage actively, collaboratively and at times independently in negotiation of meaning while participating in meaningful tasks in real time'. As the available online tools permit transmission of speakers' voices in real time, together with information presented visually through images or text, the interactions in a wide range of web conferencing applications can now mirror very closely those in face-to-face teaching situations.

Increasing experience in teaching language with the help of online synchronous conferencing tools has helped practitioners to develop a better understanding of working in such an environment. In a 2009 in-house survey of thirty language teachers working at the OU, respondents suggested that, in their view, the learner experience was enhanced and interaction was supported by multi-modal exchanges via audio, video, visual aids and other tools in the Elluminate conferencing system, which was being used. During a pilot using iLinc in 2010 involving fifteen teachers at the Goethe-Institut in Glasgow and Munich, participants reported that some learners tended to speak more and took on more responsibility for making communication work than they would in face-to-face sessions. They also maintained that some learners liked the fact that they could not be directly observed when attempting to speak. This was interpreted as a comfort rather than a problem. A further advantage stressed by both groups was that, since such conferences were available twenty-four hours a day, a number of learners took advantage of the opportunity to communicate with one another outwith teaching session times. This in turn allowed them to develop a stronger sense of belonging to a group in the blended learning context.

The purpose of this chapter is to demonstrate how teachers can most efficiently plan and prepare synchronous online teaching sessions as part of a blended teaching programme as outlined in Chapter 7. The chapter covers both technological and pedagogical aspects and explores the roles and conventions in online synchronous interaction that affect the planning process.

Key pedagogical considerations

Although language teaching via synchronous online conferencing has many similarities with teaching in a classroom context, some features are different and may share some similarity with teaching by telephone (see Chapter 8). This section covers the main issues that have an effect on planning and teaching in synchronous online conferencing.

Conference type

The term 'synchronous online conferencing' actually comprises a variety of formats of conference types, in a continuum ranging from basic text chat to complex multi-modal conferencing environments.

At one end of the spectrum the text chat (or 'instant messaging', 'IM', or 'chat') solely relies on the input of short text (or possibly simple images such as emoticons). Although the term suggests a rather informal mode of communication, chatting may be used for teaching purposes. It can be managed, structured and moderated; whole teaching sessions can occur through chatting, although typing speed and accuracy are two critical factors. While text chat is mainly based on fast written reactions in short and sometimes simple language, there is also the so-called 'expert chat' where an invited expert is available for a question-and-answer session. Messages then tend to be longer and more complex. Most virtual learning environments have a built-in text chat facility which is available at all times. The technology notifies users of who logs on and who is online. Learners can spontaneously 'meet up' and give each other study support or practise the L2.

At the other end of the spectrum are complex web conferencing applications incorporating a range of functionalities (such as text chat, audio, video and interactive whiteboards and avatars). In this chapter, the authors concentrate on that type of complex conference to outline the scope of such multi-user and multi-functional web-based communication tools for language teaching.

Technological constraints

Whereas face-to-face teaching allows for high degrees of spontaneity and flexibility with regard to timing and task design, as outlined in Chapter 11, synchronous online sessions require more detailed planning in these areas. The challenges for learners and teachers are varied. Learners have to negotiate the L2 within the settings for interaction that the online tool affords. Some learners may even find that the technology gets in the way of their language learning. Planning for synchronous online conferencing is generally based on 'ideal' conditions that rarely occur. Many challenges cannot be predicted, yet they will affect the quality of the session. These could include technical problems, poor sound quality, the different IT skills base of teachers and learners, variations in the capacity of the hardware and software, fluctuating connection speed, varying bandwidth, unexpected disconnection and the like. Teachers need to plan for the unexpected and take account of what might go wrong in order to create circumstances that offer a valuable learning experience nonetheless. In addition, lack of familiarity with the mode can lead both learners and teachers to perceive the communication as artificial because of the absence of visual cues such as facial expression and gesture. Everyone needs to learn to make the most effective use of the tools available in the particular conference type that they are using.

Focus

In many blended language programmes, synchronous online conferencing is primarily used for speaking practice, as it is felt that synchronous teaching time is better spent in helping learners build their confidence and skills in various forms of spoken interaction and in pronunciation and intonation. In blends where synchronous teaching is used for consolidating what learners have worked on in their self-study time, the teaching of new grammar points is likely to be kept to a minimum in this mode, although contextualised grammar practice via speaking activities may be a key feature of such teaching sessions. Where the synchronous online conference is a more substantial component of the blend, the focus may shift towards greater teacher input of new language points and teacher-led presentations, explanations and exemplification of these points as well as interactive speaking practice. Synchronous online teaching sessions as part of a blend also offer an ideal environment for revision, enrichment and extension work. In addition, the discussion of study and learning skills pertaining to learning and using a language can, as in other modes, be usefully integrated into synchronous online teaching sessions.

Time

Time is precious in synchronous online teaching. Sessions cannot be as lengthy as in a face-to-face environment because the multi-tasking, the need to look at a screen, to sit for the entire duration of the session and to listen and speak through a headset can be exhausting for those involved. Therefore, teaching time needs to be carefully planned and managed. Synchronous online conferencing relies much more on turn-taking than is the case in face-to-face contexts where spontaneous, polite interruption may be possible. This means that communication may take longer. In addition, turn-taking in synchronous online conferencing is not supported by facial expressions, gestures or body language, and an equivalent cue may have to be expressed verbally or through the use of on-screen emoticons.

Group support

Synchronous online teaching sessions can play a vital role in the development of communication within groups and in helping to promote positive group dynamics. This is significant for a number of reasons. Learners may be new to blended learning and therefore not familiar with working in groups that do not frequently meet face-to-face. Much of the regular communication in the group may be carried out in asynchronous formats. Teaching learners how to use the synchronous conferencing tool confidently facilitates and encourages groups to meet outside teaching session times and work together independently. This in turn allows learners to carry over discussions from asynchronous to synchronous modes and vice versa, as suggested in Chapter 2.

Netiquette

This term refers to 'network etiquette', that is, the expected code of conduct of participants. The first rule in many netiquette guides is '"remember the human" to encourage more tolerant and considerate behaviour among internet users' (Sturges, 2002, p. 209). In the context of web conferencing, adhering to a code of conduct requires the teacher to introduce ground rules and to establish with the group what action signifies which stance. The following list may help teachers define such ground rules for their group:

- remind learners to indicate when they want to speak (which could be done by clicking on buttons such as 'raise hand' or 'join the queue');
- remind learners that all messages in the chat may be read by moderators; that the chat is part of the teaching session work and can distract when used for extensive chit-chat; that chat can be saved; and that others will be able to read the messages after the session;
- remind learners to maintain a friendly tone in spoken and written output, as they would in other contexts;
- ask permission from participants of a particular session before recording any part of a session to adhere to rights of privacy;
- establish when the use of L1, as opposed to L2, is acceptable (e.g. in connection with technical problems and functionalities of the tool or depending on the nature of the group as explained in Chapter 3);
- establish what to do when technical problems arise (e.g. notifying others via text chat);
- establish when learners ought (or ought not) to use tools such as video and when (or when not) to alter screen contents, since any change, even just resizing an image, may affect the entire group.

Tools and their pedagogical uses

This section provides an overview of the most commonly used tools for synchronous conferencing such as Elluminate, FlashMeeting, iLinc or Skype. A summary of some typical tools and their pedagogical uses is given in Figure 9.1 (see p. 132-3). Many web conferencing software packages are based on the division of roles into participant and moderator. In addition, some allow for a third and fourth role, the assistant and the administrator. Although not all tools have this division of roles (for example, FlashMeeting, Skype) this overview concentrates on the participant/moderator distinction, because it has the biggest impact on the management of teaching sessions. However, it is important to note that these conferencing tools were developed originally for purposes other than language teaching. The role of learner is not an exact equivalent to the role of participant, and the role of moderator is not identical with that of teacher. These roles can shift and be adjusted during individual sessions as outlined in the discussion below.

What follows is a list of the most common tools in synchronous online conferencing. The letters 'm' and 'p' indicate which tools may be manipulated by moderators (m) and/or participants (p):

- audio (m/p);
- audio set-up (m/p);
- video (m/p);
- interactive whiteboard (m/p limited);
- text chat (m/p);
- list of participants with activity indicators (m);
- hand/join queue button (m/p);
- voting/polling (m/p limited);
- away or time-out button (m/p);
- gather/follow moderator button (m);
- moving between screens (m/p limited);
- moving between rooms (m/p sometimes limited);
- opening/removing/saving materials/screens (m/p limited).

A number of software packages also offer the following, more complex tools:

- file transfer (m/p);
- application sharing (m/p);
- desktop sharing (m/p);
- integrated web browsing (m);
- recording (m);
- multi-media store (m);
- breakout rooms (m);
- timer (m);
- quiz (m);
- personal settings, i.e. picture/icon/avatar/sounds (m/p);
- personalised greeting/absence indicator (m/p);
- preloaded content (m).

Tool	Description	Pedagogical uses
Audio	Transmits audio from one or more speakers at a time; the sound level can be adjusted.	Facilitates oral communication, interaction, collaboration and practice.
Text chat	Instant messaging which may be enhanced by emoticons such as ☺ or ☹. The communication happens between moderators and learners but the settings may also allow for messages to be sent to specific users only. Text chat can be saved during or after the session.	Written communication for comments, asides, adding a personal reaction and vocabulary help without interrupting the flow; for writing brief utterances or short stories together in real time; messages between moderators can assist organisation in team teaching; useful when participants encounter audio and other technical problems. Review contents/vocabulary after the session.
Emoticons	Allow participants to show emotions, reactions or to make comments which in face-to-face situations are expressed by gestures and facial expressions.	Allow all participants to express themselves non-verbally; facilitate communication; make non-verbal 'asides' quicker and less intrusive.
File transfer	Sharing files from other software applications with participants.	Allows information sharing; facilitates collaboration.
Gather/follow moderator button	Enables the teacher to ensure everyone in one room is looking at the intended visual materials simultaneously.	Helps to avoid confusion and allows easy management of visual materials; group management.
Raise hand button	Indicates that a person wants to speak (is visual but can also be set in connection with an audio signal).	Managing spoken interaction, polite interruption; useful for activities where the numbering of the raised hand indicates the order in which learners wish to speak; time-saving device as the main facilitator (possibly the teacher, though not necessarily) does not need to indicate whose turn it is to contribute — providing this convention has been established.
Recording	Entire sessions or some parts can be recorded and later made available online with the participants' consent.	Learners can listen again to sessions or part-sessions; teachers can set specific listening tasks or tests as a follow-up activity after the session; recordings can support self-reflection/evaluation and can be provided for those who missed teaching sessions.
Rooms including breakout rooms	Whilst each conference has a main room by default, many applications also have so-called personal rooms. Many packages allow the creation (and deletion) of additional breakout rooms, generally with the same functionalities as the main room. Participants can move from room to room but the moderator can also control this movement. Rooms can be created and prepared (generally by the moderator) by uploading content in advance.	Allows learners to work in pairs/groups (without hearing the communication in other rooms). Use of these rooms supports learner control and collaboration, facilitates more unconstrained learning experiences, and maximises speaking practice and learners' active involvement.

Tool	Description	Pedagogical use
Time out/away button	Usually changes the appearance of the participant's/ moderator's name on the screen and indicates that this person is currently not taking part.	Helps teachers keep an overview of who is active and allows moderators and participants to indicate that they have to leave the session briefly, without logging off.
Timer	Can function either as a timer or a stopwatch, generally set by the moderator and visible to all participants in all rooms. Once the timer has run out it can also send an audio signal to all users. It can be paused, stopped and cancelled.	Supports time management by indicating when groups ought to finish their tasks. It can also be used in assessment situations with time limits.
Integrated web browsing	The tool opens websites from within the web conference and allows guided and independent web surfing. The web addresses can be published and saved in the text chat.	Facilitates access to authentic and up-to-date materials online. The 'guided web tour' helps learners to find specific information fast. It can be prepared by the teacher allowing more control of material and assumes less ICT skill on the part of learners. Caution is needed however, since the linguistic level and the presentation of materials on many websites is not designed for teaching purposes.
Video	Provides streaming of video images via webcams. Many applications now facilitate simultaneous streaming of more than one video. The tool allows the placing of video snapshots on the whiteboard and adjustment of the image settings and quality.	Allows moderators and participants to see each other in real time and add a more personal note to a teaching session. Use with caution however, since it can be perceived as distracting or even intimidating.
Voting and polling/feedback	Facilitates voting by means of x (no) and ✓ (yes) as well as selecting answers in multiple choice questions. The system shows all votes in conjunction with participants' names and publishes overviews of the multiple choice answers.	Allows participants to cast votes or to confirm whether they understand instructions. It supports the teacher's time and group management, in that it provides quick feedback and an overview of answers within the group.
Interactive whiteboard	Facilitates drawing, uploading of images, prepared whiteboards or PowerPoint presentations, and the placing of objects, visuals as well as text. Objects can be layered, moved and fixed. Whiteboards can be saved, labelled, copied and pasted.	Provides visual stimuli for activities and discussions etc.; allows collaboration in groups and in the plenary; serves as a place for gathering and noting ideas, structures tasks; and affords creative interaction with the tool.

Please note that the personalisation tools and preferences settings available in a particular conferencing system are indispensable in order to help learners to tailor the use of the software to their individual needs and to promote learner control. This means that teachers need to ensure learners are familiar with and can manipulate these settings.

Figure 9.1: Overview of some typical synchronous conferencing tools and their pedagogical uses

Roles and settings

Teacher or moderator

The role of the teacher in synchronous online conferencing is not very different from her/his role in face-to-face teaching sessions, although there can be a tendency for the teacher to become more dominant during synchronous online teaching sessions. This is partly due to the configuration of the conferencing software, which may allocate more 'rights' and 'privileges' as well as access to more tools to the moderator than to the participants. Teachers consequently have to plan to stimulate learners' spoken interaction as effectively as possible and consider how to teach the group to become more independent. The planning stages can appear to require more input from teachers than the actual teaching sessions, where learners are often encouraged to take control. The teacher nonetheless needs to be in charge of the event and will need to master several challenges, such as keeping track of the multiple communication channels (chat, audio input etc.) and developing strategies to compensate for the lack of body language such as gesture and facial expression. The following aspects can help in planning to meet these challenges.

A gradual introduction to the tools for learners

Although most institutions provide preparatory materials and help for users, teachers cannot expect learners to master the conferencing software fully in the early teaching sessions. An effective way to address this is to introduce one new feature (for example, 'voting') in each teaching session. In this way learners can gradually familiarise themselves with the different tools and understand their purpose.

Maximising participation

Teachers who facilitate tasks where learners can take control tend to achieve a higher degree of engagement between learners. However, participation should not simply be measured by the amount of spoken output from each learner. The synchronous online environment allows interaction on many other levels such as written output, use of symbols or emoticons and manipulation of the whiteboard.

Individual teaching style

Teachers will want to familiarise learners with the way in which they prefer to use the tools and intend to run the interactive teaching sessions. This can be done by explaining to the group why certain tools are used in particular ways in certain parts of sessions and how these can support interaction. Such a strategy will make the organisation of the teaching session more transparent and can increase learner engagement.

Code of conduct

By establishing ground rules and protocols (for example, about turn-taking), the communication can become more fluid. Learners can more easily take control of sections of the teaching session and become more independent in the way they interact and build up the interaction further. Because there is a set of ground rules and protocols, learners can keep the session going should the teacher encounter technical problems or even be disconnected. Part of the planning for each session can therefore include the teaching of new phrases in relation to such rules and protocols.

Detailed task instructions

Teachers need to consider in advance how they want to introduce a new task. Do they want to present learners with a model dialogue or do they want to give everyone the necessary information and leave learners to create a dialogue on their own? In addition to spoken instructions, teachers need to plan how the material they use can complement the instructions, especially when learners are asked to work in separate breakout rooms. A reminder of how to find the material they want in the breakout room will help learners become more independent, confident and familiar with certain procedures.

Developing routines

An element of predictability in the structure and conduct of an online teaching session can be a major advantage. After a few sessions, learners can anticipate what to do if they or the teacher get disconnected. The activities can still go on. A routine can also be a time-saving device as learners will not need repeated explanations: for example, that breakout room work is followed by a plenary session with a spokesperson from each sub-group summarising the discussion.

Learner or participant

Despite the seemingly 'hierarchical' configuration, learners can take control of the session as effectively as in face-to-face settings, if not more so, but this requires an effective use of the software and possibly a shift from the default setting. In most web conferencing software the default setting is that participants are not given access to the same range of tools as the moderator, but this contrasts with an ethos of learner empowerment, which is important in many blended contexts. Moving from less to more involvement in the online learning situation can help bolster learners' confidence in speaking the L2. The fact that mastering the technology is not directly linked to the mastery of the L2 also allows some learners (the ones who are more familiar with the online environment, that is the 'digital residents') to play a leading role in guiding the whole group, including the teacher, on some aspects of the technology. As mentioned earlier, the accessibility of online synchronous conferencing within a blended programme can also enable learners to meet and establish strong group dynamics outside teaching sessions and without being dependent on teacher presence.

What has become more and more apparent to practitioners is that online learning can have an impact on learner identity (Nicolson and Adams, 2008, p. 106). The online mode can provide some learners with a 'safety net' in the sense that they can create a new persona, to whatever degree they desire, and use this in activities more readily than they could in a face-to-face context, where visual identity markers can result in stereotyping on the part of others. Some learners will be accustomed to such reinvention via social networking sites such as MySpace, Facebook or Second Life, which allows people to 'live a second life online', for which they create their own 'avatar', their new identity. The absence of some visual cues (for example, the lack of spontaneous facial expressions and body language, which can sometimes be unsettling in face-to-face settings) can also be perceived as an advantage. Some other learners, however, may see the online mode as an obstacle to communication, particularly those who rely on visual cues and feel the need to be able to see the person with whom they are communicating. Some may go so far as to find this form of communication artificial and refuse to engage.

When planning sessions it is important to remember that taking part may already represent a substantial psychological effort for some learners. Put another way, their presence itself may be taxing for them, even before the start of the session. Simple acts such as explicitly acknowledging/welcoming each learner by name are very important. Experienced teachers always allow time at the start of each session to create and strengthen the sense of an online community of learners ready to interact with one another.

As in telephone conferencing (see Chapter 8), silences in web conferencing can be perceived as more significant because of the lack of accompanying cues, such as facial expressions and eye contact, which, in the face-to-face context, allows others to interpret silences more easily. As suggested by Stickler *et al.* (2007, online), silences are not necessarily negative, but may be just a gap indicating necessary 'thinking time' for the communicator. When planning sessions, extra time must therefore be allocated to tasks that in face-to-face contexts may not take as long, and teachers need to be ready to allow learners to respond in their own time.

Task design for synchronous online teaching sessions

Klapper (2003, p. 35) defines tasks as: 'Meaning-based activities closely related to learners' actual communicative needs …, in which learners have to achieve a genuine outcome … and … effective completion of the task is accorded priority.' To design tasks that fulfil these criteria it is necessary to take account of the following four aspects: form of interaction; content focus; material; form of feedback. In web conferencing, a fifth dimension is added: the functionality of the software. All planning therefore has to determine in what way the software can facilitate the task. The pedagogic purpose of a task determines content and form. The interaction in the online context is governed by the configuration of the software and the way the settings are employed to support engagement and communication.

Feedback in online synchronous conferencing takes on a slightly different form from that in face-to-face settings. Feedback is determined partly by software settings and partly by their use during a teaching session to indicate understanding, attention, (dis)-agreement, emotions etc. as well as the verbal expression of learners' views.

Some practical examples

While it would be impossible to provide an exhaustive range of guidance, the following examples may highlight the potential and possible pitfalls in planning tasks for interactive teaching sessions. The four examples highlight planning issues and also show that, despite different approaches and solutions, the teacher's role is to select what is most appropriate for each specific group and conferencing tool.

Example 1

Learners are asked to discuss a question in the 'snowball' format where they start by speaking in pairs and then move on to an exchange in larger groups. In a face-to-face context, it is possible to move around the room and to provide the instructions on the board or a handout, but online the teacher has to think about how the breakout rooms can be set up with relevant materials, and how movement between those rooms can be organised to allow for the most effective interaction and smooth running of this part of the session.

Example 2

The teacher is planning to use a website during the session. Does s/he want learners to explore it on their own or be guided in a plenary session? If s/he chooses the plenary, s/he can open a browser and guide the search. If s/he decides that independent surfing is more beneficial, s/he would have to set up breakout rooms for groups and start the browser her/himself manually in each room, as learners in the role of participants do not have access to this function in many conferencing applications. Another solution would be to grant participants temporary moderator status. This makes the initial organisation of the activity easier but brings a number of pitfalls, since learners will then have access to the same tools as the moderator and be working with less familiar settings.

Example 3

The teacher plans to start the session with an ice-breaker during which learners are expected to speak without prompts from the teacher. But how can interaction be organised to ensure the aim is achieved without confusing learners and causing long gaps in the interaction? The teacher could ask the entire group to raise their hand at the start of the activity. This automatically puts all speakers in a 'waiting list'. Learners then speak taking turns according to this order without the teacher having to manage this or even speak her/himself.

Example 4

The teacher is planning to incorporate visual materials produced by learners. Can learners upload their own materials? If so, they need to have the material ready and have to be told/shown how to upload. If this is not the case, the teacher has to gather the materials from the group before the session and upload everything in advance or use file transfer during the session. Alternatively, participants could again be granted temporary moderator status to facilitate the uploading during the session either in the plenary or in breakout rooms.

Visual aids

Visual aids can contribute to the success of synchronous online teaching sessions: although material production is initially time-consuming, the digital format makes reusing and adapting very easy. Often it appears more difficult to narrow down the choice than to find interesting and stimulating material. One can distinguish between three sources, described below.

Designed by the teacher

Material may have been previously designed by the teacher for a different group and purpose. This may mean adapting material that worked well, for example, in a face-to-face context, although this can prove difficult because of the different nature of the environment.

Produced by colleagues

There are many resources freely available online, and more and more institutions are establishing repositories where colleagues can share digital resources. However, all prepared materials designed for different contexts may need careful adapting. Possible pitfalls include standardisation of format and copyrights.

Produced by learners

Material produced during previous sessions, for example, can be used in order to involve learners in the preparation of *their* teaching session.

Guidelines for planning and task design

As maximising interaction is a key success factor in online sessions, the following guidelines for planning and task design are essential:

- Be aware that tasks tend to take longer than in face-to-face settings.
- The best session plan often includes a move from highly structured and closed tasks to more creative and open-ended ones, which is why the beginning-middle-end teaching model outlined in Chapter 7 is a highly suitable format for online synchronous conferencing.
- Employing too many different tools during one online session may be confusing for participants; using fewer tools keeps the focus on interaction in the language rather than on mastering the technology.
- Using and modifying a limited number of materials during a session tends to be beneficial for time management.
- Visuals may support interaction, but they need to be carefully tailored. Showing video clips in the L2 can have a disheartening effect if the level of the language spoken is too complex for the group.
- Each task should have a clearly defined beginning and end, with outcomes that can be visualised by the learners.

- Time planning for tasks needs to take account of extra time needed for managing screens, moving between rooms or using interactive features.

The following task types may be particularly appropriate for online synchronous sessions:

- brainstorming;
- role-play;
- dialogue;
- working with visual images;
- reviewing core vocabulary;
- information gap or 'jigsaw' tasks;
- storytelling and retelling.

Synchronous online teaching sessions can offer much scope for creative, open-ended tasks that foster learner control and individualised learning experiences, despite the formalised configurations of the technology and the turn-taking nature of much of the communication.

Conclusion

Having explored the role of synchronous online conferencing within a blended language programme and identified key planning issues for teachers, this chapter has shown the importance of understanding how technological features of synchronous online conferencing can best support teaching practice to achieve intended learning outcomes. Synchronous online teaching sessions can maximise learners' exposure to the L2 and facilitate speaking practice by providing opportunities for interaction among groups. They can foster group cohesion and collaboration as well as allowing learners to take more responsibility for their learning. However, they also require both teachers and learners to acquire new skills in mastering the tools and putting them to the most effective use.

The scope of the communication and interaction supported by the range of tools available in the synchronous online mode is vast. In view of the time constraints and the nature of the tools, the planning stages of synchronous online teaching sessions may be even more crucial to the success of the teaching sessions than in the face-to-face context. The adoption of online communication may result in the learner and teacher roles being different from traditional patterns. Teacher input is likely to be more extensive during the preparation stages and learner input will be required more and more during teaching sessions in which interaction becomes 'visible' through codes and symbols as well as through the spoken word. Supporting learner control over both the L2 and the technology necessitates skilful planning and design of the task components and material on the part of the teacher to achieve effective and creative teaching that inspires learners to interact and develop their language skills, both during the teaching sessions and beyond.

Chapter 10:   **Delivering Synchronous Online Teaching**

Loykie Lominé, Sylvia Warnecke and Elke St.John

Introduction

Following the discussion of preparation and planning for synchronous online sessions in the previous chapter, this chapter will examine key issues affecting the delivery of such teaching sessions, with a focus on the logistics, facilitation and evaluation of these sessions within a blended language teaching programme. Particular attention is paid to the nexus of technology and pedagogy, with the ultimate aim of ensuring they complement each other in effective and enjoyable online teaching sessions. The chapter will aim to provide advice and suggestions to help teachers deliver sessions successfully.

Learners participating in synchronous online teaching sessions may bring a diversity of skills and experience that affect their approach to both the L2 and the technology, as noted in Chapter 9. Moreover, that experience may mean that both teachers and learners may be used to a particular 'power balance' in teaching sessions, often based on a view that the session is controlled by the teacher who takes a lead throughout. However, in an online environment that 'power balance' may shift: for example, where the learner may be more competent in use of technology than the teacher, thereby contributing knowledge and expertise of a different kind. The learner may then take on a 'teaching role' with regard to technical skills while the teacher continues to take the lead in the language learning aspects of the session. This shift can have a positive effect on learner confidence, encouraging learner control and group cohesion.

In the context of synchronous online language teaching sessions, the 'digital divide' referred to Chapter 9 can have a crucial effect on the success of language learning activities, since learners will need to feel sufficiently at ease to engage successfully in multi-layered interaction with others. As Bennet *et al.* (2008) confirm, in the context of education settings in general, the more familiar learners are with the functionalities of non-subject-specific web-based interactions the more they will be inclined to employ these in a teaching session, and even show others how such functionalities can be appropriately used.

The issues affecting the delivery of synchronous online teaching sessions fall into five categories: interaction management, group management, time management, communication flow management, technology management. This chapter examines each in turn, ending with consideration of some forms of evaluation that play a vital role in shaping successful teaching sessions. Before focusing on these elements, some essential logistical and practical aspects of managing synchronous online teaching sessions are outlined.

Logistical and practical aspects

Logistical aspects during the planning phase

This section focuses on introducing learners to the mode prior to the teaching sessions. During the planning phase the teacher will want to focus on two aspects:

- managing learner expectations through contact via email, in an asynchronous discussion forum or in a face-to-face session (in some blended teaching programmes, there may be an initial face-to-face contact, which gives the opportunity to demystify future online work; some online participants may also feel more comfortable if they have met their peers before engaging in online interactions);
- anticipating possible technical challenges by providing relevant information to learners in advance.

Learners need to know well in advance where, when and how to access their online teaching session, whether they have to install software or follow a web link, and what other hardware (for example, headphones with microphone or a webcam) is necessary. Teachers will want to make the web link, together with a step-by-step guide explaining how to access the synchronous online teaching space, available to the group several days before the first teaching session. The guide could include screenshots, where appropriate, and information about where learners can get additional help (for example, from the institution's technical helpline). If new software for an online application has to be installed, the software should be made available before the beginning of the course, either on a CD-ROM or via the internet, together with detailed instructions of how to install it, thus giving learners sufficient time to familiarise themselves and to obtain a headset and webcam if required.

There are several possible ways to address expectations and uncertainties and therefore reduce learners' apprehension before the first online session. Liaising with learners in advance via email, through a forum or face-to-face is advisable, as it provides the opportunity to raise and address possible concerns. It may also be an opportunity to do some ice-breaking before the synchronous online teaching session itself. The teacher can also email or use a forum to post netiquette guidelines, the session plan and any preparation documents to manage possible anxieties and thus give learners more confidence to attend. For subsequent teaching sessions, as suggested in Chapter 7, the teacher may invite learners to make suggestions about the content, pace or intended outcomes, thus giving them a sense of ownership, while encouraging communication between teaching sessions and hence providing continuity. Where the pattern of teaching sessions is irregular, it is also good practice to send reminders of forthcoming sessions, including their intended aims and outcomes, a few days beforehand.

Another possible approach is to introduce informal online 'drop-in' sessions before the first 'official' teaching session or, if there is a face-to-face element, to organise a demonstration of the conferencing system. This also helps the teacher to get to know her/his learners. Some institutions offer centrally organised training sessions, thus removing responsibility from the teacher. Learners may feel more at ease in training sessions together with other learners but without their future language teacher. Furthermore, these training sessions can encourage the formation of self-help groups where learners can meet informally online to chat, discuss the course or revise the work done.

Practical aspects just before and during the teaching session

Some of the practical issues to be considered immediately before and during an online teaching session are in many ways similar to those in a face-to-face setting. Others, however, are specific to the online environment. To ensure that things run smoothly, especially in the first teaching sessions, the teacher will want to log on early in order to:

- upload the necessary materials in all the teaching spaces that will be used (i.e. the main room and breakout rooms, if appropriate);
- check the sound (some platforms such as Elluminate and Wimba have audio set-up tools) and possibly upload some information showing learners how to do this;
- acknowledge and greet learners as they start arriving (just as in face-to-face settings, some learners are likely to arrive early).

Other practical tips for the teacher to ensure the teaching session runs smoothly are:

- have a printed copy of the session plan to avoid having too many on-screen windows open and juggling between them;
- have a printed copy of the class list with at least names and phone numbers, should there be a sudden need to contact one learner, as well as the phone number of the institution's IT helpline (if there is one);
- have a drink nearby, as well as pen and paper, so that there is no need to leave the computer;
- check emails shortly before the teaching session in case some learners have emailed about connection or other problems.

Interaction management

During a synchronous online teaching session, learners have to display a range of skills for interaction in the field of language learning and beyond:

- technical skills (e.g. to cast a vote, change rooms or check sound quality);
- cognitive skills (e.g. to deal with multi-media materials and a range of

inputs, including disembodied or distorted voices in a language with which they are not familiar);

- social skills, especially when working in different groupings where the participants often cannot be seen, moving from plenary sessions to smaller groups or pairs and back;
- listening and speaking skills in the L2;
- reading and writing skills in the L2, should the teaching session involve such activities, either via formal text-based tasks or informally in the text chat, for example.

Although all these skills may be required at different times for language learning in face-to-face, telephone or self-study settings, their combination in the context of an online teaching session may make the experience particularly intense, if not difficult, for some. This is why online sessions, like telephone teaching sessions, tend to be shorter than face-to-face ones, with sixty to ninety minutes a suitable length. Any challenge, such as a sound problem, the inability to understand one task, or missing some instructions while typing a text message may be potentially detrimental to the participant's overall experience. The gradual building of the ability to multi-task will increasingly enable teachers and learners alike to make such sessions work for them, and encourage learner control. Establishing some initial principles is useful, especially for users who are new to online and teaching contexts, as summarised below.

Principles for interaction management

Some useful principles include:

- prioritise speaking activities. The online environment lends itself well to a focus on the spoken word, given that the synchronous online teaching session is an audio event;
- use a small set of tools in an individual session. Establishing regular teaching session procedures (e.g. always starting by asking one student to read the learning outcomes on the screen) and routines (e.g. always having a warm-up activity in a plenary session before working in breakout rooms) may help learners develop a sense of familiarity and confidence.
- establish a group 'netiquette'. Defining ground rules in initial sessions tailored to individual teaching styles and group needs (e.g. regarding turn-taking or the use of the chat/instant messaging function) will make participation in such sessions more relaxed and less time-consuming;
- it may be counter-productive for teachers to prepare tasks that expect learners to engage with a wide range of stimulus materials at the same time. Using one channel of interaction at a time (e.g. audio or text) will focus attention on the language task rather than on the technology.

These principles apply not only to teaching sessions focusing on speaking skills development through interaction but are also all relevant for contexts where new grammar points or new vocabulary are taught during synchronous online sessions, and where interaction may then be facilitated straight away in order to practise these points. As in all teaching modes, pedagogical considerations related to the intended learning outcomes have to come first. The choice of the most suitable tools will follow. For example, if an intended outcome is to revise and consolidate use of a specific language structure, a teacher-led recap of a grammar rule supported by a visual presentation may lead to a controlled activity in the plenary group room, followed by more practice based on learners' input and ideas in pairs in breakout rooms where minimal visual prompts are provided.

In summary, the key to interaction management is for the teacher to make the most effective use of the interactive technology so as to enable genuine communication and collaboration. An important aspect of the teacher role is ensuring that learners are aware of how they can best employ the interactive functions to support their language learning. Another part is to facilitate their creative, confident and independent use of the software in a step-by-step approach, which in turn allows them to participate in a way tailored to their own needs. Interaction management is the basis for all other aspects discussed in the following sections, as it has a strong impact on how effectively the teacher can assist language learning in this environment.

Group management

With regard to group management, the challenges for teachers and learners alike are similar to the ones encountered in other settings: creating and maintaining rapport and group cohesion; working with plenary or smaller groups; involving everyone as much as possible while remaining aware of how far learners are prepared to go; moving from teacher-led towards learner-led activities; and dealing with unexpected numbers or groupings (for example, if a smaller than anticipated number of learners attend). There is nonetheless a major difference between group management in face-to-face teaching sessions and in online sessions where the 'group' may not see each other. The participants may be just a list of names/images on a screen or, at the most, a set of videos streamed from webcams. Learners have to familiarise themselves with the different ways of communicating within their virtual groups (for example, by using the microphone, chat box, emoticons and voting tools); and they have to develop a sense of community in an environment that has more similarities with a telephone than a face-to-face teaching session (see Chapter 8). Teachers therefore have to teach not only the language in question but also strategies that can compensate for the lack of visual cues, which are a significant form of communication in face-to-face interaction.

In this respect, interaction and group management are closely linked. Learners can take control only once they have established what the symbols and signals of the software mean with regard to communication (for example, a 'raised hand' with a certain number associated to it in the list of participants means that the learner has to wait for her/his turn). Chapter 9 has listed the most common and most frequently used features that help teachers and learners manage the interaction in such environments (for example, emoticons to express spontaneous reactions). As facilitator and organiser, the teacher will want to manage the group in the least intrusive but unambiguous manner. The teacher can monitor frequency of interaction as well as actions of individual participants using some indicators provided by the software (for example, to see who may be writing in the chat box or on the screen, even before their words appear).

Group management also covers breakout room management, if such rooms are available. Working in breakout rooms requires more careful preparation than working in a plenary room where all the learners are together. In a face-to-face situation, when learners work in pairs, for example, it is possible to interrupt the entire group with reminders or further clarifications if necessary. When learners are working in online breakout rooms during a synchronous teaching session, doing this would be very disruptive as it would mean bringing all participants back in the main room for the announcement. It is therefore important to ensure that groups know exactly what to do, with whom and for how long, before they leave for the breakout rooms. Most systems have a timer which can be set before groups leave the plenary room if this is helpful and does not distract from the activity. The breakout rooms also need to be prepared in advance with the appropriate materials. Once learners are in their breakout rooms, the teacher will want to monitor learners' presence and contribution. For example, if learners are in pairs and one gets disconnected, the remaining learner may not be able to continue with the activity. Therefore if connections are found to be unreliable, activities in threesomes rather than in pairs may be advisable. Some teachers will want to visit all breakout rooms to check on progress while others will let the groups work on their own while using the visual display or activity window on screen to monitor participant activity. They will also want to remind learners that they can call for assistance or ask questions by sending a text-chat message to the teacher. As in face-to-face teaching sessions, this is a matter of teaching style and appropriateness to the task.

What follows are some practical ideas for teachers related to group management in online synchronous teaching sessions. Some of these points would also be relevant to other synchronous modes.

Tips for group management

- Use the polling/voting tool regularly in order to check that the entire group can hear and understand. This may feel unnatural at first, but in the absence of other visual cues it is an essential tool to monitor learners' understanding and satisfaction.
- Encourage spontaneity and a positive atmosphere; this can be done in a number of ways, including by:

— helping learners to get to know you as well as one another;
— using humour and letting others hear when you/they are laughing (but note that although humour can help to relax the atmosphere, it can also misfire when participants lack other cues. It is therefore important to encourage forms of interaction where the meaning of cues and signals is established and understood by everyone);
— showing spontaneous reactions via the emoticons;
— showing images;
— using the video at times;
— writing brief comments in the chat.

- For turn-taking, remind learners to make use of the 'raise hand button' (or similar tool) to indicate intentions, rather than interrupting or talking over someone else. This also helps to manage discussions more smoothly and allows everyone to participate.

- Make sure the names and activity indicators of all learners are visible at the same time. This might involve resizing windows, changing the view layout or changing the number of pixels in your desktop settings. If you don't see participants, you are less likely to actively involve them!

- Try to involve everyone. It tends to be easier to overlook quiet learners in online than in face-to-face sessions (e.g. keep a list of names, and tick those who have spoken).

- As in face-to-face sessions, ask learners to chair parts of a session, or use task types such as chain questions. In these activities, one learner starts asking another one a question. The next learner will then have to answer and move on to ask another participant either the same question, or one that builds on the previous one. Such activities can be supported by the use of the 'raise hand button' and the automatic 'waiting list' initiated by the system.

- Use visuals to help explain tasks and to prompt learners to remember them when they are in breakout rooms. Use colours and images, not just black and white text.

Time management

Time management in online synchronous teaching sessions needs particular consideration for two reasons.

First, as noted earlier, such sessions tend to be shorter than their face-to-face counterparts. While it is possible to have a face-to-face intensive day/weekend course or a programme lasting several hours, including breaks when everybody may practise and communicate in the L2, online teaching sessions rarely last more than ninety minutes. The need to multi-task and the concentration required by both teachers and learners can make the experience physically and psychologically tiring.

Sitting at a computer desk looking at a screen for any extended period of time also presents potential health and safety risks. The teacher is likely to log in up to thirty minutes before the teaching session itself in order to prepare breakout rooms, check materials or even support learners with technical problems in advance, which may mean two hours of online work, often without a break.

Second, particularly for people new to the environment, teaching can seem less flexible, and interaction may appear more stilted, because of the formalised turn-taking and the need to use technical features to replace the visual cues familiar in face-to-face interaction. It often takes longer for learners to get to know their teacher, each other, the software, its interactive potential and the most productive approach to activities. However, online teaching sessions may occur at more frequent intervals than face-to-face ones (for example, twenty hours' teaching could be either ten face-to-face sessions of two hours or twenty online sessions of one hour). Although it may take time to build a rapport at the beginning, the more frequent meetings may help in building relationships in the long term.

So as to make the most effective use of teaching time, the teacher will deploy both technology and methodology. From a technical viewpoint, several approaches may be employed: for example, a noticeboard where the teacher can announce where, when and what is happening for the benefit of late-comers; or a sound check facility to which learners with sound problems could be directed, since trying to sort out a participant's sound problems could potentially waste a lot of valuable teaching time and be frustrating for the other learners. From a methodological viewpoint, several techniques may be employed to make the best use of limited time: for example, sending preparatory tasks in advance or explaining tasks precisely and providing clear task instructions on screen for reference so as to avoid repetition. Technology and methodology can also be effectively combined: for example, by teaching learners how to use the specific tools through the activities so that they develop confidence. Some key principles for time management in synchronous online teaching sessions are summarised below.

Time management principles

- Establish a set of common teaching session procedures, such as plenary explanation and instructions followed by practice in breakout rooms. This will help learners become confident and independent, which in turn will allow them to work faster, and will reduce the need for frequent instructions on how to use the software for specific tasks.
- It can take up too much time if activities draw on a range of different types of materials or use a variety of different tools, since learners may need to spend time familiarising themselves with the technology. Some of this time could be spent more effectively on spoken interaction or on teacher presentation, as appropriate.

- Let the technology help with the time management. Many synchronous online environments provide timers, which take the pressure off the teacher to carry out time-keeping. Other features such as the 'waiting list' of participants can save time since they reduce the need for teacher to say who should speak next. Materials can also be put in a particular, predictable order, so as to avoid additional explanations and instructions.

- Establishing regular group management procedures can save time (e.g. doing a sound check at the beginning of each session, or sending announcements/central messages to all participants to indicate different stages in the session).

Communication flow management

Although the numerous tools available in synchronous online conferencing systems may be a source of distraction or perplexity, they provide mechanisms for giving reactions or feedback on performance and documenting events that help learners improve their motivation and confidence, accuracy, fluency and pronunciation. As part of providing an effective stimulus for spoken interaction and confidence building, the variation of task types is essential. Wherever possible, learner-centred tasks can be used in differing combinations. The task types described below are particularly suitable for synchronous online teaching sessions.

Communicative tasks

Chain activities in a plenary group

To make interaction less stilted and faster flowing, it is advisable to remove the focus from the teacher wherever possible, with activities that allow learners to take more control. The aim is to engage all learners as much as possible, even if they are not speaking, and the variety of interactive tools available plays an important role in this respect. Chain activities, where learners ask or respond in turn, include giving definitions or describing, asking yes/no questions to guess famous people from countries where the L2 is spoken, matching words/ideas, chain questions (see above), games such as bingo, call my bluff and taboo.

Group/pair tasks

In group or pair tasks, it is easier for learners to express themselves in longer statements. They can also take on different roles or work on different tasks (for example, reading dialogues aloud and expanding on them; creating new dialogues from notes and questions; making plans for presentations and discussions; brainstorming, gathering or summarising information; or debating a topic).

Error correction and communication flow

When they want to give feedback on matters of accuracy, teachers often use the text chat box for corrections (for example, to give the correct gender of a noun or an appropriate grammatical form), as well as for brief comments or reactions, or to show the spelling of new vocabulary. This avoids interrupting the flow of conversation or an individual contribution. Errors common to many participants can be gathered and explained in a plenary session, or it can be sent to participants later in the form of a follow-up email with an explanation and perhaps a task for revision and reflection. During the teaching session, as in any other setting, if the focus is on development of fluency and confidence in speaking, it may be better to ignore errors that are not significant and do not impede understanding, rather than correcting them and interrupting the flow of the session. As in other modes, the aim is to help and encourage learners to communicate and making mistakes and taking risks is a crucial part of that process.

Synchronous online teaching sessions therefore have much in common with synchronous teaching in other settings. This includes the use of techniques to facilitate discussions and interaction among learners, or to stretch more competent learners by encouraging them to express ideas in different ways. However, the perceived artificiality of the online environment adds a particular challenge. Online discussions may not flow as naturally as those held face-to-face because turn-taking procedures can make the process more formal and a little less spontaneous, even with learners fluent in the use of the L2 and with IT-proficient participants. In some conferencing systems it is possible for more than one person to speak at a time and interrupt spontaneously, but this may result in sound distortion for other participants and it may therefore be avoided. As a result, the flow of communication may not appear as smooth and natural as in face-to-face interaction; discussions may appear as a succession of short monologues, with people, consciously or not, exploiting the fact that they have control of the microphone before handing over to the next person who has indicated a wish to speak.

Developing good pronunciation

With respect to pronunciation, audio and video conferencing presents both advantages and disadvantages. The main advantage is that such environments favour the spoken word, thereby giving learners the opportunity to improve their speaking and listening skills, by practising with others and learning from them. Teachers can include specific pronunciation exercises using audio supported by visual images and textual representations, exploiting the multi-modality of online conferencing systems. However, voices can occasionally be distorted and sound quality may not be clear enough for learners unfamiliar with the sounds of a particular language. Although webcams can be used to show the teacher's mouth, it is not easy to show learners how to move the tongue and mouth to articulate and pronounce particular sounds. Live video-streaming is currently not advanced enough to provide naturally moving images and it may also substantially slow down the transmission and operational speed of the software. Key principles for communication flow management in synchronous online teaching sessions are summarised below.

Communication flow management principles

- Resist the temptation to correct every linguistic flaw or error. This will help learners to focus on the discussion rather than just reading text chat messages. It is pedagogically more appropriate to gather points into a focused feedback session where common errors are corrected and typical problems in the group highlighted and explained, thus taking pressure off individual learners who might otherwise feel put on the spot.

- Accept that discussions may not feel the same as in face-to-face sessions. Encourage learners to master this new and different form of communication with the tools at hand as best they can, and to be creative in using them.

- Articulate even more clearly than you would normally do in face-to-face interactions. This can make up for sound distortions and give particularly good examples of pronunciation that learners can revisit by listening to a recorded session.

- Interrupt the communication as little as possible. Interventions can be kept to a minimum using the tools such as text chat and emoticons. The fact that the teacher cannot 'be seen' moves the focus from the teacher to the participants who will tend to feel the need to take responsibility for the interaction more strongly.

- Use L1 where it helps to avoid diversions and distractions. With regard to technology the use of L1 can help the group deal with problems swiftly. However, the names of the tools should gradually be taught in the L2, as should instructions in how to use the tools, as this is another opportunity to learn the language through regular practice.

- Use task types that support interaction at different levels. This involves exploring the potential of the technology and making sure that, when learners are not speaking, they have something to do other than 'just' listening. They can take notes, read, look at images and take on different roles and tasks when contributing to group activities.

Technology management

Technical problems can be a significant issue in synchronous online teaching sessions. No matter how well prepared the teaching session is, how technologically literate the participants or how powerful their computers and how reliable their internet connections are, there are likely to be occasions when the teaching session is interrupted by technical glitches. A participant may be disconnected at some point or her/his sound may break up for a few seconds. The impact might be minor, with the learner just asking the teacher to repeat a sentence they could not hear, or it may be major, with participants/the teacher being disconnected several times, for a few seconds or several minutes. The teacher needs to reassure learners, prepare some strategies to cope with these eventualities, and ensure that learners are also prepared, as suggested below.

Technology management principles

- Ensure learners are aware that technology is fallible and that problems may well occur. Being psychologically prepared is important, so as to limit levels of anxiety. Although technology problems can be frustrating, it is crucial to keep them in proportion.
- Keep an eye on the list of participants. When learners lose connection and reappear, acknowledge they have returned, welcome them back in an unobtrusive way, and update them with what has been happening (e.g. with the help of a message in the text chat).
- Remember that a language teacher is not expected to be a technology expert. Do not spend a lot of time trying to help learners who have sound problems or who do not understand some technological aspects, but redirect them politely to appropriate sources of support.
- Apply the use of the technology as creatively as possible. Enable as much interaction and learner control as possible, but at the same time do not utilise more tools with potential technical challenges than is necessary to foster lively interaction.

Forms of evaluation

To define and measure the quality of synchronous online teaching sessions, observation of learners' reactions and monitoring of their performance together with teacher self-evaluation are useful approaches. The previous sections have stressed the importance of giving and gathering information continuously during the session about how well learners are following the session, understanding what is happening and engaging with others, with the materials and with the activities. At the end of the session, learners can be asked for their views (for example, they can be asked to identify three things they have learned or will take away from the session). This approach is not unique to online sessions, but the method of gathering learners' comments will be different. Learners might write their views in the chat box or work in a small group in a breakout room to produce a joint list of the top three points. Alternatively, learners could later be asked to fill in an (online) questionnaire about their learning experience. It could be a set of simple questions with a poll taken, the results published on screen and then discussed either in the session or on a forum afterwards. From time to time, a more detailed individual survey by email might be carried out, covering both pedagogical and technological aspects. For example, if a learner mentions that they struggled with some activities, it could be due to sound problems, not to the quality or appropriateness of the activities themselves. A range of external factors may also influence the results (for example, the number and grouping of learners who took part, or the preparatory work they had or had not done). Teachers will also pick up useful information during the online session itself as they observe reactions and responses.

Chapter 7 identifies several interrelated questions that may guide teacher self-evaluation after any teaching session, and they can also be used with some adaptation to encourage learners to reflect on their participation and progress in the online teaching session and to provide some feedback to the teacher:

- How did the session go overall? How did I feel afterwards and why?
- Were the intended learning outcomes achieved? How do I know?
- What worked well or less well? Why might that be so?
- How active was I during the session?
- How well did I manage the technology?

Self-evaluation by the teacher could be systematic or impressionistic. Teachers may look at slightly different aspects when reflecting on their online teaching sessions compared to reflecting on their teaching in other modes. All categories and aspects of management discussed in this chapter are useful indicators of the success of a synchronous online teaching session. The key is to establish whether the combination of technology and pedagogy produces interaction and satisfaction. A rough guideline may therefore be that a teacher who is less visible and audible during a session online tends to be an effective facilitator of such events. As most teaching session software offers the possibility to record the session (subject to learners' permission), some teachers may seize that opportunity to observe themselves teaching using the principles in this chapter as parameters.

The ultimate aim of the approaches described above is to enhance the quality of the next online teaching session. Teachers might draw precise conclusions from an individual teaching session (for example, 'remember to check that all the break-out rooms have the same screen with the instructions' or 'allow five minutes for debriefing at the end') or they might decide to take part in further professional development (for example, attending online workshops or practising on their own). Teachers new to synchronous online teaching may set themselves fresh goals each time (for example, incorporating use of more tools); experienced teachers may aim to vary their approach to the use of specific tools.

Conclusion

This chapter has highlighted the role and importance of the interplay between pedagogy and technology in synchronous online teaching. Although such environments may seem more formal and rigid than face-to-face settings, they can encourage a high degree of learner control and move the focus from the teacher to the learner. Knowing how to interact online is a skill that teachers and learners can develop as they create their own individual communication strategies within the particular conferencing system they are using. The chapter has signalled the importance for successful online learning and teaching of recognising the different nature of communication in this setting and of not simply attempting to replicate face-to-face interaction. This involves, for example, accepting that not every silence needs to be filled at once, that continuous monitoring and explicit information is essential, that technical problems are common, and that, as a result of the need to communicate via a multitude of channels, short breaks or thinking time can help learners relax and focus. A further aim is to establish a flow of multi-channelled communication that is as natural as possible. Teachers have a key role to play in minimising anxieties about technological problems, and reassuring that interaction need not be hampered by temporary technical glitches, while building in procedures for checking that learners have understood what to do and can hear each other. Teachers working in the synchronous online mode are creating a virtual reality. They are combining their pedagogical expertise with the affordances of the conferencing system to produce the conditions for effective language learning.

Chapter 11:   Face-to-Face Teaching in Blended Contexts

Margaret Nicolson and Sylvia Warnecke

Introduction

To many adult learners, face-to-face teaching will be one of the more familiar elements of any blended language programme. As outlined in Chapter 7, face-to-face sessions, like other synchronous teaching sessions, may assume different purposes in blended contexts. They may involve brand new input which the teacher has to present and develop with learners before they study this further independently after the session. Alternatively, the sessions may rely on a facilitative rather than didactic approach, particularly in open and distance settings, where the aim may be to enhance and develop learning that has already been undertaken independently using course materials, often in line with study calendar deadlines or assessment demands. If independent or distance learning forms a *large* part of the blend, then the practice of speaking skills and group discussion and the support of study and learning skills development will be important in these synchronous teaching sessions.

It is also the case that the focus of face-to-face teaching in the blended context will as much reflect and build on key aspects of contemporary teaching practice as teaching in any other mode in the blend, and involve concepts such as particularity (Kumaravadivelu, 2006), individuality, creativity, open-endedness and simulation in a context of inter-cultural awareness (Fenner and Newby, 2000).

The authors' understanding of face-to-face teaching is based on a fluid and creative concept of planning, with varying teaching models possible. The planning and teaching phases overlap and can at times be less easily separated than in other modes. This is because face-to-face teaching often has a higher degree of flexibility inherent in its use of time and space, so, at times, outcomes may be less predictable. This is a positive issue as it allows for greater learner input and negotiation of how tasks will be carried out before and during sessions.

In this chapter, the three key stages in the development of any teaching situation, planning, implementation and review, will be examined with regard to the face-to-face context, and practical examples will be provided along the way.

Planning considerations

Planning for face-to-face teaching in the blended environment has to take account of all generic planning issues referred to in Chapter 7. Ideally, the teacher will aim to establish communication about planning with learners in a way that best suits the specific group in question. One method of dealing with this, where time and the institutional setting allow, is to distribute the teaching session plan in advance, with an outline of what individual tasks will involve. This allows learners to flag up issues that may be of concern, such as access to the venue, getting there on time, managing the physical environment, or what they should do about tasks they may find problematic. This also gives teachers time to take account of these concerns and to modify the plan as appropriate and within the realms of possibility. Where time is at a premium, learners may simply be asked to indicate what they would ideally wish to see incorporated. The final decision about what will be included has to lie with the teacher, who ultimately has control over the amount of compromise and concession.

Four specific issues may particularly affect planning and task choice in the face-to-face environment and these are outlined below.

Use of time

The length of face-to-face sessions will vary depending on the nature of the blend in operation and the institutional context. Face-to-face sessions are often likely to be longer than those in online synchronous or telephone modes (see Chapters 8–10), and, where this is the case, they give greater scope for a more fluid plan and for longer and more complex tasks/activities. There is also the opportunity to make space in the plan for episodes which relieve pressure or intensity (for example, language games or informal conversation in L1). Breaks in the session for refreshments, or a move to another part of the building such as a café or outside the building for some air, can also be built in more readily than in shorter more intense virtual or telephone sessions where movement away from the computer or telephone during the session is unlikely.

Interaction

In face-to-face teaching there are a range of variables at work in the interaction, both human and material. The connections between them can result in the need for fluidity. This is because the nature of the interaction may result in these connections developing and changing. The mind map (Figure 11.1) indicates several of these variables. Some clearly overlap with all teaching modes. Others, such as physical space, facial expression, body language and gesture, the use of physical objects and movement in activities, will be particular to this mode. In planning for face-to-face sessions, it is advisable that these be taken into account.

In the face-to-face setting, because the whole group is within sight and earshot in the one space, it is perhaps easier to switch the combination of variables more efficiently. Shifts (for example, from groupwork to plenary, from one part of the room to another, or from a visual resource to an audio stimulus) may require only a turnaround of body or chair and cause less apparent disruption and take less time than in

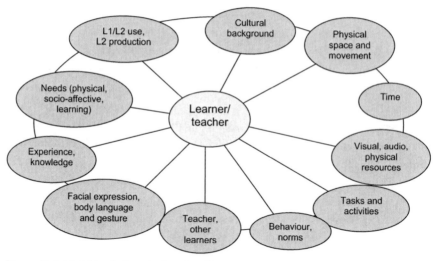

Figure 11.1: Variables in face-to-face teaching

online environments. Different means of managing the interaction, not necessarily available in other modes, are also at the teacher's disposal in face-to-face teaching (for example, eye contact and gesture). However, while such cues are common to human interaction in any social face-to-face scenario, they are nonetheless subject to interpretation and assignation of meaning. While this may make face-to-face teaching more situational, it is nonetheless helpful to achieve some common understanding so that physical, gestural and visual cues work in the teaching and learning context. For example, the discreet raising of a hand may be established as the indication that someone needs to be invited to speak as they do not feel confident about interrupting. A discreet shake of the head may indicate that someone does not wish to be asked to speak but wants simply to listen. In many ways, determining such common cues among the members of the group pre-empts differences that may exist in terms of levels of courtesy and confidence, with a common set of cues being a leveller. However, as with all such conventions, they do rely on the same people attending regularly so that they understand the conventions.

The physical environment

The physical environment can be an enhancing element in task planning: objects can be used as props, texts can be physically handled, cut up and reassembled and movement can be incorporated into tasks. Working in the physical environment may also have the advantage of being more familiar to learners than the virtual one. However, this can give a false sense of security. External noise and visuals, such as signs or posters in the room, which are nothing to do with the session, may distract. Learners may not feel familiar or 'at home' in the physical space, particularly in cases where providers use other institutions' premises, with the location or room sometimes changing from one session to the next. The impact on confidence and on learner participation and language production should not be underestimated where individuals rely on psychological comfort from surroundings to function at their best. Some learners may not be used to working well when there is noise around them, such as from pair or group conversations. Lighting, colour, smells or temperature in rooms may affect others. Physical obstacles and hazards are also an issue for some learners and teachers. Negotiating objects and moving around, if that is to be part of the plan for the session, have to be carefully managed or even avoided with some groups. In this respect, the physical environment may lend itself to task choices that do not, in fact, always suit all learners. Miming, acting or presenting 'up-front' is not comfortable for learners who are anxious about standing or speaking in front of the whole group or simply shy in face-to-face group contexts. Circulatory tasks can cause issues for those with mobility challenges as the following learner's experience highlights: 'In fact I found it quite a shock the amount of activity of moving around. I just couldn't take it. I didn't realise it was going to be like that' (Adams and Nicolson, 2010, p. 111).

This learner's experience of a face-to-face session was a negative one because he was unaware of what would happen during it. He really needed either an early warning and time in advance to contact the teacher to negotiate his participation, or the chance to opt out of the activity altogether without exposing his problem in front of other learners. This highlights the need to inform learners in advance of what might happen and to invite them to discuss with the teacher any specific cognitive, physical or interactional issues. Some learners, for example, may not have covered some of the work to be practised in tasks featuring on the plan, and will need to be reassured that they still have something to learn and contribute by attending.

Language output and communication

Several points emerge here with regard to face-to-face teaching sessions. The absence of the need for structured turn-taking (necessary in a virtual environment) allows more scope for the incorporation of spontaneous language functions, such as polite interruption, disagreement, or *ad hoc* humour and therefore more scope for maximum creativity of the individual learner and for the immediacy of communication.

Teachers and learners can also take advantage of the face-to-face context to approach classroom tasks with the full gamut of communication in mind, demonstrating that it is often reliant on gesture, facial expression, miming and so on as much as on the component parts of the language, such as grammar and lexis. The face-to face setting can help learners to understand that, in human communication, getting the message across successfully by a variety of means may at times be more crucial than absolute grammatical accuracy. Improvement in grammatical accuracy can follow, but be approached inductively rather than deductively. This allows both teacher and learner more choice and can help build their confidence to make choices according to a specific context and situation.

Communication in face-to-face sessions can become more natural since it incorporates all levels of day-to-day interaction such as gesture, sound, facial expressions and humour. However, teachers will have to take into consideration that learners may be studying the subject with different aims in mind. Some may want to improve communication, while others will want grammar improvement and the rigour of absolutely correct language as an academic exercise. Reasonable compromise, explanation of aims and mutual understanding will help to reconcile both positions.

Types of teaching plan

Here, the main focus will be to look specifically at the teaching plan models, referred to in Chapter 7, along with examples that work well in the face-to-face session within the blend, sometimes because physical movement or facial expressions play an important role. As in all teaching modes, the type of teaching plan will be dependent on the level of language proficiency concerned, and teachers will have to adapt as necessary. The authors also seek to highlight that the follow-up work in the first two models can either be continued in or transferred to asynchronous discussion forums, wikis, blogs or other asynchronous online contexts that are part of the blend, after the face-to-face session.

In the face-to-face environment it is possible to adopt the *beginning–middle– end model*, with a traditional move from closed to open-ended discussion over a period of two to three hours. Sequencing is then built on a model of language and skill accrual where, usually, each task on the plan, or its development as an activity, becomes more complex linguistically and structurally.

In the *rolling model* the gradient is not a linear one but accrues laterally, for example through extended role-play via the development of scenarios that build in layers, adding more complexity of content and different areas of language en route. The face-to-face event is also suitable for this. Language and skill accrual happens here perhaps in a freer way with more linguistic creativity and more individuality, since development of scenarios via role-play, for example, does not have to be predetermined or dependent on turn-taking in the same way other modes would demand. For the same reason language input and output can also be freer because time and the nature of the face-to-face context allow this.

In face-to-face teaching, a third model also works particularly well. This is often referred to as the *workstation or carousel model*. Learning and skill accrual during the work may happen in a more individualised and in an even more unpredictable way than in the rolling model. To a certain degree the teacher can structure learning accrual through the design and set-up of the different workstations, but at activity stage s/he may not be able to influence how learning happens as much as in the other two suggested models. The language used as learners advance through workstations is multi-layered in that it can relate to more than one conceptual area simultane-ously: the content of the theme and the skills used to work on the theme. (See the workstation plan on p. 161 and 164.)

Suitable task types for use in the context of all three models might include:

- role-plays/simulations;
- improvisatory tasks;
- open-ended discussions in plenary and small groups;
- activities with props (e.g. stories around objects, producing poster responses, cutting and pasting text, board games, jigsaw sentences);
- tasks that involve judicious use of movement where appropriate (e.g. mar-ketplace activities to collect information from the wider group);
- tasks based on more complex use of a variety of pictures and on drawing;
- workstation activities;
- pronunciation exercises that rely on observing lip-speaking (more likely to be used in the beginning–middle–end type plan);
- tasks that involve swift changes between a variety of groupings and formats (e.g. snowball or marketplace activities);
- audiovisual tasks (e.g. listening to a song, watching a short video clip, or presenting/listening to a PowerPoint presentation via smart boards or other audiovisual aids).

A sample plan for the 'beginning–middle–end' model

As outlined in Chapter 7, the session plan can be held together either by one of the following links or by a mixture of any two to four of them. Specific suggestions for one particular session are set out in Figure 11.2:

- thematic link (e.g. traditional festivals in different countries);
- language function link (e.g. describing, discussing, comparing, giving your opinion);
- grammar link (e.g. present tense for description, adverbial clauses, com-parative adjectives);
- skill link (e.g. vocabulary development, note-taking, reading skills, sum-marising, reporting).

A sample plan for the 'rolling' model

Rolling models generally revolve around role-play and are largely based on the most advanced of its improvisatory forms. They also involve the physical context as a 'staged setting' with designation of parts of the classroom as places used within the role-play, such as reception/hotel room/taxi/shop. Other rolling models may involve process drama as described by Kao and O'Neill (1998) or simulation as exempli-fied by Tompkins (1998) or García-Carbonell (2001). The role-play model in Figure 11.3 (pp. 162–3) derives from Cockett's work (2000) on drama-based role-play. The

Phase	Aim	Format	Time (minutes)
1. Ice-breaker/ Warmer	Social; confidence-building; vocabulary building; formulation of simple phrases; introduction of thematic link	Circulatory; learners gather information on traditional customs in the countries/areas where L2 is spoken as well as on experiences of fellow learners with these festivals	20
2. Closed and more structured tasks	Vocabulary building in specific areas; describing topic-related images; sharing, reporting and summarising information	Groupwork; learners gather information on one traditional celebration by scan-reading newspaper articles or texts to collate information on festivals/ customs	40
3. Break or downtime	Social and peer-support (allows learners to talk about their experience of course study in L1; to speak to the teacher or one another in private)	Informal outside the classroom (in café or outside area)	20
4. Discursive tasks	Hypothesising on aspects of the topic; preparing interview questions for a role-play on the topic; inventing a scenario for a group discussion on the topic; gathering arguments for and against on the topic	Groupwork	40
5. Discussion	Applying vocabulary, information and structures from previous activities in a more complex context	Plenary/large or small groups; roles are assigned and a time limit is set; the teacher observes, gives and gathers feedback following the discussion; expressing and discussing personal opinions; agreeing/disagreeing; polite interventions; asking and answering questions	20
6. Open-ended and creative follow-up tasks	Collaborative writing; elaborating facts and points of views	Pair/groupwork; role-playing as journalists, preparing a newspaper article; reporting on the debate	30

Figure 11.2: Sample plan for the 'beginning–middle–end' model

central aspect here is that the teacher acts as a facilitator, motivating and organising the collaborative development of the narrative through role-play. Learners can choose and develop their roles individually and are involved in all stages of the role-play, including preparation, acting out and feedback phases. In their research on the uses and benefits of role-play in distance learning, Brash and Warnecke (2009, pp. 101–2) state that:

> The aspect of playing is as central in this context as the fact that learners tell a story together … This may in turn benefit their psycholinguistic development because learners … can … 're-invent' themselves as somebody very different … acting 'out of character', without risking censorship from others or even being seen to be 'acting'. This opportunity may increase the learners' willingness to take risks.

As the scenarios are entirely imaginary, and at points even far-fetched, learners may also experience role-play situations as a 'safe' way of acting out emotions. Cockett's concept of drama-based role-play revolves around what Neelands (1990, p. 68) labels the 'hook'. Cockett, following Bentley (1965, p. 229), defines such 'hooks' as 'disturbances of normality' and suggests that learners are:

> enticed not by representations of normality but by the *disturbance* of it, by things beyond the normal, those parts of everyday life we prefer to play down or hide: awful mistakes, unfortunate coincidences, extremes of behaviour, embarrassments, secret thoughts and passions (Cockett, 2000, p. 18).

According to Cockett the incentive 'to speak springs from tension between what happens on the surface level of speech and action, and the inner level of thought and feeling' (ibid). A role-play such as this can be planned and carried out as illustrated in Figure 11.3.

A sample plan for the workstation model

This model is particularly suitable for the face-to-face context for several reasons:

- Different areas of the physical environment can be used clearly to demarcate each station.
- Physical action enables the use of different types of materials including objects.
- There can be a more flexible use of time. Learners can explore the different tasks better and in a more in-depth way. This is necessary since the linking of the discussion of skills with language work can be challenging and complex for learners.
- Workstations in the face-to-face context promote individualisation since activities are more open-ended and allow for diverse ways of working on them.

To ensure that learners can capitalise as much as possible on the face-to-face contact when learning at workstations, it is useful to have learners work in pairs or groups of three. The teacher has to build in time for movement between different workstations and to ensure safety in terms of physical space. The following example, which is loosely based on a model presented by Stork (2006), is designed to highlight how the discussion of study skills can become a key focus of L2 teaching sessions for intermediate to advanced learners.

The room is set up with seven workstations. All tasks provided at these stations revolve around strategies for learning and noting vocabulary. Learners are asked to carry out the individual vocabulary training tasks, and then in the group reflect on this particular strategy. Learners work in small groups of three or in pairs.

Phase, aim and time	Format	Procedure	Scenario
Phase: Setting the scene 1 Aim: Preparing learners for role-play; assigning roles to learners Time: 10 minutes	Plenary work where learners and teacher describe and develop the setting of the role-play together and where the teacher outlines the basic scenario and the hook that will be further developed.	Learners describe in the L2 the worst hotel they can imagine. During this phase learners do not write down any words: all vocabulary/ideas are gathered and explained orally. The teacher then describes the hook/conflict.	A person is on a winter vacation in the UK. When s/he arrives at the pre-booked hotel, s/he finds that the online brochure did not reflect the true qualities of the accommodation. The heating does not work, there are rodents in the rooms, loud music is coming from the ball room, and the windows do not close properly. The guest complains at the reception but the receptionist does not accept the complaint and describes these flaws as the charm of an old British country hotel.
Phase: Role-play 1 'At the reception' Aim: Learners develop the scenario further in a short role-play using L2 intuitively and expressing personal feelings about the scenario when taking on a role Time: 5 minutes	Pair role-play work	Learners are split up in pairs. They move to their designated area in the room and can set up their space with props according to their impression of the scenario. The teacher then gives a signal for the so-called 'freeze frame' (Cockett, 2000, p.19). This is a moment when learners take their positions and stop chatting. The teacher signals the start of the role-play and quietly observes the different pairs. After a set time during which the pairs do not need to fully exhaust all possible avenues of the dialogue, the teacher signals the end of this first scene. It is important that all learners start and finish at the same time.	
Phase: Setting the scene 2 Aim: See setting the scene 1 Time: 10 minutes	See setting the scene 1	Learners describe in L2 the best hotel they can imagine. Then the teacher describes the hook/conflict.	The guest decides to leave the old hotel and to find better accommodation. She can only find a room at the most expensive and luxurious hotel in town. At check-in, the staff mistake the guest for a member of the royal family travelling incognito, whom they have been expecting all day. The guest is ushered into the best suite and despite efforts to query this misunderstanding the staff do not listen.

Phase, aim and time	Format	Procedure	Scenario
Phase: Role-play 2 'Mistaken identities' Aim: See role-play 1 Time: 5 minutes	See role-play 1	See role-play 1	The member of the royal family arrives shortly after 'our' guest. The staff are angry and try to remove 'our' guest forcibly from the hotel.
Phase: Setting the scene 3 Aim: See setting the scene 1 Time: 10 minutes	Teacher narration	Teacher describes in L2 the hook/conflict of the final scene.	
Phase: Role-play 3 'Persuasion' Aim: See role-play 1 Time: 5 minutes	See role-play 1	Learners act out the dialogue that might develop and decide how the story could come to a conclusion.	
Phase: Follow-up work Aim: Reflection on the role-play; error correction; use of theme-specific vocabulary in different contexts and different genres Time: Open-ended	Individual work, group work, plenary	The teacher and learners give their feedback on the role-play experience. The teacher talks specifically about: learners' use of L2; errors; further work on the role-play on linguistic forms, vocabulary, pronunciation or other aspects. Learners could then engage in writing within the fictional frame, telling the story from a different point of view, developing a play script, 'examining similar *hooks* in real life: situations where people have tried to hide the truth, been mistaken for somebody else, or have persuaded somebody to do something to get them out of a difficult situation' (Cockett, 2000, p. 21).	

Figure 11.3: Sample plan for the 'rolling model'

Station 1

Learners write a 'word net' or 'word map' similar to a mind map to practise gathering topic-related vocabulary and discuss whether this would be helpful for essay preparation since it may not only gather words but offer a text structure as well.

Station 2

Learners play a card-matching game. Some cards contain a word or phrase. Others show an explanation of the word or phrase. This exercise is an effective way of learning to rephrase vocabulary. Learners discuss whether this way of looking at vocabulary is preferable to translation with a dictionary, and why.

Station 3

Learners write labels for as many items in the classroom as possible. On the labels there can be the word, the article and gender (if appropriate) as well as an exemplar sentence. This activity highlights how some learners will learn vocabulary best if they are constantly surrounded by visual examples of vocabulary.

Station 4

This introduces learners to the 'key word method', which asks learners to find words that are similar in L1 and in L2. Learners need to find as many words as possible and compare spellings, varying meanings and identify 'false friends'. To make this task more demanding, learners are asked to find similar sounding words that have very different meanings: for example, 'eye' (English) and 'Ei' (Geman.). A way to help memorise these words would be not only to write the word but also to draw the item, too, if this is suitable for the learners in question.

Station 5

This introduces learners to the concept of contextualising vocabulary. Learners find as many words as they can on the theme of 'detective' in two minutes. Then they start writing a detective story together using the words they have found. They will understand the difference between types of words such as nouns and verbs and their role in sentence structures. They will also experience that this way of gathering and learning vocabulary is creative and can bring about the production of highly individual texts and ideas in the language.

Station 6

This highlights the importance of the connection between the spoken and the written word. Learners read out poetry as well as a short story to each other. Then they discuss how much they took in and what helped or distracted them, and why. Learners discuss in which situations and contexts speaking words aloud supports learning vocabulary in particular.

Station 7

This highlights that categorising vocabulary can be a useful exercise. Learners are asked to think of a word field: for example, 'work'. They brainstorm vocabulary relating to 'work', then find categories that fit the words and phrases gathered in the brainstorm (for example, workplace, colleagues and jobs). Alternatively, they are asked to think of categories first (for example, 'professional', 'practical' or 'emotional'), and then find words from the word field 'work' that match these categories.

The tasks at the workstations illustrate and suit different learning styles and at the same time develop learners' reflective skills. They are also designed to encourage learner choice in terms of matching their individual learning needs to particular study skill methods that work for them. It is important in this context, however, to stress that a 'learning style' is a fluid entity that can change from time to time through the period of study. With increasing knowledge of strategies and approaches, learners' learning styles can be transformed to become more adapted to their needs at particular stages of the language learning process.

Managing the face-to-face session

Chapter 7 has outlined generic issues to be considered when managing any synchronous teaching session. In the face-to-face context the following specifics will be particularly relevant.

Protocols/rules of game/approaches

In the face-to-face context, teachers need to establish with the group when certain potentially distracting behaviours (for example, individual consultation of dictionaries) are acceptable and when learners ought to refrain from these. In the case of dictionary use, the distraction affects the individual as well as other learners and considerably disrupts the interaction, especially in activities such as role-plays. Other factors that may distract or be unacceptable to the majority of the group in terms of behaviour norms can be the use of mobile phones or other devices, or eating and drinking during a session. Further aspects specific to this mode which need to be considered are, for example, teacher movement within the classroom, the way in which a teacher can manage interaction through eye contact, procedures for the teacher sitting in on pairwork and groupwork, and the teacher listening in and taking notes for later error correction.

Knowledge of the particularity of the environment

In the face-to-face sessions this will rely on knowing the physical context, so that it can not only be used to maximum effect but also, as previously mentioned, make it safe and welcoming for learners. Physical obstacles may need to be removed. This can involve a reassessment of what an obstacle is and the teacher partly putting her/ himself in the minds of the learners. Seating may need to be changed to make it more inclusive (horseshoe or circle, for example). Workstations or resources, if these are to be used, are best set up prior to the learners' arrival to a great extent, to save time and disruption.

Teacher knowledge of and reaction to learners

This will be crucial particularly with regard to facial, gestural and physical cues. These can be helpful, but may mislead if knowledge of individual learners is not fully formed. For example, learner Y may always frown when concentrating, but this is not to be interpreted as a sign of unhappiness. Learner Z may be uncomfortable with circulatory activities but not declare this because s/he does not wish to reveal a health problem. Complex needs and reactions of this kind need to be considered by the teacher during the session, as well as before and after. What cannot be pre-empted at planning stage in terms of learners' comfort or vulnerability in this face-to-face environment has to be considered at the teaching stage, since it is highly dependent on the particular group of learners who attend that day. So again, flexibility, this time in terms of implementation of the plan, is paramount. Another crucial point is the management of learners' expectations regarding the amount and intensity of spoken input and the use of L2. A further aspect, outlined in Chapter 3, is the acceptance of silences and peripherality as a positive choice and the unpicking of marginality, as outlined by Norton (2004), as a negative position.

After the session

Clearly the time frame covered by 'after the session' can range from the immediate end of the formal session to days or perhaps weeks after it, depending on the frequency of contact dictated by the particular blend and its timetable. In some blended programmes there may be less frequent contact face-to-face, with most sessions occurring online. It is important therefore that learners are made aware of the continuation, via the variety of teaching sessions, about issues raised. Issues can be varied, ranging from the thematic focus, the grammatical focus, social interaction, learning skills discussions to personal observations/comments/problems. Post-session work can take various forms (for example, error correction, generic/personal feedback, individual support, follow-up tasks and online asynchronous discussions) and can be communicated in different ways (for example, face-to-face, by telephone, email, forums or wikis).

Feedback

An advantage of face-to-face contact is that teachers can quickly ask learners to fill in a feedback form at the end of the session. Some teachers and indeed learners may prefer that learners fill this in later when they have time to reflect more analytically. They then return it by post or email. This of course relies on learners remembering and having time to do this.

It can also be useful, particularly for those learners in the group who have not attended the face-to-face session, to receive a summary of issues or learning points from the teacher via email or in an asynchronous group discussion forum, if the time and salary so allows. In addition, such feedback after a face-to-face session can function for all learners as a support for their progress and situate their work in relation to other elements of the blend. The teacher can suggest ways in which learners can continue their work until the next teaching session. The teacher's views on how well learners did, on their general progress, on the challenges they still face, can prompt learners to reflect on their work as a whole. This form of feedback can either be given quickly after the session and informally to individual learners or more formally afterwards during follow-up work.

Follow-up work

An asynchronous forum as well as learner support groups are also ideal places for learners to continue debates begun in the face-to-face session and to undertake further role-plays or follow-up work. This will create a sense of belonging to the group, including for those who missed the face-to-face session, and can highlight the advantages for some of collaboration. It might in turn encourage more learners to return to the next face-to-face session and engage actively with other learners there.

Individual support

Immediately after the session it is helpful to pick up serious issues that have arisen for individuals and need urgent attention so learners do not go away feeling defeated or upset. This may involve speaking to individuals who have struggled badly or seemed uncomfortable, despite the teachers' best efforts. The teacher should ask such learners to stay behind in a discreet way so that they do not feel targeted in front of others. Sorting out any issues on the spot may also encourage them to return to face-to-face sessions.

Conclusion

With teaching environments changing and blended teaching becoming increasingly common, many teachers and institutions will want or indeed have to take a fresh look at their face-to-face provision and its place within any blended programme. This chapter has aimed to add to the discussion, indicating that, while aspects of the face-to-face environment will not change, the teaching and learning that happen within it may be radically different from older forms of face-to-face teaching. The increased learner input and control at all stages of the teaching and learning process in the teaching models advocated here can promote learners' reflection on their individual learning process and raise awareness of their own responsibility for progressing in their studies.

What may have also emerged throughout the chapter is a potentially demanding role for the teacher in this part of the blend, as in the other teaching modes. Though this is true, it can at the same time lead to a highly rewarding professional experience in teaching and learning, involving teachers and learners alike in creative and intuitive language work. This creativity is facilitated by the greater openness of planning and task design in this component of blended teaching, which allows more scope for learners to contribute and relate to their individual experiences and worldviews.

Interaction has to remain a key objective in the face-to-face session in many blended programmes, with scope for variation and development but not to the detriment of learner comfort or need. This is a prerequisite which may require careful negotiation and understanding from all concerned. Undoubtedly the move to confident, autonomous learners, at ease with blended learning and in control of their own progress and development, will be greatly enhanced by enlightened approaches of institutions and individual teachers to their teaching practice in face-to-face as in other modes. What the authors have described in this chapter constitutes an ideal and life is rarely like that, particularly in the classroom situation. The complex social picture in learning at present, however, makes moves toward this ideal a necessity in adult learning today.

Chapter 12:   **Asynchronous Online Teaching**

Hannelore Green, Elke St.John,
Sylvia Warnecke and Vikki Atkinson

Introduction

Asynchronous online tools are frequently a key component of blended language programmes. They offer a support framework for teaching and learning, which learners can access in their own time at a place convenient to them. Some asynchronous tools, for example email, have been used successfully in language teaching and learning for more than fifteen years (St.John and Cash, 1995). Since then, a myriad of asynchronous tools including forums, wikis, computer-marked quizzes, audio, video or microblogs, podcasts and a vast number of social networking sites such as Facebook, MySpace and Kaioo have become available to supplement language teaching sessions. These sophisticated multi-media features all exploit potential learner enthusiasm for communication. Asynchronous tools connect people and allow exchanges between teaching sessions, thus providing continuity of access to a learning community. Combining synchronous work, whether face-to-face, by phone or online conferencing, with tasks and activities carried out asynchronously can be a good way of drawing together modes in blended language teaching. Obvious advantages are that, unlike in synchronous work, learners can choose the time of their contribution having had the opportunity to reflect, for example, on its content and style. Moreover, with asynchronous work a sense of belonging and cohesion can be strengthened in learner groups. From the ever-increasing number of online and mobile technologies that fit into the category of asynchronous online tools, this chapter will concentrate on the more established and tested forums, wikis and blogs, which can enable learners to use the L2 in interaction with one another (and a teacher) and can also facilitate collaboration.

A wide range of language learning skills can be developed via asynchronous tools: for example, Macdonald (2008) suggests that these may include reading, writing, peer review and translation skills. However, the decision regarding the planned use of the tools has to be based on more than linguistic aims. To be fit for purpose, they must form an integral part of a language learning experience that is underpinned by sound pedagogy taking into consideration socio-cultural, psycho-linguistic and cognitive issues affecting learners as well as the affordances of the specific tools.

The following list provides an overview of the key pedagogical aspects and learning outcomes that may impact on the planning and implementation of teaching with asynchronous tools:

- developing L2 learning (e.g. accuracy, fluency, communication);
- exchanging concepts and ideas, including inter-cultural aspects;
- collaborative co-construction of knowledge;
- integrating ICT skills into courses;
- developing transferable skills;
- utilising realistic, up-to-date forms of communication (integral to language teaching);
- applying constructivist pedagogies, i.e. in producing learner-generated content;
- supporting teaching and studying for all learners including those unable to access other teaching modes.

A further crucial difference between teaching in asynchronous and face-to-face contexts is the role of the teacher. In asynchronous communication the configuration of the tools often distinguishes between the roles of moderator and participant, as in synchronous online conferencing outlined in Chapter 9. As explained in that chapter, the roles of teacher/moderator and learner/participant, however, are not identical and can shift; learners can become moderators of discussions. In fact, in the asynchronous mode the teacher generally facilitates and oversees the interaction rather than primarily 'imparting knowledge' to learners. In view of this significant aspect of asynchronous teaching, this chapter aims to illustrate how learner control, creativity and independence can be promoted in this environment.

Planning for teaching in an asynchronous context

This section provides an overview of the features of asynchronous environments and describes which aspects of language teaching and learning are best served using forums, blogs and/or wikis. It examines the role of the teacher, considers task design and provides examples of tasks. Figure 12.1 outlines those characteristics of forums, wikis and blogs that are specifically relevant to language teaching and learning and shows that these tools can serve multiple uses in blended language teaching.

The planning framework

Before deciding on a particular asynchronous environment and planning a task, a framework needs to be clarified. The following questions can help the teacher to develop a framework that is tailored to a specific group and purpose:

- What functions do I want the tool (forum/wiki/blog) to perform?
- How do I want learners to use the tool?
- How much time can I afford for reading and responding to contributions?
- How much time do I want learners to spend reading and submitting contributions?

- How should the tool be used for groupwork?
- How can I motivate learners to participate?
- How can I keep the space structured and organised?

In the subsections below, further issues related to the respective tools are highlighted and contrasted where applicable. A certain degree of overlap between the tools is unavoidable.

	Forum	Wiki	Blog
Working definition	Structured/organised discussion of one or more topics with a small or large group of people	Working collaboratively towards a jointly/mutually authored product	Individual or group diary that allows comments to be made by readers
Technological competence	Low/moderate	Moderate	Low/moderate
Authorship	Open multi-authored discussions; author clearly identified; often only moderator has editing rights	All contributors have editing rights; negotiated final version; name of contributor not displayed, but author can be tracked	Authorship remains with the primary author(s)
Status of content	Topic often provided by moderator/teacher; all contributors share information	Topic(s) normally negotiated; all contributors combine information	Primary author decides topic and shares information
Nature of interaction/ contribution	Moderator/teacher-led multi-party open discussion; new topics can be added; new topics often arise from existing discussions	Group-led interaction/ communication happens in the actual editing as well as in the use of the comment feature; sub-topics can be added as new pages	Blogger-led series of dialogues through individual comments by secondary authors
Structure/ organisation	Organised chronologically within a thread	Organised on a dividing tree through different pages	Chronological structure determined by tool
Number of participants	Group size varies; all sizes possible	Can cope with large groups	Individual blogger is sufficient
Pedagogical features (usefulness and disadvantages)	Teacher can see who reads the postings and establish who the active and passive contributors are; statistics (e.g. of individual contributions) are available; summarising function allows overview of long threads in a discussion	Teacher can see when and what participants have contributed; passive contributors cannot be identified	Teacher can comment positively/encourage publicly as comments are visible with dates
Learner appeal	Ease of use; high interest if learners are motivated by discussions, tasks or the opportunity to strengthen the group dynamics	Ability to change and modify a document; everyone can contribute according to her/his own strengths	Suitable for learners with high levels of confidence as they can become creative with multiple media

Figure 12.1: Characteristics of forums, wikis and blogs and their potential use in language teaching.

Teaching via forums

In conjunction with the generic framework above, further forum-specific issues need to be considered:

- In addition to learner interaction in response to set tasks, forums might be helpful for providing extra documents. A separate section for learning aids (e.g. examination revision materials, vocabulary lists, grammar help, writing tips or handouts from face-to-face sessions) can be included.
- Forums may be set up to support discussions between peers, questions for the teacher and other learners, general conversations and debates, which allow for more creative use of the language for all types of learners and encourage the use of critical thinking to develop arguments and provide opportunities for writing practice in the L2.
- Forums can be used for social purposes as well as for language learning. In fact, the additional provision of a social forum may greatly aid reflection on the language learning process.
- Planning the overall forum structure in advance will save confusion when more material is added.

The most difficult aspect of planning is predicting how to motivate participation in asynchronous activities, when the unpredictable diversity of the language learners in a group with different backgrounds needs to be taken into account (see 'Addressing diversity', p. 182). One motivational strategy suggested by Macdonald (2008) is to link forum and wiki activities to specific assessment tasks and integrate them into an overall assessment structure. The relevance of assessment-framed activities in near-synchronous settings, that is, where learners have only a short period of time to complete their tasks on the forum/wiki, is seen as especially compelling as a preparation for tests or examinations. However, incorporating assessment and time frames into asynchronous teaching creates a whole set of different considerations which are not the focus of this chapter.

Teaching via wikis

A wiki is a constantly changing written text in which all active users participate in the process of reading, drafting, revising and editing. It is in effect collaborative writing between all users. Since many people may contribute to the wiki, exposition, understanding and interpretation is a continuous joint process. Not only do many of the issues outlined above also apply to wikis (for example, when planning reading and writing tasks) but wikis also actually combine quite naturally with forums. The forum provision can be used for social purposes and clarification or discussion of matters related to work on the wiki, since it is often important to have a space for users to ask questions, to discuss their collaborative writing. Many wikis already incorporate forums in the form of discussion or talk pages on which users can interact directly with each other.

Wikis can promote learner autonomy through collaboration with others by means of pairwork and groupwork without the teacher being present. Earlier studies, such as one by Stickler and St.John (2001), have demonstrated that once learners have been introduced to learning more independently it increases their motivation to study and their engagement with the subject. As noted previously in the context of forums, linking wiki activities to assessment can also motivate participation.

For learners to derive the most benefit from independent learning in asynchronous environments, it is important that the teacher acts mainly as the facilitator by providing a general topic at the beginning of the project and encouraging learners to add further sub-pages according to the aspects of the topic *they* decide to work on. Thus, at the end of the activity, learners have an extensive collection of meaningful texts produced collaboratively on the initial stimulus from the teacher. Such tasks are also designed to accommodate a variety of learners. The detailed planning of the structure of a wiki is not as crucial and therefore probably less time-consuming for the teacher than in a forum, since learners develop the activity independently.

In a wiki, content and organisation can be modified and owned by the community. Weaker or less confident learners should feel encouraged to participate because the name of the individual contributor is not prominently displayed, thus affording them a sense of anonymity within the wider community. For this reason, wikis are likely to support an almost entirely learner-centred environment, in contrast to forums which, as already discussed above, generally involve contributions from and moderation by the teacher/moderator of the learners' contributions. In addition, interesting intercultural exchanges and discussions may be fostered in this community.

An additional benefit of employing wikis is that they can provide an authentic opportunity to concentrate on reading and writing rather than speaking and listening skills. Wikis focus on the written output, although the basic written record can be enhanced with integrated images, web links and audio files. Therefore, while using the wiki to develop analytical and research skills, participants are inevitably practising the skills of (critical) writing and reading. Negotiation of meaning and content is achieved either through commenting on the original text or through editing respective wikis entries.

Teaching via blogs
Blogs are web diaries and similar to forums and wikis in terms of their use for social and academic purposes, but with a tendency to be more personal. One use may be as a learning journal, which can be helpful as an individual learning space or, if made public to the entire tutor group, for peer review purposes and commenting. Blogs, in contrast to wikis, offer the opportunity to express opinions and thoughts on a topic of personal interest and to publish them online. Bloggers often reflect on aspects of their choice and express their personal views. Everybody who reads them can in turn

post comments. Blogs support the use of different media such as images, videos, text, hyperlinks or audio. It is even possible to invent a new (fictional) identity that reflects the blogger's creativity: for example, through their postings, their writing style and use of images.

Blogs are similar to forums and wikis where writing practice is the primary focus. Here too additional documents such as vocabulary lists and grammar aids can be included either to add emphasis to certain points made or just to provide more background information to the blogger's own reflection. A good example of enthusing learners to get involved is the Royds Languages Department blog (http://roydslanguagesdepartment.typepad.com). It offers information in French, German, Spanish and Italian on many topics such as comics, songs, sports, religion. Learners and teachers alike leave comments on the materials. Here too a diversity of learners is addressed as ideas from learners of many different backgrounds are shared and reflected on.

Learners can use blogs not only as tools for communication and written exchanges but also as resources. In this respect, they are a means of finding information on particular subjects and issues. As bloggers plan their blogs very carefully, readers will find that content is updated regularly. Class blogs can be used for discussions among learners, as exemplified in the Sans problems!-blog (http://mmeperkins.typepad.com) on all matters French. The compilation of examination revision material blogs can be motivational for both the blogger and the learner.

Task design

The more the teacher knows about the target group the better. However, the composition of any given cohort, the group dynamics and cohesion, the levels of active participation, technical competence and confidence may be difficult to anticipate. The main design focus must be to elicit contributions, to promote and facilitate communication. Therefore, the teacher needs to consider how each of the asynchronous tools might best achieve these purposes and how they relate to other components in the blend.

Points to consider in the task design for the use of asynchronous tools in blended language learning are:

- the linguistic competence of the group, especially in written communication;
- the nature of the intended learning outcomes. This is likely to determine which asynchronous tool is used. Furthermore, determining whether a variety of blogs, wikis and forums throughout the course can make the activities more interesting or prohibitive is vital;
- the relevance of the learning outcomes, i.e. whether learners will be able clearly to see how the use of the respective tools and the activity benefits their learning;
- the group size, in that small groups moderated by a teacher will find it easier

to work on a collaborative task compared with a plenary group, which may consist of a large number of learners and be moderated institution-wide. The task in large groups needs to provide enough scope for all members to add their own contributions;

- the use of a 'hook' (see Chapter 11) in an activity. This should encourage the learner to want to respond. Such a 'hook' can be an image, puzzle, short text or question prompts. Ice-breakers are useful 'hooks' at the beginning of a course. Long input texts requiring extensive preparation before a contribution can be made are less useful in this respect;
- the expected length of contribution. To make efficient use of teachers' and learners' time, it is advisable to avoid tasks that require learners to produce and comment on long texts;
- the frequency with which learners and the teacher are expected to check for new responses or make contributions. This has to be clear since, apart from being tiresome, the need to log in frequently may reduce learner motivation and willingness to contribute further, particularly if there is little new to read or respond to;
- the use of the L2 for task instructions, subject-specific terminology and metalanguage. This could be beneficial but may be off-putting to some learners;
- the technical skills and experience of learners. This may influence decisions about which tools to use and whether help with technical aspects needs to be provided;
- the number of asynchronous tasks in the blended language course overall. Too many optional asynchronous activities may spread the contributions thinly and participants may end up with disappointingly few or no responses to their postings. On the other hand, too few tasks jeopardise the sustained engagement with the asynchronous mode;
- the timing of tasks. This is vital and questions such as 'Will feedback arrive in time for the next assessment point?' or 'Will an activity fall into a holiday period/coincide with religious/cultural festivals?' have to be considered accordingly;
- the assessment strategy for the course. If the learner response to the task forms part of the course assessment, the success criteria need to be communicated to the learners in advance.

Research has shown (Murphy, 2005) that learners are least likely to engage in self-study activities that involve open-ended writing tasks and therefore have no clear-cut solutions, and some learners may omit them altogether. Even when model answers are provided, they are often not seen as helpful, as learners' uncertainties regarding their own versions cannot necessarily be addressed. Willingness to engage with model answers requires self-direction, reflection and autonomy that many learners lack or find too time-consuming. It would therefore seem beneficial to embed this type of writing task in an asynchronous teaching setting where feedback by peers and the moderator is provided. It would be interesting to ascertain whether learners feel that generic feedback (for example, in a forum) is seen as valuable and meets their needs, thus providing enough incentive to engage in such open-ended tasks. There is a clear need for further research in this respect.

The examples below, which have been extracted and adapted from a variety of OU languages courses, demonstrate a number of approaches. They illustrate how tasks can be used at different levels of L2 proficiency to stimulate communication through reading and writing in conjunction with the planning issues discussed in the previous section, as well as to foster reflection on the language acquisition strategies themselves.

Examples of forum tasks

German beginners' task

The task in Figure 12.2 seeks to encourage learners to use the recently-learned vocabulary and structures on the topic of hobbies. Learners need to read and respond to others' contributions, as well as add their own details. Familiar L2 vocabulary and structures are consolidated and new ones encountered.

This is a chain-reaction task. Read the chain of messages from fellow students and reply to the latest one in the chain. Include:

- a response to their question about hobbies;
- something about your own hobby/hobbies;
- other hobbies you might be interested in;
- a question about a specific hobby.

You can make up any details if you wish. I'll start the chain with my message:

Hallo,

mein Hobby ist Basteln. Ich möchte aber neue Hobbys ausprobieren – was ist Barfußlaufen? Was braucht man dazu? Welche Hobbys haben Sie? Kann mir jemand ein neues Hobby empfehlen?

Danke,

Figure 12.2: Beginners' German forum task.

French intermediate task

The example in Figure 12.3 illustrates how the task designers not only set the scene in order to help learners 'recall an amusing or bizarre anecdote', but they also instruct the contributors to use past tenses as well as relative clauses, i.e. create an additional focus on grammatical learning outcomes.

Racontez une anecdote, quelque chose d'amusant ou de bizarre qui vous est arrivé. Utilisez les temps du passé (passé composé et imparfait)

- Si possible, essayez d'inclure aussi un exemple de *qui, que* ou *où* et une description d'un objet.
- Postez votre contribution en réponse à ce message.
- Revenez régulièrement pour lire ce que les autres étudiants auront posté, poser des questions ou faire des commentaires.

Figure 12.3: Intermediate French forum task.

Examples of wiki tasks

The intention of a wiki is to collect numerous pieces of information about a broad topic to arrive at a consistent, ever more objective entity that is written collaboratively. Topics can range from a wiki on French recipes to grammar rules. Within the context of the continuous reviewing process, the personal perspective of one individual is superseded. Thus the basic aim of a wiki project is to create an ever-evolving knowledge base through ongoing collaboration.

The wiki tasks shown in Figure 12.4 aim to collate a wide range of support mechanisms and to guide contributors towards reflection on their learning, thus engaging them in constructivist pedagogies. In the first, learners exchange ideas for effective learning and memorising of L2 vocabulary, and in the second they establish a grammar rule by researching a topic, using appropriate resources (such as grammar books) in order to produce learner-generated content.

Task to collate memorising strategies	Contribute your own successful strategies for memorising vocabulary and grammar rules. Share and compare the different learning styles in your group.
Task to develop a grammar rule	Gather examples of the use of *ser* and *estar* in Spanish and try to formulate the rule.

Figure 12.4: Two reflective wiki tasks.

Example of a blog task

Blogs too are valuable tools for reflection and for practising L2 writing skills. Blog readers will not only be able to practise L2 reading skills but can also initiate a conversation by posting comments to the blogger, as they are able to give feedback via a comment box. This can lead to meaningful dialogues between the blogger and those who comment on her/his blog. Despite the individualised nature of a blog, readers can become interactive participants.

The personal blog task for an upper intermediate German course, shown in Figure 12.5, asks participants to reflect on a definition of art, to state their own preferences and to list links to artists and their work that they have found. Concepts and ideas are exchanged by way of inviting readers to add their comments.

Die Einträge in Ihrem Blog zum Thema ‚Kunst' sollen dazu dienen, dass Sie die folgenden Aspekte diskutieren:

- Ihre eigene Definition von Kunst;

- was Sie daran interessiert;

- welche Kunstwerke Sie besonders gut/schlecht finden und warum;

- Links zu Künstlern und Künstlerinnen bzw. deren Werken angeben, über die Sie schreiben;

- ...

Vergessen Sie nicht die anderen Teilnehmer(innen) im Kurs. Sie sollten so oft wie möglich gegenseitig Ihre Blogs lesen und natürlich kommentieren.

Figure 12.5: Upper Intermediate German blog task.

Management of the online learning environment

Role of the teacher in asynchronous environments

Teachers possess many transferable skills from their experience in face-to-face teaching that can be applied in asynchronous environments. However, there is a clear need for teacher development, as identified by Hampel and Hauck (2006), Hauck and Hampel (2008) and Salmon (2003), since the role of the teacher as moderator requires a number of additional skills and qualities. The teacher/moderator needs to:

- introduce learners to the environment and address possible technical problems;
- post a welcome section to the forum/wiki with clear parameters for time frames to manage learner expectations (e.g. when tasks are to be posted and when feedback is to be expected);
- act as mediator dealing with group dynamics and appropriateness of individual contributions;
- acknowledge postings, mediate, reinforce netiquette, praise;
- give clear objectives and explain the rationale of the task;
- encourage contributions by carefully balancing support against early content-related intervention;
- employ question techniques to prompt reflection that encourages follow-on contributions;
- weave and summarise forum threads to elicit further postings;
- provide feedback that is generic, depersonalised and feeds forward (e.g. target setting);

- promote learner autonomy by gradually removing scaffolding and handing responsibility for collaboration over to the group.

Fostering learner autonomy (Chapter 4) in an asynchronous learning environment confronts the teacher with new challenges. It means allowing learners to have the opportunity to learn from mistakes and helping them to recognise this learning. This concept may be incompatible with some socio-cultural backgrounds and furthermore may be even more difficult to accept in an environment where mistakes are visible for all to see. Posting contributions in the L2, when the learner is unsure about her/his linguistic competence, or trying out new structures and vocabulary 'in public', can be the cause of great anxiety and may prevent some learners from participating. Affective factors in asynchronous online language learning have to be acknowledged and sensitively dealt with by the teacher/moderator.

Macdonald (2004, p. iv) points out: 'The conventional tutor group [is] often too small for sustained online discussion', hence issues of rapport between moderator and the forum/wiki group in the context of possible anxiety and reticence need to be examined. The question arises whether moderators who also teach the participants in synchronous settings are preferable to separately appointed moderators for a larger, merged plenary group that has enough of a critical mass to maintain momentum in the online setting but where the contributors have never met the moderator.

Mediation

Asynchronous online tools rely on the written word, and this can be open to a variety of interpretations and misinterpretations by participants. To minimise the need for mediation, it is crucial to establish a code of conduct before engaging in asynchronous activities. Having to address issues that are unconnected to linguistic content and task completion threatens an environment that has to be conducive to participation and collaboration. Adhering to an online netiquette means that learners should:

- respect each others' opinions;
- not judge their fellow learners;
- use polite and respectful language that is constructive and helpful to the group;
- respect different approaches and ways of learning.

While the teacher/moderator has to exercise control over the type of identity the group develops, this can present challenges. A group may be the same as the sum of its individual members and can be rational, democratic and/or supportive, but group dynamics can sometimes acquire their own momentum leaving the most skilful teacher/moderator perplexed.

Moderation

Moderating the asynchronous online environment presents the teacher with a dilemma. S/he has to decide between desirable frequent intervention that may be needed to generate a sense of group identity — to invite, to motivate and sustain momentum — and a 'willingness to "let go" of control and content presentation approaches to teaching' (Siemens and Tittenberger, 2009, p. 15). Siemens and Tittenberger (2009, p. 20) list further challenges:

> Teaching in online environments increases the workload and responsibilities for many educators as new conceptual views and technical skills are required. Isolation and depersonalisation impacts [on] educators as well as learners, creating concerns about burnout.

Moderator expectations clearly need to be managed too. Participation may vary despite the moderator's best efforts. An over-ambitious moderator, expecting full engagement of the group, might find figures by Macdonald on participation levels reassuring. Writing in an internal OU moderator training course (Macdonald, 2010), she comments, '[Group] viability depends on a nucleus of active students which varies from 30% of the population to less than 10%. A larger group will benefit from reading the contributions.'

Online participation as a form of social interaction relies on a sense of the identity of the group and familiarisation, which take time to develop. Forum/wiki tasks and the frequency of interaction may not be conducive to generating sufficient cohesion in the time available. Participants may have to be weaned off the desire to produce a perfect piece of L2 writing based on detailed, individual corrections by the teacher. An examination-led culture, where the result matters more than the insights gained during the learning processes, may be a hindrance to self-reflection and self-direction. Generic feedback, rather than individual correction, requires the learner to apply metacognitive analysis and, more importantly, to engage again with a subsequent draft. The learners' growing independence afforded by the interaction in the asynchronous learning environment may not be immediately apparent to the individual or be valued. The nature of the information cycle, time delays in responses (by peers or moderators) and the unfamiliarity with learner-centred pedagogies that expect the learner to become increasingly independent may frustrate initially willing participants and prevent them from contributing again. Having to reflect on and apply generic feedback to their contribution may not constitute sufficient 'reward' for their efforts. The familiar teacher–learner interaction of task submission and subsequent detailed error correction has to be re-evaluated and replaced. Scaffolding mechanisms for students to develop the envisaged autonomy need to be put in place.

Whether moderation or task feedback should employ L2 is a further consideration. Using L2 can support language acquisition, but if insistence on L2 causes paralysis in forums/wikis it may not be the best way forward. As learners progress through the different levels of linguistic competence, the L2 will increasingly become the norm. At intermediate levels the decision is not as straightforward and the moderator's judgement is essential. In contexts where learners do not share a common L1, however, no such language choice is available.

Collaboration between learners

The concept of the teacher no longer being the expert to whom the learner turns for all the answers (Siemens and Tittenberger, 2009, p. 3) is still alien to many participants in asynchronous environments. Even with an active nucleus of learners, who regularly submit their individual contributions, collaboration on forum tasks remains relatively rare and postings stand in isolation from one another. Wikis may fare better, as collaboration is a built-in design feature, but here also learners are hesitant to 'spoil' contributions from peers and often simply add further text without editing what is already there.

White (2003) points out that 'feedback plays a critical role for distance learners, not only as a response to their performance but also as a means of providing support, encouragement and motivation to continue'. However, motivation may be affected negatively by feedback given for all to see, and even more disconcerting if feedback is supplied by peers who are not experts themselves. The learners' initial anxiety about posting publicly, especially in the L2, is equalled by their anxiety about commenting on someone else's work in case the comment is incorrect.

The idea that assessment of collaboration might combat forum/wiki fatigue has been mentioned. Using assessment as a motivational tool, even as a carrot-and-stick approach, raises questions about clear assessment criteria, the proportion of the overall result and issues of quantity versus quality of content. Learners have been known to forego this online element of assessment as their anxieties are greater than the perceived reward.

Murphy *et al.* (2009), in a language teacher development project, clearly identify the difficulties of establishing meaningful, active and productive collaboration asynchronously. They establish that aspects such as the lack of detailed guidelines, intervention by the moderator or the availability of synchronous sessions to support asynchronous work were important factors that hampered successful collaboration. However, specific factors could be deemed beneficial *or* detrimental by members of the same group. Lack of guidance can, for example, open the possibility of creativity with impressive outcomes or lead to the collapse of the working group and no outcome at all.

Hauck and Youngs (2008) question the ways in which telecollaboration, that is, working together in online environments, differs from collaboration in a face-to-face classroom. The following points need to be borne in mind:

- There is a time delay in support mechanisms being applied.

- Teachers/moderators are not present to witness communication breaking down, to re-explain instructions, to iron out misconceptions.
- Failed communication attempts in emails due to a lack of non-verbal signals are well known. Online environments have seen a rise in using emoticons in order to overcome the missing cues from body language or to aid the interpretation of silence.
- Teachers who are willing to relinquish control may nevertheless feel the need to step in with comments if collaboration between students is not forthcoming.
- The greater a learner's autonomy and willingness to collaborate, the more intimidating s/he may appear to the rest of the group. The role of the moderator in praising and welcoming the contributions without stifling the shy members in the forum/wiki demands much sensitivity.

Addressing diversity

When working with diverse groups of adult language learners in blended settings, teachers using asynchronous online tools face challenges that are both similar to and different from those in other modes (see Chapter 3). The range of backgrounds, learning and writing styles, personalities and levels of confidence will vary from cohort to cohort. It is therefore crucial for the teacher/moderator to have a high level of awareness of possible issues in order to manage the asynchronous tools effectively.

Learners have differing needs and expectations when they use forums and wikis. For example, some learners want constant recognition for their hard work in the form of positive comments. Others want to observe what their peers are contributing, so they may glean not only what to do in the asynchronous mode but also learn from their peers' ideas in general. Some may never engage beyond actually reading the contributions but it can be argued that learning still takes place, just as learners who remain silent in the face-to-face classroom can benefit from the experience. Others want to gain assistance from, as well as help, their peers. Then there are those learners who never visit the online environments, no matter what the consequences might be. Participation levels may vary from under-participation, where the teacher constantly needs to remind learners to use the forum, to over-participation, where the teacher cannot even manage to keep up with everything that is happening there.

Part of the described behaviour is attributable to the diverse range of technical skills learners have. If they are new to the use of these tools, they may need further instruction to guide them. Although many educators will endeavour to guide students through some of the early hurdles they face online, some might not have that expertise themselves. It cannot be assumed that teachers and learners have progressively moved towards becoming 'digital natives' (Prensky, 2001) during the time these online facilities have been available to them.

Academic confidence varies. Many learners only ever had to share their work with the teacher. In forums, wikis and blogs, learners are 'going public' with their ideas and their work. Some will be extremely confident, sometimes to the point of intimidating the less self-assured learners who may have perfectly good ideas and work to share but who are nervous about posting in a public domain. The over-confident learner may get to the point of overpowering the group or even giving people the idea that s/he knows more than the teacher or has more control over the forum than the teacher. Equally, there may be a plethora of messages from a weaker learner which go off at a tangent or add little to advance the discussion, and will need to be skilfully summarised by the teacher. Those who feel vulnerable and exposed by placing their thoughts or work online may shy away from posting if someone is being overly aggressive, but learners who do not feel that their work is good enough to be posted are denying themselves the opportunity to receive feedback to improve their skills in addition to depriving the rest of the group of their own knowledge and expertise. To promote further participation the moderator needs to strike a fine balance between tactful, sensitive intervention and allowing time for observation before stepping in.

Language questions arise from differences in styles of address, the hierarchy and authority of learners (Salmon, 2003). For example, some learners come from cultures in which a teacher would not be directly questioned. Some may have problems with offering criticism of another's work, while others could have problems receiving criticism depending on how they view themselves and their work.

The skilful management of respectful peer approaches to commenting is required when conflicts arise, because although some learners are open to new ideas others may feel that there is only one correct way of doing something. For example, with regard to the use of Standard English some students may consider only one form to be 'correct'. They may feel that dialects have no place in languages and be unaware that dialects have their own strict standards of grammar, vocabulary and pronunciation. It is important to be open to different ways of using language so that the learner, whose posting it is, is not devalued.

Critical reflection after asynchronous teaching

Chapter 7 has set out some questions that teachers can ask themselves to determine whether asynchronous online teaching and learning have been effective. However, the variables between different learner cohorts over a number of course presentations can make this evaluation a difficult task. Adjustments made from year to year may simply result in different issues arising with a new group. Nevertheless, the teacher will want to do the following:

- evaluate her/his own level of participation in the asynchronous learning environment (Macdonald, 2008). It is essential to look back at feedback offered to see if there was too much or too little. S/he will need to check that advice and feedback was positive and constructive. The feedback needs to be expressed in a way that helps learners who are posting work and receiving responses publicly to maintain face;

- re-assess online tasks in view of the number and quality of responses (i.e. overall participation and the quality of contributions) and gauge whether or not the tasks were effective in meeting the intended learning outcomes;
- review learner contributions in the light of the intended learning outcomes to assess where additional support is needed.

Conclusion

Asynchronous online tools are valuable assets in blended teaching contexts that strongly support the development of learner control and independent learner activity. They allow learners to work both individually and together and are ideal for providing continuity between synchronous teaching sessions as well as contributing to a flexible teaching and learning environment. It is important to stress that asynchronous online tools are not a substitute for synchronous teaching and that the two work best in conjunction with one another, each offering specific strengths. While acknowledging the differences between asynchronous and synchronous learning, it is equally important to appreciate how the two complement each other within blended language teaching.

Further study is needed to establish the most suitable exploitation of online tools, to identify the most appropriate forms of professional development which can support teachers moving between the roles of facilitator and moderator and to devise strategies that motivate learners to participate. Many teachers and learners still see asynchronous tools as bolted-on extras rather than integral parts of the learning experience.

The availability of an interactive tool does not mean that learners will interact, nor does it mean that it must be used at all costs. Pedagogical considerations have to be the driving force. The speed of technological advance, which in turn impacts on teaching and learning, suggests that a host of new asynchronous tools will soon become accessible. Fragmentation into too many different components within a blend — and the potential disorientation of learners (and educators) — could result in a reluctance to engage with them. The affordances of new tools and their use will need to be carefully matched with learners' needs to create a coherent and pedagogically sound blended learning experience.

Section 4:
Community and Indigenous Celtic Languages

Chapter 13

Teaching Community Languages in Blended Contexts

Helen Peters and Lijing Shi

Introduction

Substantial groups of speakers of languages not originally indigenous to the UK have lived here for centuries. In the last decades considerable resources have been made available for the teaching of English to these communities. However, provision for the teaching of their community or heritage language to second and subsequent generations of these communities has not developed in parallel. Although the value of multilingualism is gaining recognition in the school sector, there is perhaps less recognition of the skills of multilingual adults. Where there is provision for teaching the languages spoken in the various communities, it is often aimed at those studying them as a foreign language rather than at community learners. There is also little recognition of the pedagogical differences between teaching these two groups or of the needs analysis necessary to cater for the range of learners wishing to study the language of their community. This chapter will consider some aspects of community language learning from the perspectives of teachers and learners, and some of the options open to them in the context of blended learning.

The nature of community language learners and learning

What is a community language?

The terminology in this area can vary. Fishman (2001, p. 81) uses the neutral term 'heritage language' to cover all indigenous, colonial and immigrant languages, whereas Hornberger (2005) favours the term 'community language' for all of these. McPake and Sachdev (2008, p. 5) define community languages as 'all languages in use in a society other than the dominant, official or national language' and distinguish community language learning from foreign language learning on the basis of two major factors. First, the community language learner has generally spent time learning or using the language in informal circumstances, at home or socially and is therefore a 'user'. Second, the learner may have different goals such as developing an identity, cultural engagement or a career with communities who speak the language (for example, in interpreting and translation). For the purposes of this chapter, the term 'community languages' will refer to languages that have been introduced to the UK through migration in the last few centuries. Chapter 14 will focus on the teaching of older Celtic languages which are indigenous to the UK and Ireland. Some issues addressed in this chapter with regard to community languages will, however, be equally relevant to teachers of indigenous Celtic languages.

One of the chief characteristics of a community language is that it binds together those who use it both vertically between generations and horizontally across national boundaries 'as a crucial identifier and bond to the immediate and wider diasporic group' (Mills, 2005, p. 253). Using the community language enables people who grow up in the UK to forge links with relatives and friends of all generations in the UK, in the country of origin and in other countries where speakers of the language have settled. Mills points out the importance of language 'as a marker of identity in maintaining group boundaries ... and maintain[ing] a group's sense of its ethnicity' (Mills, 2005, p. 259). This is borne out by the importance parents attach to their children learning the language of their country of origin and the efforts made by communities to establish complementary schools (for example Saturday schools, although not exclusively for children) and to organise activities where language and culture can be maintained, developed and enjoyed. The relationship to the language of study in terms of emotional investment may thus be very different from that of a foreign language learner.

Why do people study community languages?

People who regularly use a language other than English in the UK, acknowledging it as one of their own languages, may have a number of reasons for wishing to study it in a formal context.

First, young people may be encouraged by family to maintain a language so they can remain linked to their community of origin. Adults may be motivated by the desire to maintain their culture, the respect of their community and their identity within it, because: 'You're alienated if you don't know the language and, although you might look the same [and] dress the same, if you can't speak the language you are not the same as they are' (a Pakistani mother cited in Mills, 2005, p. 267). Adults who have not developed a broad or in-depth knowledge of the language may therefore be motivated to remedy this so they and their children can feel part of the community and gain status within it. For example, Comanaru and Noels (2009) found that community learners of Chinese were strongly motivated by feelings of obligation to the community as well as by the feeling that it was an integral aspect of their self-concept. However, the role of language learning in the construction of identity is difficult to quantify, since so many other factors such as class, gender and the status of an individual in the community also come into play. Block (2007) concludes that insufficient research has been undertaken in this field at present. Nevertheless a learner with links, direct or indirect, to a country or community where the language is spoken is likely to have a different engagement with the language from that of the foreign language learner.

Second, learners may have vocational motives such as obtaining a formal quali-fication in the language, at school or as part of a degree programme. This may be because they think a qualification will serve them well in gaining employment in the future or because they are aiming for a specific career that requires in-depth know-ledge of the language to equip them for teaching, community work or social work. Many universities now offer language electives and these can be perceived by com-munity learners as a way of consolidating and gaining credit for skills that they have acquired through other means.

A few examples in specific languages are of interest. Speakers of Sylheti may undertake study of Bengali to open up work opportunities beyond the Sylheti community. Speakers of Latin American varieties of Spanish and Portuguese and varieties of French from francophone countries around the world may also wish to gain knowledge of varieties sometimes accorded a higher value. Arabic, for which learner numbers in the UK are increasing (CILT survey, 2005, cited in Anderson, 2008), is also frequently studied for religious purposes in its classical form by users of other forms and other languages.

Where a language is spoken in several countries, the existence of different vari-eties makes the job of teacher, interpreter or translator complex and sensitive. A speaker of a regional or informal form of a language might be seeking to learn a formal or standard variety, although learners might not agree with the way varieties are classified. A learner in London is cited as saying:

> Our teacher who taught us to read and write Greek often stressed to us that we should not speak Greek with a Cypriot dialect and try to speak it with a Hellenic accent as this was regarded to be 'proper Greek' … I feel the teacher was wrong in trying to stop us from speaking with a Cypriot dialect. The Cypriot dialect is part of the heritage and culture of Cyprus and to try to discourage us from using it is only contributing to the destruction of the culture (ILEA, 1990).

The issue of language varieties will be further discussed under 'Catering for differing needs among community learners' on p. 193.

Third, most non-indigenous language communities in the UK have active organ-isations that bring people together and serve to maintain cultural and social ties. A common motivating factor for language study may be engagement in voluntary or paid work within such communities. McDermott (2009) describes the setting up of community Sunday schools in Polish and Lithuanian in Dungannon, North-ern Ireland, by immigrants who became aware that their children were growing up without knowledge of the language and culture of their country of origin. According to a CILT survey (cited in Anderson, 2008) such schools exist for more than sixty-one languages in the UK, with 500 in London alone.

Addressing the needs of community language learners

Although sometimes the motivation of community language learners may be similar to that of those learning an L2, such as to find employment or gain a qualification as mentioned above, the knowledge base from which the community learner starts is invariably different from that of the L2 learner. Among community language learners the range and nature of the knowledge of the language varies from one individual to another, in terms of variety, knowledge of written and spoken forms and cultural background. Particularly in the case of languages not using the Roman alphabet, such as Bengali and Urdu, learners who have grown up in the UK may be fluent speakers but have a much less developed knowledge of the written language. On the other hand, in the case of Mandarin or Cantonese, for example, learners may have a sound knowledge of the characters but little familiarity with the spoken form. It can be difficult for Cantonese speakers to master the pronunciation of Mandarin Chinese, and they may experience high anxiety when they cannot perform well, as they are often perceived as 'native' speakers by other learners in the group. Teachers need to take care with these learners to build on their strengths and avoid making them feel that they have not lived up to expectations from themselves and peers.

Community learners may therefore have very different needs from one another as well as from L2 learners. Anderson (2008) suggests that for the majority of these learners, especially those born and brought up in the UK, it may not be appropriate to consider them as mother tongue learners, although he implies that a foreign language teaching approach would be equally inappropriate. He found in his own study that the majority of community language learners are also users and that teaching them separately from those learning the language as an L2 is preferable, taking what he calls a 'modified second language' approach (ibid., p. 295). Teachers who are required to teach community and L2 learners together will therefore need to be aware of confidence issues for both groups, and develop appropriate differentiation strategies to meet the needs of each.

Other studies of children learning languages have also found that separating them into groups of community learners and L2 learners has been more effective than teaching both groups together (Valdés, 1995). Hornberger and Wang, cited in Lawton and Logio (2008, p. 138), suggest that the difference between community language learners and L2 learners cannot be clearly defined but lies on a continuum ranging from the learner who is 'linguistically proficient and culturally immersed [to] ... the learner who has no language proficiency, cultural or historical ties'. Lawton and Logio (ibid.) found that many schools considered separate classes necessary to teach groups at different ends of the continuum because of the different needs of the learners. In the case of adult learners, there may be classes provided exclusively for community language learners in some community schools and adult education, but in higher education and in a blended context these are not generally available. Chapter 3 discusses diversity issues in general, and Chapter 14 considers some implications of motivational diversity for teachers of indigenous languages, which may also be relevant in a community context.

Dlaska (2009, p. 105), however, sees grouping community and L2 learners together as a positive aspect of language teaching and learning because 'language classes tend to address the cultural and national diversity of students in the UK and make it the very topic of discussion'. Dlaska sees language centres in universities as bringing together learners from different disciplines as well as different language backgrounds, and facilitating the adoption of collaborative learning practices. She points out that when learners are studying a language for academic purposes, both native and non-native speakers are acquiring new repertoires (ibid., p. 108). Additionally, learners benefit from contact with peers who are familiar with the target culture, and exchange information about cultural backgrounds. In terms of facilitating this cultural exchange, both Harrison and Thomas (2009) and Dlaska (2009) emphasise the potential role of new technologies in meeting the needs of different learners, by facilitating peer collaboration and involving learners in new discourse communities (see 'The use of technology in the blend' on p. 197). Harrison and Thomas (2009) point out the value of web-based applications in integrating the four skills of listening, speaking, reading and writing, particularly important in the context of mixed groups of learners. They also relate social networking to Vygotsky's view of the importance of social interaction between learners, particularly rewarding where learners have different areas of strength and different levels of cultural awareness. These issues need to be taken into consideration in the community language learning situation, where blended learning has much to offer.

Issues raised by teachers in a survey of blended community language teaching

As mentioned earlier, in spite of differences in their backgrounds and aims, learners of community languages and L2 learners of those languages with no community background are generally taught together in further and higher education in the UK. In order to gain a teacher perspective on the teaching of these two types of learner together in blended contexts, the authors of this chapter conducted a small in-house survey (Peters and Shi, 2009), asking teachers what the implications were for their blended practice. Questionnaires were distributed to language teachers at the OU, most of whom were also teaching the language in other contexts as well, such as Saturday schools or evening classes. Responses were received from teachers of Chinese (Mandarin), French, Spanish and German. Although in the UK these languages may be largely viewed as foreign languages, there are significant communities of immigrant speakers in some parts of the country, and all respondents said they had community language learners in some of their groups.

Most of the teachers saw the presence of community learners as an advantage for themselves as well as for the other learners, because it raised the level of spoken language in synchronous sessions, where the community learners helped others in pairwork, for example. Some saw it as neither advantage nor disadvantage and found community language learners not particularly eager to help. However, all the teachers felt that the combination of different types of learners required a change in approach to teaching, and often involved extra work and the provision of differentiated materials. They felt that the learning situation needed careful management, so that community language speakers did not feel exploited and foreign language learners did not feel disadvantaged and uncomfortable. Teachers said that some foreign language learners felt it was 'intimidating' and 'unfair' for community learners to be on the courses. In a separate survey of learners on an advanced French course (Peters, 2008) a learner said: 'Although it was good to hear them converse and converse with them … I felt that they would be at an unfair advantage when marks were given.' However, teachers reported that francophone learners on the course, who came from Algeria, Martinique, Seychelles, Mauritius and Senegal as well as metropolitan France, generally did not have prior experience of higher education, and there was a considerable gap between their spoken and written competence (ibid.). This was also true of learners on an advanced Spanish course (Peters and Shi, 2009), who had 'an oral proficiency way beyond their written proficiency [and were] often unaware of differences in register'. Some learners of German (Peters, 2008), who had grown up in Germany or lived there a long time, also 'often found grammar and spelling difficult'. Teachers of Chinese (ibid.) found that Cantonese speakers learning Mandarin wanted to focus on the spoken language while learners new to characters needed to learn to read and write as well.

Teachers felt that it was important to have a good range of materials to draw on and that teaching face-to-face was an advantage, although all of them also used online modes either as a supplement to face-to-face teaching or as the main form of delivery. One teacher said that:

> Such [community language] students often have multiple questions
> which only arise in the group. With a self-teach method there is not much
> spark to questioning and no on-hand tutor (Peters and Shi, 2009).

The survey (Peters and Shi, 2009) implies a rich and potentially rewarding teaching and learning environment, albeit one that makes particular demands on teachers and learners.

Level of teacher experience

Chapter 14 will consider some of the issues that might arise where volunteer L1 speakers are used to support learners of indigenous languages or when L1 speakers who are not professional teachers are employed in a teaching capacity. Similar difficulties may be faced in the community language context. Those working with learners may have little teaching experience but sound knowledge of the language, and would find development in pedagogy for blended teaching useful. A further factor is that teachers in these settings may come from a range of backgrounds. Anderson (2008, p. 287) discusses students on a Postgraduate Certificate of Education (PGCE) course in community languages who:

> described vividly the difficult transition they had made ... from a traditional, didactic approach to teaching that they themselves had experienced to one based on active involvement of the learner and the opportunity to engage in meaningful communicative tasks.

Teachers coming for the first time to blended provision may therefore find that they have to make modifications from the traditional methods they are used to, since they do not lend themselves easily to a blended teaching approach.

Teaching and learning community languages in the blended context

This part of the chapter will look at blended teaching and its potential in the context of community language learning, and examine the implications for teachers and learners of situations where community and L2 learners are studying together. The range of teaching strategies and tools offered by new technology may provide some solutions to the questions posed by the variety of motivation and needs presented by learners. However, learners react differently to different ways of teaching and learning, and this may depend on age and background as well as the way in which methods are introduced and learners supported.

Advantages and challenges of blended teaching for community languages

Does blended teaching have solutions to offer where learners do not have the same learning requirements across the four skills? Many of the obvious advantages of blended teaching (for example, flexibility and independence of the learner, the possibility of communicating with fellow learners online, or opportunities for one-to-one communication with the teacher) are of benefit to all learners, whatever their linguistic background. Likewise the challenges (for example, restricted opportunity for spoken communication or face-to-face contact with teachers and fellow learners, or lack of familiarity with aspects of technology) affect all equally. What therefore are the implications for teachers of different types of learners with regard both to language learning materials and to cultural content and background? Two issues are worthy of consideration here, namely how to cater for the various needs of different types of learners and how to foster learner autonomy to facilitate the meeting of such needs.

Catering for differing needs among community learners

To meet the needs of community language learners, teachers in blended contexts need to understand how the learners perceive their own language and knowledge, and to recognise the values attached to different languages and varieties. Some may be considered more beautiful, while others are perceived as ugly or bad. Some varieties may be more appropriate to particular functions than others. The example given above of a teacher's attitude to Cypriot dialect illustrates this. Another example is that of Sylheti. At Bangladeshi independence Bengali was made the official medium of education, with the result that the Sylheti script is not officially recognised or taught. However, most Bangladeshi children in the UK are Sylheti speakers and there are campaigns for the recognition of written Sylheti in areas where the language is dominant. Teachers who are native speakers of the language they teach will have their own perspective and will need to be wary of letting this influence their attitude towards learners. Teachers also need to be clear about what they are intending or are able to teach and whether this meets the expectations of the learners in terms of the variety, the degree of formality and the skills to be covered. As part of the teaching process teachers need strategies for exploring the expectations and needs of learners, and resources to cater for these.

One approach is to start with a language history activity. Questions such as those shown in Figure 13.1 could be used, although teachers may need to modify them to suit their students and avoid any distress or embarrassment.

Your language history

- Which languages do you speak?

- Where do you use your languages?

- Where did you learn your languages?

- Did you speak another language as a child?

- If you have children, are you bringing them up to speak more than one language?

- Do you speak a different language from your parents or grandparents?

- Can you speak a language better than you can write it?

- Can you read or write a language better than you can speak it?

- Which language is most important to you?

- Have you had a job which involved using more than one language?

Figure 13.1: Language history questions

In a blended context, responses could be written in the form of a blog, where learners could choose whether to share their writing with just the teacher or with the whole group. Alternatively, learners could be given the option to respond by private email to the tutor alone, or to post their answers in a forum or a wiki, where they could also respond to other learners' messages. Questions can be designed to suit the particular learner group in order to raise the awareness of both learner and teacher with regard to learners' linguistic experience. The learners' responses could lead into a discussion at the next synchronous session of implications for language learning, and how best to cater for the strengths and weaknesses of the group and of individuals within the group.

Fostering learner autonomy

Learner autonomy, recognising learners' diverse goals and enabling them to realise these in whatever way suits them best, may be the ideal approach in a community language learning context and a blended learning environment. For example, learners who want to develop writing skills can be directed to elements of the blend that will be most useful, such as an asynchronous forum or online practice resources. Those wishing to work on speaking skills would focus on synchronous sessions and might look at strategies to engage with local speakers (see Chapter 14) or post short recordings in a blog or forum. However, the concept of autonomy may be new to some learners who may be expecting a more traditional approach, particularly if they are older or have been educated in a more teacher-centred mode. Auerbach (2007, p. 53) suggests that:

> students' learning histories shape their trajectories as language learners; thus, in order to take control of their learning, they need to name/make explicit prior learning experiences and reflect on them.

As this approach may be unfamiliar to learners, teachers will need to encourage and support them in the process and ensure they have the confidence to recognise their own requirements and to make choices, and the skills to take advantage of the possibilities open to them. Auerbach (2007) also found that if learners are engaged with the content of learning because it helps them make sense of their lives outside the learning context, they will become involved in autonomous learning. This implies that topics covered in the teaching sessions and/or learning materials should be relevant to the learners' aims, whether these are related to future careers such as teaching and interpreting or to day-to-day family and community issues. See Chapter 4 for further discussion of issues associated with learner autonomy.

Using published written course materials

Published written materials, which often form a key part of blended programmes, may not always be suitable for community language learners because of the difficulty of meeting the need for differentiation. In the preparation of sessions, care needs to be taken to be inclusive of the range of needs present in the group of learners. Where teachers are designing their own materials it may be easier to bear the needs of their particular group in mind, whereas published material may require more adaptation if course writers are targeting a general audience. Web-based material may be more easily adapted, supplemented or used flexibly than textbooks and CDs or DVDs. Where written materials are presented electronically on websites there is the potential for adaptation and flexibility of use, and they can be supplemented as the need arises. Whatever the balance of the components in a particular blend, the teacher will want to consider the issues outlined below in framing a response to the diverse needs of her/his learner group.

Just as it will not always be possible to import face-to-face material into online or telephone teaching, Anderson (2008) warns against importing materials produced for the teaching of L2 learners of languages into the community language context, because of the assumptions made about the nature of the learner group who will use the materials. A multiple challenge therefore has to be faced when teaching community languages in blended programmes. First, the material may not be suitable for the blended context. Second, the topics covered may fail to engage community language learners, since they often relate to tourism or study abroad, which may not be relevant to community language learners' goals, although the exploitation of internet sources using web tours in a synchronous online teaching session (see Chapters 8 and 9) may provide one possible solution. Third, teachers will also need to take account of language varieties in material used for listening activities so that learners can feel that the spoken variety they use is valued, but can also learn about other accents and dialects. Fourth, they will need to consider the cultural and linguistic knowledge of learners and their relative speaking and writing strengths. In Figure 13.2 an example of the written form of French Creole as spoken in St Lucia (ILEA, 1990) illustrates the difficulty a speaker might have in tackling standard written French:

St Lucian Creole	Standard French
Leonard Jones ni swasant an. Ek kon tout lôt mizisyen ki ka jwé mizik twadisyonal, i pa ka bat tanbou tousel. I ka alé lanmè, I ka fé ti jaden'y, èk lé I ni tani ka fènas pouf è an ti lavi.	Leonard Jones a soixante ans. Et comme tous les musiciens qui jouent de la musique traditionnelle il ne fait pas que battre tambour tout seul. Il va à la mer, il fait du jardinage, et quand il a le temps il fait la pêche pour gagner sa vie.

Figure 13.2: St Lucian Creole compared to standard French.

Raising awareness of language varieties

As shown in the survey (Peters and Shi, 2009) discussed above, community language learners may be stronger in the spoken language than in the written, although in the case of Cantonese speakers learning Mandarin the opposite is the case. Being clear about what different forms have in common, as well as about specific differences, can help learners build on existing knowledge. The text in Figure 13.3 from an OU Spanish course (The Open University, 2010) gives examples of differences in pronunciation, grammar and lexis between Spanish as spoken in Spain (Castellano) and in Paraguay, acknowledging the influence of the other main indigenous language in Paraguay, Guaraní. This information would help speakers of Paraguayan and other

Latin American varieties of Spanish to recognise the differences, and would help learners new to the language to familiarise themselves with these. Rather than the information simply being presented, a discussion between community and L2 learners in a synchronous session could begin to explore learners' awareness of different language varieties. This might lead to individual internet research to find written and audio examples, after which findings could be brought together in a wiki task (see Chapter 12), resulting in a shared resource similar in content to the one mentioned in Figure 13.3.

Así se habla en ...

Paraguay: Rasgos específicos del español paraguayo

(a) Pronunciación

El español paraguayo comparte algunos de sus rasgos de pronunciación con el resto del español de América:

(i) La conservación del 'lleísmo', cuando en el resto del mundo hispanohablante el 'yeísmo' es más predominante. Por ejemplo, en Paraguay 'lleno' no se pronuncia / yeno/.

...

(b) Estructuras gramaticales

...

(iii) El uso del voseo en forma similar a como ocurre en la región del Río de La Plata, en Argentina, por ejemplo, 'vos tenés', 'vos sós'.

(c) Léxico

El español paraguayo, como el del resto de Hispanoamérica, incorporó voces de otras culturas indígenas de América.

...

(iii) La mayor influencia léxica en el español paraguayo viene del guaraní. Existen muchas voces de origen guaraní en el habla cotidiana del Paraguay ('agatí' (libélula) y 'ñahatí' (tábano)).

Figure 13.3: Extract from an OU Spanish course summarising features of Spanish as spoken in Paraguay.

Access to information and examples of different forms of most languages have become accessible through new technology, and its uses in the teaching situation will be discussed in the next section.

The use of technology in the blend

Technology can support a range of invaluable activities in community language learning. The following are some examples that may be integrated into the blend to complement formal face-to-face or online teaching, or used by learners independently. The implications and challenges for language learners and teachers of integrating technology are discussed below, together with some practical suggestions.

Word processing

This offers many advantages to learners struggling with literacy in the language being studied, and can help to sustain motivation. In Chinese, for example, the learner can type in pinyin to elicit a range of on-screen characters, as shown in Figure 13.4, from which the learner then chooses by typing its number rather than having to draw the characters by hand. Different varieties of a language can be selected for word-processing purposes. For example, Microsoft Word offers twenty varieties of Spanish, sixteen of Arabic, fifteen of French and five of Chinese. The software provides help with spelling, grammar and accents for learners less familiar with the written form.

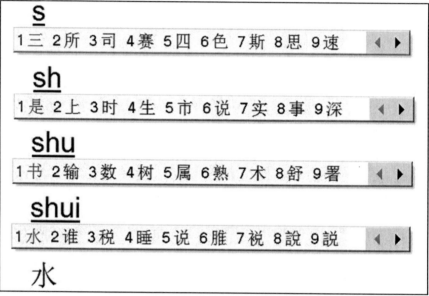

Figure 13.4: Conversion of pinyin to Chinese characters in Microsoft Word.

The worldwide web

Earlier sections have suggested some specific uses of the internet in blended teaching to meet the needs of a diverse group of learners. The web offers access to relevant and stimulating material and can be used as a means of independent learning or in conjunction with face-to-face or online teaching. At the time of writing the BBC languages site offers material in Polish, Urdu, Japanese, Russian, French, German, Spanish, Greek, Chinese, Italian and Portuguese as well as a 'quick fix' in thirty-six other languages (bbc.co.uk/languages). There are also online dictionaries and translation software, although inexperienced learners need to be advised to use these with extreme caution. Learners can be referred to such sites to accomplish tasks individually or in groups. It should be borne in mind, however, that searching the Web can be time-consuming for both teachers and learners. Most useful, perhaps, for learners of community languages is the potential to find information about their country of origin and explore its culture.

Computer-mediated communication (CMC)

Tools such as email, online forums or messaging services, which are commonly used for social purposes, can be incorporated into the language learning blend. Communication can be in real time, as in audiovisual conferencing, or asynchronous as in email and online posts. For example, through a Routes into Languages (www.routesintolanguages.ac.uk) project in London, university students of French were put into contact with pupils preparing AS levels in French, acting as their mentors for ten weeks through online written and spoken communication. Some of the school students were community users of French and more fluent speakers than their mentors, so a fruitful exchange took place with mentors offering advice on aspects of language learning in higher education, and both benefiting from valuable speaking practice. This helped build confidence for mentees and mentors and provided valuable recognition of the bilingual school students' skills. It is appealing to set up collaborative activities of this kind via CMC tools. However, organising collaboration requires management skills and careful planning. Many projects of this kind have failed due to cultural, institutional and technical differences (O'Dowd, 2006).

Online forums

Intercultural communication such as that described by Dlaska (2009) can be encouraged and fostered in online forums where students can raise questions, clarify and discuss information, as in the examples given on p. 191. Written and spoken assessment tasks can be completed online, and forums provide a useful platform for preparatory discussions with fellow learners or teachers prior to the submission of an assessment task. Learner confidence needs to be built, since some learners may be reluctant, particularly if they are less confident writers, even though many of them are already used to online communication on Facebook, blogs or Twitter. One way of stimulating learners to start participating is to integrate online forum discussion into a language history activity as outlined in Figure 13.1 (see p. 194). See Chapter 2 for further consideration of integrated tasks using more than one mode of communication.

Audiovisual conferencing

Internet-based systems such as Elluminate create a virtual classroom for distance learning, where learners can carry out activities in listening and speaking, working in pairs or groups in breakout rooms and interacting with material provided on the whiteboard, which can include prepared presentations, interactive worksheets, visual and audio stimuli and access to web pages (see Chapters 9 and 10). Confidence building for teachers (see Chapters 15 and 16) as well as learners may be needed, both in using the technology and in becoming comfortable with the mode of communication. The environment lends itself to collaborative work in which learners' different strengths can complement one another, if the teacher bears such strengths or weaknesses in mind when allocating learners to pairs or groups. It may be useful to pair a community learner with an L2 learner. Someone who can speak well but has weak literacy skills, for example, can convey ideas orally for another to put in writing. One who is shy about speaking can participate in discussion in a pair or small group and leave presentation tasks to a more confident learner. Learners can also meet independently for discussion and practice to complement each other's skills and knowledge.

Interactive screens and whiteboards

Interactive screens in synchronous conferencing applications such as Elluminate are key tools in the blend. Interactive whiteboards have also been demonstrated to be extremely effective in motivating language learners in a face-to-face context (Anderson, 2008). Both can be used for introducing stimulating visual material such as videos, images and interactive tasks and games in connection with language learning, facilitating active learner involvement rather than a teacher-focused presentation.

Social networking sites (SNS)

Harrison and Thomas (2009, p. 110) have described the advantages of SNS for language learning and their 'potential to enhance opportunities for language exchange between native and non-native speakers'. They perceive this as a device whereby native speakers correct and inform non-native speakers. Lam (2007, p. 23), however, has researched how teenagers of Chinese origin in the United States used SNS 'to maintain simultaneous affiliations with their local immigrant community, larger affinity groups with other Asian Americans, and transnational relationships with their peers and families in China'. She describes how participants developed different identities and concepts of Chinese-ness through communication with the different communities. This was not perceived as a teaching situation but one similar to Facebook, where participants were involved for their own interest and enjoyment rather than for specific learning purposes. This suggests that new, more independent ways of learning are developing and it seems these are being used by learners of all ages (TNS Market Research Digital, 2008, cited in Harrison and Thomas, 2009). Some sites where learners can meet native speakers and practise are listed in Figure 13.5. Teachers may want to consider how SNS might be harnessed as a means of providing extra practice in particular skills that learners wish to develop, and whether it would help to sustain learner motivation to have regular social contact with native speakers or learners of the community language.

Virtual worlds

Virtual environments can also provide a stimulus for learners. The OU has been using the 3D virtual world Second Life for a course on networked living since 2006. Here students can 'meet' each other in a 'classroom' or 'café', for example. Another

italki www.italki.com	Users can find people and resources to help them learn a foreign language. Members from 200+ countries use 100+ languages. Free to join.
Livemocha www.livemocha.com	Social network service where users can learn languages through audiovisual lessons and peer tutoring tools that allow native speakers to help one another. Users aid others in learning languages they are proficient in, while learning other languages themselves. Achieved through peer reviewing of submissions, live text and audio conversations, and other learning systems.
Language Exchange Community www.mylanguageexchange.com	Users find a partner in the online community and practise any language with a native speaker who is learning their language. Provides online practice with lesson plans and text chat rooms.
Conversation Exchange www.conversationexchange.com	Users find a partner for face-to-face, correspondence (pen pal) or text or voice chat communication in a range of languages.

Figure 13.5: Social networking sites for language learners

virtual world is Zon, an online role-playing game designed for learning Mandarin Chinese (Zhao, 2008), in which the user/learner practises language skills and acquires cultural knowledge during the process of evolving from 'tourist' to 'citizen'. Teachers may simply wish to encourage learners to explore the possibilities of extending their linguistic skills and cultural awareness by interacting in a virtual world of this kind. On the other hand, they may want to consider integrating interactions in a virtual environment into the blend, either by setting tasks for learners to complete there, or by inviting those who choose to engage with virtual worlds to report their experiences back to the group via another component of the blend.

Mobile technology

The rapid growth of smart phones such as the iPhone and Google Phone further blurs the boundary between learning and day-to-day life. Mobile technology offers learners even greater flexibility for language learning, although issues of cost need to be taken into consideration. Learners can receive and complete homework using mobile phones (Levy and Kennedy, 2005), download applications demonstrating, for example, how Chinese characters should be written stroke by stroke, and share their thoughts with a greater community. This can take place at any time and anywhere.

Some final observations

In integrating different forms of technology into their teaching, teachers need to be aware of issues of time, cost, technical know-how and pedagogical expertise. Many learners and teachers will need time to become confident in using applications, and teachers require pedagogical expertise if they are to integrate them appropriately into their teaching (see Chapters 15 and 16). They will want to ensure that learners are aware of the possibilities, and are equipped to plan their use of the most appropriate tools for their needs. Teachers will also wish to evaluate learners' progress in utilising such tools, understanding that there could be considerable gaps between learners in terms of skills and attitudes towards using ICT.

Conclusion

In the teaching of community languages, whatever teaching modes are included in the blend, and whether it includes a face-to-face element or not, sensitivity is needed in understanding the variety of needs learners may present and in catering for them in the most appropriate way. Issues of identity with the community in the UK, the broader diaspora and the country of origin, the interrelationship of the language with the society and culture of the community, relative proficiency in the different skills in the language and the status of different varieties of the language need to be taken into account. Materials that were designed for L2 learning may not be appropriate linguistically or culturally, and learners may find them alienating or feel they devalue their own background. Learners who consider themselves native speakers may find their confidence undermined if they do not get good assessment grades because of poor literacy, use of a different variety of the language or lack of experience in the more academic use of the language.

Community language learning and teaching has an important role to play in validating and valuing the linguistic and cultural communities that make up society in the UK today. New technology and the ever-increasing possibilities for blended learning offer advantages for both teachers and learners. Where the range of backgrounds, levels of language and motivation is potentially very broad, technology offers a number of possibilities in terms of activities and access to resources which can benefit learners, and teachers need to keep abreast of developments so they can guide learners in the best possible way. As a result of technological development the world is getting smaller and communities need no longer feel isolated as they link up and form closer ties with others around the world and in the UK. It is hoped that this will lead to greater recognition of the wealth of linguistic diversity and the importance of maintaining it through educational provision.

Chapter 14:   **Teaching Celtic Languages in Blended Contexts**

Lynda Newcombe and Margaret Southgate

Introduction

Recent decades have witnessed an increased interest in the global preservation of indigenous languages, sometimes also termed heritage or community languages (see Chapter 13). In New Zealand more adults are learning Maori, and in North America there is renewed interest in preserving some of the languages of the First Peoples. In Europe intensive programmes have been set up to teach languages such as Basque and Catalan, and in the British Isles and beyond there is increasing demand for Celtic language provision (Newcombe, 2007).

While there are issues common to the learning of any language, some additional issues specific to the learning of indigenous Celtic languages will be outlined in this chapter. The chapter will first provide an overview of Celtic language learning in the UK and Ireland, before examining some significant motivational and cultural factors. It will highlight a number of practical individual and group management issues that teachers may face when working in a blended context, and will consider how teachers might deal with such issues. Finally, it will suggest some resources that could usefully be integrated into the blend to support and extend the experience of learning a Celtic language.

Celtic languages in the UK and Ireland

Official recognition

Despite bleaker times for the Celtic languages in the mid-twentieth century, Gaelic, Irish and Welsh have survived, and goodwill towards the Celtic languages has increased alongside an increase in the numbers of learners of all ages. Irish is now an official language of the European Union (EU); Welsh and Gaelic are co-official languages. In the case of Wales, and to a lesser degree Scotland and Ireland, legislation protects and promotes the use of the language (Aitchison and Carter, 2000; Ó Murchú, 2008). The Welsh Language Board, established in 1993, has promoted and facilitated the use of Welsh, while in Scotland Clì Gàidhlig (formerly Comunn na Luchd-Ionnsachaidh) has promoted Gaelic learning since 1987. Bòrd na Gàidhlig was established as a public body by the Gaelic Language Act of 2005. This legislation was designed to promote the use of Scottish Gaelic in order to enhance the status of the language and secure its long-term future as an official language enjoying the same respect as English in Scotland. Since 1999, Foras na Gaelige has promoted the Irish language throughout the island of Ireland. A further example of official moves to develop and support the use of Irish can be seen in Fiontar's twenty-year strategy, which suggests that 'language maintenance is enhanced when the conjunction of three processes is supportive: the ability (or capacity) to use the language; opportunities to use it; and attitudes towards its use' (Fiontar, 2009, p. 5). Teachers of Celtic languages may be engaged therefore not only in helping learners to acquire linguistic skills but also in promoting or guiding learners towards opportunities to use their language skills to maintain the language more widely. In doing this they will need to understand learners' own attitudes towards the L2, and work with them to consider how they might respond to a range of attitudes they could encounter in others.

Census data

The main indigenous Celtic languages taught in the UK and Ireland are Gaelic, Irish and Welsh, all living community languages. Although no longer extant community languages, Cornish and Manx have become the subject of revival campaigns, Manx was reintroduced as an option in Isle of Man schools in 1992, while a Manx-medium primary school was established in 2001 (Wilson, 2009).

The 2001 UK Census gathered information on language competence, which is summarised in Figure 14.1 (Aitchison and Carter, 2004). The 2006 Ireland Census reported 1.66 million Irish speakers, approximately 42% of the population, compared to 1.57 million in 2002 (CSO, 2007). In Ireland all children learn Irish at school, but many rarely use it again.

2001 UK Census: % of population aged 3+	can speak the language	have some knowledge (understanding speech, reading, writing, and/or speaking)
Welsh in Wales	20.4%	28.4%
Gaelic in Scotland	1.2%	1.9%
Irish in Northern Ireland	7.0%	10.4%

Figure 14.1: Knowledge of indigenous Celtic languages in 2001

Language competence is a difficult area for measurement, however, since the definition of a speaker may be influenced by subjective issues, such as confidence levels (MacCaluim, 2007; Newcombe, 2007). It is unfortunate that census questions do not differentiate between native speakers and learners, making it difficult to estimate how many people are learning a Celtic language, or their level of competence.

Adult learning

The promotion of Celtic languages by the bodies mentioned above has led to a general interest and growth in the number of adult learners. However, McLeod *et al.* (2010) note the difficulty in obtaining accurate data on the *extent* of adult provision and the number of learners. The informal voluntary sector plays a major role in Celtic language teaching, but statistics in this area are even more difficult to gather. As long ago as 1995 it was estimated that there were more than 8,000 adult learners in Scotland (Galloway, cited in McLeod *et al.*, 2010, p. 9). McLeod (2006, p. 4) notes that 'learners of Gaelic are relatively rare, probably comprising 5–10% of the speaker population', although numbers are now increasing. The introduction of an Ùlpan course in Gaelic in June 2007 has attracted many new adult learners (Grannd, 2010). Since the academic year 1996/7 there have been more than 20,000 registrations each year on Welsh for Adults courses provided by universities and local authorities. The Irish government plans to increase the number of active users of Irish from about 72,000 to 250,000 by 2026 (Fiontar, 2009, p. 7), which will inevitably require a substantial increase in the numbers of adult learners. In Northern Ireland use of the language is also increasing, and most adult education institutions will provide Irish classes if demand can be demonstrated (Willemsma and Mac Póilin, 1997, p. 15).

The growth of Gaelic- and Welsh-medium schools (Nicolson and MacIver, 2003; NicNeacail and MacIomhair, 2007) has provided a further incentive for others to learn. As education from nursery through to secondary becomes more widely available through Celtic languages, increasing numbers of adults who are not L1 speakers but who want a bilingual education for their children are learning the language in which their children are being educated (McLeod, 2006, p. 4). Growth is also associated, in part at least, with changes in teaching strategies in the western world, which as a result of communicative language teaching (CLT) have encouraged spoken communication as a key element. The development of intensive courses has also played a part.

The blended learning context

As blended learning has increased in popularity, the Celtic languages have availed themselves of this useful learning context. Where learners are dispersed, blended teaching can help to create viable groups and to give learning opportunities to a greater number of adult learners.

The BBC and Acen are prime examples of online course providers in Welsh, with Acen providing tutor support online for some of their courses. Sabhal Mòr Ostaig (SMO), the Gaelic college on Skye, runs Gaelic courses using blended teaching operating in distance programmes as part of its commitment to the development and enhancement of the Gaelic language, culture and heritage. There are many opportunities to learn Irish online, for example via Raidió Teilifís Éireann (RTÉ)'s Easy Irish website.

The OU offered a blended beginners' Welsh course in 2008 for the first time, attracting more than 350 students, about half of whom were from outside Wales. Such blended courses are a usual part of the OU's delivery pattern, but increasingly are also employed by conventional universities and colleges. In 2008, Cardiff University's Welsh for Adults Centre presented its Wlpan course in blended format for the first time, followed by an intermediate course in 2010. The University of Wales Trinity Saint David offers an e-learning degree in Welsh. Edinburgh's Telford College has offered Gaelic open learning courses over the past forty years, with progression from beginner level to Scottish Higher level possible. Blended learning of this kind may include monthly study meetings and a designated regular online drop-in or phone-in session. Course materials may be available in conventional paper and audio formats as well as online. Audio recordings are also used for spoken homework, to discuss queries and conduct dialogues between teacher and learner.

Understanding learner motivation

Teachers will need to appreciate that different motivations (see also Chapter 4) may be at work among learners. For some Celtic language learners the main motivation may be similar to that for learning any other language, where the ability to understand and communicate with others is their primary goal, but there may often be other underlying issues that need to be taken into consideration. Some of the issues raised in Chapter 13 with regard to community languages are equally relevant here, and this section will therefore focus on areas specific to Celtic languages in the UK and Ireland.

Culture and identity

Learning an indigenous language is, for many, a link with past generations and their culture. The dominance of the integrative motive (see Chapter 4) is associated with the search for a cultural identity. A study of Scottish students' attitudes to language noted that some had grown to recognise in early adulthood the role of language in defining who they were. One student commented 'Now, after studying Gaelic ... I feel that it is part of who I am and where I come from and I feel proud to be able to speak it' (Nicolson, 2003, p. 132). Amidst the anonymity of modern life the world of the indigenous language can provide a sense of belonging. It can act as a conveyer of culture, opening doors to new worlds where hidden treasures surface to captivate, inspire and even disturb the learner (MacCaluim, 2007; Newcombe, 2009; McLeod et al., 2010)

Political identity

The association of language with a political cause may also be a motivating factor. As Macdonald points out, heritage languages can 'lie at the heart of a deep-seated identity ... Language use is conceptualised not so much as a pragmatic matter as an affective, symbolic and political one' (Macdonald, 1997, p. 219). For example, supporters of the Scottish National Party (SNP) may want to learn Gaelic, even though they have no individual cultural links with the language. Similarly, Plaid Cymru sympathisers may wish to learn or improve their Welsh language skills to make a political statement rather than a linguistic or cultural one. Conversely, learners of indigenous Celtic languages could be aggrieved if they are assumed to be nationalist sympathisers when they may have an entirely different motivation for learning the language.

Language regeneration

For others again, the desire for regeneration of an ancestral language, a unique feature of indigenous language learning, is the main source of motivation. No one learns English, French or Spanish to keep those languages alive, but for some indigenous language learners the main motivation is to safeguard the language for future generations. Even where this is not the primary reason, an element of such motivation exists in many learners (MacCaluim, 2007; Newcombe, 2007).

Interest in specific skills

Since all the Celtic languages have a strong oral and written cultural and literary tradition, some learners may want to focus on listening or reading skills to access songs, poetry or stories whereas other learners may initially wish only to get by in speaking the indigenous tongue so they can interact with speakers of the language. Those with some prior knowledge of the language may have already learned to read, write and understand the Celtic language relatively well, but want to improve their speaking, while others who have already learned to speak the language may wish to develop their reading and writing skills (see also Chapter 13).

Extrinsic and intrinsic motivation

Extrinsic factors (Ehrman *et al.*, 2003, p. 320) are a significant source of motivation for an increasing number of learners. The desire to learn in order to use the indigenous language in the workplace is important for some: for example, in Wales many employers, particularly in the public sector, now require or at least give preference to job applicants with some knowledge of or qualification in Welsh. Still more are learning so they can socialise with family and friends or because their child is being educated through the medium of a Celtic language, whereas for others the intrinsic desire to read literature and sometimes even write in the Celtic L2 is the motivating factor (Newcombe, 2002; MacCaluim, 2007; Newcombe, 2007; Ó Murchú, 2008).

Some learners do not know why exactly they expend so much time and effort, sometimes even enduring financial hardship to become fluent, but they simply feel they must (Newcombe, 2009). There is quite an emotional overlay therefore in the learning of indigenous languages that may not exist for a learner of other languages. However, teachers should be aware that motivation can change over time depending on learners' circumstances and time available for learning, as well as on the support received from the L1 speaking community and teachers, and on levels of interaction with other learners.

Implications for teachers of Celtic languages

Motivation is the key to success, and the teacher need not be overly concerned about the diverse reasons for learning if s/he can sustain learner motivation by providing sufficient and relevant opportunities for progress. Whatever the type of motivation, learners need to be encouraged to gain a wide general vocabulary and have a good grounding in the workings of the language. The section that follows will consider some implications of motivational diversity from the teacher's point of view, together with some additional issues that a teacher of a Celtic language may have to face.

Task design/selection

The varying degrees of competence and type of motivation in the real or virtual classroom may have implications. In pairwork it may be helpful for teachers to prepare differentiated tasks (see also Chapter 13) for learners in the same group. When practising the past tense, for example, those wishing to support their children who are in Celtic-medium education could be given a different communicative task from those learning to use the L2 at work, while using the same verbs and adverbial expressions of time. Online it may be possible to send learners into separate virtual rooms to practise (see Chapters 9 and 10). In working on a prose text, those who want to improve reading and writing skills can be asked to summarise and note in writing, while those who want to improve speaking skills can be asked to present a spoken summary.

Group management and learner relationships

As mentioned in Chapter 13, a mix of motivations and backgrounds can enrich learner relationships and help group dynamics, but these need to be managed sensitively by the teacher with respect for individual learner perspectives. Sometimes there may be cultural reasons for grouping those with a family background in the language together for any one task so they can better understand each other's viewpoint and compare experiences from their own lives. Alternatively, there will be tasks in which cultural knowledge from a learner from the L1 background is helpful to those who are coming to the language with no background in it at all, so they can better understand viewpoints and cultural sensitivities.

Those coming to the language as a new L2 experience may have false expectations of learners from an L1 background, and be unaware that for reasons beyond their control those learners may not have been given an opportunity in the past to achieve native speaker competence. The teacher will have a key role in ensuring that inappropriately critical statements are not made in this regard, and that respect underpins all group dynamics and relationships.

In skill terms, careful group management will also be important. If a teacher is setting up small groups (for example, for a task that involves preparing and presenting a short talk to other learners), s/he could allow participants to develop the skills on which they wish to focus. Someone with good reading skills, who would be able to collate information from written sources, might be grouped with someone whose strength is in writing and who would be happy to prepare slides or handouts, while a third member of the group might be more at ease giving the spoken presentation. There may, however, also be a need for teachers to point learners towards different modes of communication so that they not only develop the particular skills that they regard as most important but also have opportunities to strengthen areas of weakness, depending on their longer-term goals.

Fostering interaction beyond the formal teaching programme

The practice of spoken communication beyond formal learning sessions can help to build confidence and improve accent and intonation. In recent years researchers have increasingly viewed learners as social beings whose processing of L2 depends to a certain extent on their ability to negotiate entry into the social networks of L1 speakers (Tarone, 2004). Learners on blended programmes should therefore be encouraged to immerse themselves in the indigenous language community as much as possible, whether through face-to-face encounters or through online interactions. Learners may find, however, that this is not always easy to achieve. Teachers will need to warn learners that even if they do have access to speakers they may find that some are reluctant to communicate with them in that language.

L1 speakers as learners may have many issues of their own, such as lack of confidence, that need to be addressed by educators (Newcombe, 2009), and L1 speakers encountered by learners elsewhere may come from a culture where courtesy towards the other speaker's native language is expected. L1 speakers of an indigenous language may have many reasons for switching to English, not necessarily to do with the standard of the learners' language skills. This is often related to the all-pervasiveness of English, which is a particular challenge for learners of Celtic languages in the UK and Ireland. Nicolson and MacIver (2003) highlight problems arising from the domination of a monolingual culture in Scotland, even though the country in reality has not only Gaelic and Scots but also many community languages as well as English. Nevertheless, bilingualism or multilingualism is generally regarded as different from the norm (ibid., p. 64). Teachers will also need to warn learners that they may come across native speakers who regard the language as their cultural heritage, and who may therefore resist attempts by 'outsiders' to break into their cultural space. Others may see the language purely as a practical communication tool and may find it difficult to understand why an English speaker would want to learn an indigenous Celtic language when there is already a common language of wider communication readily available.

Factors such as difficulty with the learner's accent, intonation, grammar and limited familiarity with idiom could make mother tongue speakers outside the formal learning context wary of speaking to learners. L1 speakers may even feel ill-at-ease with learners, who often speak so correctly as to appear unnatural, perhaps because they may use neologisms in preference to borrowed words with which the L1 speaker is more familiar. Irish, Gaelic and Welsh are witnessing the growth of lexicons and databases of specialised neologisms. Unlike other European languages, which generally use English for media and computer terminology, Welsh, for example, has coined its own words for television (*teledu*), computer (*cyfrifiadur*), internet (*rhyngrwyd*) and mobile phone (*ffôn symudol*), and in 2006 the Welsh Language Board launched a glossary which includes words for all essential IT usage such as laptop (*gliniadur*). The use of loan words rather than neologisms by L1 speakers is an area of particular sensitivity that has to be faced and dealt with by the individuals concerned, but teachers could help by preparing learners for what to expect from L1 speakers.

Learners may have chosen to study a blended course at a distance precisely because they live in an area where there are few or no L1 speakers. The availability of online synchronous and/or asynchronous communication tools can provide communication channels for isolated learners, as well as for those who may have met with resistance from native speakers in their own area. Such modes of communication can enable learners to communicate with sympathetic users of the language as well as to gain valuable independent speaking practice with other learners, including those outside their own learner group, in a range of online settings (see 'Useful websites' on pp. 264–5).

Where face-to-face interaction is an option, learners in Wales, for example, will find that some learners and even L1 speakers wear badges to indicate that they wish to use the language. On a practical level L2 learners could be given phrases, such as 'Speak more slowly please' or 'Please can we speak Gaelic/Irish/Welsh?' They might be alerted to the fact that persistence with an L1 speaker may sometimes be inappropriate and potentially damaging to the relationship. Groups of learners that include those who come from the indigenous language culture will be helpful in illuminating relevant perspectives.

Promoting interaction in L2

Teachers may alleviate the pervasiveness of English somewhat by making L2 the predominant language of communication in the learning situation at an early stage, albeit at a basic language level. This can increase confidence and help sustain motivation. This may not work for all language learners, some of whom may become anxious when the L2 is used extensively, as they may find such a situation threatening. Teachers will need to be sensitive to learner anxieties, recognising that some learners need to learn gradually, using a combination of L1 and L2. When teachers communicate with learners in L2 at an early stage of a blended course they will also need to compensate for the lack of facial expression and body language when communicating in synchronous online or telephone modes, and devise new ways of checking that they have been understood. An exploration of such issues can be found in Chapters 8–10.

A potential difficulty of language learning in blended contexts is that, if self-study is a major component of the blend, learners may have fewer opportunities to practise speaking and responding to others' speech than in a conventional course and will not always have the advantage of immediate teacher feedback, particularly with regard to pronunciation and intonation. However, with teacher guidance, learners can find alternative ways to practise with other learners and native speakers: for example, by using audio recordings or telephones and software applications such as Skype (where they can actually see the interlocutor), even if these are not integral parts of the blend. In a blended learning context, regular phone calls, emails, online forum interaction and the use of voice conferencing software such as Elluminate or Wimba can establish effective motivating relationships between teacher and learner as well as among learners independently to enhance speaking opportunities and develop pronunciation skills.

Although some learners on blended courses may feel that their isolation is a disadvantage for the reasons outlined above, practice opportunities for learners in traditional settings may be equally limited in the early stages. Many blended courses instigate online learner forums, which are helpful for those who may feel isolated. Learners who have an opportunity to practise L2 writing skills in forums and to make contact with other course participants in this way may be able to arrange self-help groups where speaking skills can be practised. Teachers can also encourage learners to use forums for reflection and to express how they feel about their learning and progress. This can be useful, particularly for the anxious learner who lacks confidence.

Handling a mixed group of L1 and L2 speakers

Teachers may be faced with L1 speakers as learners in their groups, an issue that also arises in community language learning (see Chapter 13). This may be because the L1 speaker wants to renew and update their knowledge of the language, particularly if s/he has not used it for a while, seeks a qualification in the language, wants to become literate in a language s/he speaks or wants to improve her/his ability to speak a language in which passive skills are reasonably good. Where L1 users are present, anxiety may hinder both spoken and written communication by others, as learners may feel that their utterances or scripts could be ridiculed if they make mistakes. The place of anxiety as a barrier to language learning is currently viewed as one of the main factors impeding effective L2 learning (Horwitz, 2001) and there is evidence from learners themselves and from teachers that lack of confidence is a hindrance to progress (MacCaluim, 2007; Newcombe, 2007; 2009). However, if the teacher thinks carefully about the role of L1 speakers, giving them communicative tasks to practise with L2 learners, it could work to the enrichment of the group. L1 speakers may not always use 'taught' language and may use colloquial forms, dialect and slang that L2 learners will not recognise. This may well cause discomfort but it can also open up discussion about varieties which may be encountered outside the teaching sessions, and prepare learners for the real world.

Skill differential

Some L2 learners will develop good spoken communication because they have regular opportunities to communicate in it in their daily life. However, the teacher may need to provide or point them towards additional resources to develop reading or writing skills (see 'Useful websites' on pp. 264–5) if this is a priority for them.

Conversely, some learners have good passive understanding of the language but have rarely communicated in it, particularly if they were brought up at a time when its use was discouraged. Confidence issues are significant factors here. The teacher can help by making the atmosphere as relaxed as possible and encouraging learners to work in pairs so that they do not feel exposed in front of a group. In a study of Welsh learners one participant said she felt she only had 'half a personality' when she spoke in Welsh and another said she felt vulnerable and like a child (Newcombe, 2009). This mismatch between identity and ability is not exclusive to the Celtic domain but is an issue learners have to face in any language. Teachers can encourage learners to read out loud at home and record themselves. Shadow-reading along with audio recordings is also a useful means of developing confidence as well as good pronunciation and intonation.

Language varieties

The teacher's approach to language varieties is key, particularly if the group consists of learners with diverse needs and interests who, if the blend consists mainly of self-study materials combined with online sessions, may be drawn from a wide geographical area. Reassurance is vital if learners are to sustain their initial motivation to learn. Learners of Welsh, for example, may become anxious if they are being taught a variety that does not match that of the L1 speakers with whom they are in contact, particularly if they meet adverse reactions from L1 speakers with a negative attitude towards other varieties of the language. However, learners do need to be confident in the basics of one variety of the language before they start using others. There may be some learners who wish to communicate only locally and may not see the need to be familiar with other registers or dialects of the language, but as they move beyond the basic stage they may need to be reminded that the media and electronic world, so useful for learners to develop their language skills, will be presenting different varieties, accents, vocabulary and syntax, so becoming fixated on one register and/or dialect may leave the learner at a disadvantage.

Resources for indigenous language learning

Useful resources are available for learners of indigenous languages in the lifelong learning and blended context, particularly at intermediate or advanced levels. Teachers of Celtic languages may wish to design tasks that draw on these resources, or may simply encourage learners to explore the world of their L2 in all its diversity to extend their language skills independently.

Visits to heartland areas

Holidays and attendance at day schools or residential courses in heartland areas where the language is used widely in the community can be of particular benefit for those in blended learning contexts, as they bring alive material that learners may have studied and practised in formal learning situations. The visit may form part of the blend, or it could be a complementary activity that learners choose to engage in independently.

Printed material

In teaching sessions teachers can use authentic material from magazine articles for discussion. *Lingo Newydd*, a magazine published by Golwg, Lampeter, for Welsh learners appears every two months in Wales. *Cothrom*, a quarterly bilingual news magazine for Gaelic learners, is compiled and issued to subscribers by Clì Gàidhlig. Teachers may also use poems or short stories from the language itself and can contact those who facilitate literature distribution, such as Comhairle nan Leabhraichean, or publishers specific to a Celtic language, such as Acair or Gomer Press which in 1998 produced a series of colourful, illustrated books in Welsh to aid beginners' reading.

Web-based reading material

Learners can be encouraged by teachers to search for 'optional extras' on the web for further independent reading or self-help group use. There are now more than 14,000 Wikipedia articles in Welsh, and almost half as many as in Gaelic, as OfCom's regional communications market report of May 2008 indicated. If at all possible teachers should 'show, not tell' to help learners engage with online material. With the proliferation of interactive whiteboards in classrooms, teachers can often take a few minutes out of a face-to-face session to whet the learners' appetites for useful websites. When teaching via online conferencing systems such as Elluminate and Wimba as part of a blended course it is quick and easy to do a short web tour as part of a session.

Broadcast media

Unlike indigenous languages in some parts of the world, Welsh, Gaelic and Irish have a reasonable amount of broadcast media provision. Broadcast media are useful for building confidence for those learning in a blended setting, particularly where contact with L1 speakers is infrequent.

Since 1982 Wales has had its own Welsh language television channel, Sianel Pedwar Cymru (S4C), and Radio Cymru broadcasts twenty hours of Welsh a day. Irish language broadcasts can now be heard daily from radio stations such as Raidió na Gaeltachta, and Raidió na Life. In 1996 the Irish language television station Teilifís na Gaeilge (TG4) started broadcasting news, documentaries, children's shows and even soap operas in Irish. In Scotland, Radio nan Gàidheal broadcasts a variety of news, discussion and music programmes, while the MG Alba television channel is now available on Freeview, supplementing some BBC broadcasting in Gaelic. Media provision is vital for Celtic languages, increasing their status and giving parity with English. Subtitling is useful for early stage learners, since they can benefit from hearing the language pronounced while obtaining help in understanding the programmes. It can help tune their ears to the rhythm of the language, and promote confidence.

Other resources

Many other examples of resources and good practice for adults learning indigenous languages have evolved over recent decades. Most are suitable to be adapted for use in a blended context: for example, by discussing in a synchronous or asynchronous mode some possibilities such as those outlined below; by inviting learners to say what they would like to take part in and why; and by reporting back on elements learners have engaged with.

Cultural organisations

In addition to organisers of major cultural festivals in areas where Celtic languages are spoken, such as the Royal National Mod, the National Eisteddfod and the Fleadh Cheoil as well as the Pan-Celtic festivals of music and film, there are a number of organisations that are aimed more specifically at learners. For example, Oideas Gael, the largest provider in Ireland for adult language learners, offers an active culture programme for learners and an online magazine.

The six designated language centres in Wales for Welsh for Adults provide programmes of activities for learners. Cardiff University has appointed an officer who arranges social events for learners and L1 speakers. There is a growing trend for interest-based Gaelic-medium hobby clubs, of which a walking club in central Scotland was the forerunner. Such clubs are useful for all levels of fluency in L2 as the participant is able to enjoy the music/sport/craft and offer language input at her/his own level in a relaxed setting.

Social networking media

In situations where learners are prepared for others to see their efforts, then blogs, wikis, online chat rooms (of which there are more than a hundred in the Welsh language alone), Facebook and Twitter could be used to publish short pieces of writing or to comment on what others have written. Some learners, however, may find such publication threatening, and may want to share their writing only with a teacher or researcher. If encouraging the use of external media, teachers need to offer the caveat that learners should try to find interlocutors at a similar level to their own. Learners will of course be less exposed if the social networking group is an integral part of the blend.

Input from volunteer L1 speakers

L1 speakers who are not language teaching professionals are often engaged in teaching and supporting the teaching of Celtic languages, often because of a shortage of language teachers *per se*. In Wales Cynllun Pontio (Bridging Scheme), which involves mother tongue speakers visiting classes to give semi-naturalistic speaking opportunities, has been highly praised by learners. Cardiff University has pioneered a mentoring system where learners are paired with first language speakers for conversation practice. Similar arrangements could be incorporated into telephone or online elements of the blend: for example, by inviting volunteers to be interviewed in a synchronous session or to take part in a forum or blog discussion, provided that the institution can grant online access to external participants.

Institutions and team leaders need to bear in mind that while L1 speakers' help may be invaluable they may be unaware of issues such as lack of confidence and anxiety that accompany second language learning, especially if they have not attempted to learn another language themselves. They may also introduce complex constructions too early or may focus too much on error correction, thus demoralising the learners. It would be helpful to offer L1 volunteers some development, making them aware of the register of language that learners use and the language patterns taught at the various levels, or the teacher would need to work with the volunteer to set up her/his involvement in an appropriate way

Conclusion

This chapter has provided an overview of indigenous language competence and adult learning in the British Isles. While acknowledging that the teaching of indigenous Celtic languages has many similarities with the teaching in a blended context of other languages, and especially with the teaching of community languages, the chapter has identified some particular issues that teachers of Celtic languages may face. It has considered a range of needs, motivations and attitudes that learners may have, and has proposed some ways in which teachers can help learners to develop their language skills, both in formal learning situations and beyond, in an appropriate way.

In spite of the potential difficulties and negative attitudes that learners may face when seeking opportunities to make use of the L2, the chapter has identified ways in which learners can communicate in a range of modes even where both L1 and L2 speakers have English as a common language, and has identified some resources that teachers and learners may wish to incorporate into the blend. As interest in Celtic language learning continues to grow, it is hoped that teachers will explore the full range of possible modes of learning, both formally and informally, so as to create blended learning opportunities that are best suited to the needs of their learners.

Section 5:
Teacher Development and Final Reflections

Chapter 15: Teacher Development for Blended Contexts

Matilde Gallardo, Sarah Heiser
and Margaret Nicolson

Introduction

The previous chapters in this book have focused on aspects of language teaching theory and practice, and on supporting learners in blended contexts. They have therefore implicitly, and sometimes explicitly, provided many ideas that will be useful for teacher development in this environment. This chapter complements these preceding chapters by offering an overview of some key issues directly related to teacher development. As in all teaching contexts, generic good practice in language teacher development will apply, but the focus here will be on aspects that specifically relate to development for teaching in blended contexts.

Different developmental needs and approaches will inevitably result from the shifts in skills and knowledge required to work in this environment. Its very multi-modality implies not only that practical knowledge of a variety of teaching modes and tools will be required but also that teachers may need to engage with learners, and with their teaching peers, in ways that are more flexible, diverse and perhaps even more demanding as a result. Teachers will find themselves potentially as members of many communities of practice (Wenger, 2000) in a way that was not always the case in the past. They may be required to become experts in technology as well as in their subject, while also assuming the role of advisers, assessors and supporters of learners and, perhaps, of teaching peers. They may have to manoeuvre their way through different types of blends and configurations of modes. At the same time, they have to understand how these can best be harnessed to achieve intended learning outcomes and meet learner needs, while working simultaneously with learners and/or peers to understand these teaching tools and modes better. They may have to reconcile their past teaching role with their new one, moving away from the role of knowledge expert and becoming facilitators of learning in a multiplicity of learning platforms. They may be subject to monitoring for quality-assurance purposes in a greater variety of ways than they previously experienced. All of this needs to be supported through appropriate opportunities for development in and professional reflection on technology, methodology and the research and scholarship in the field. Teachers will need to be aware of and reflect on their experience so they can capitalise on it

219

and adapt their current practice to the changing circumstances in which they may find themselves. Researchers such as Clandinin and Connelly (2000), Johnson and Golombek (2002) and Barkhuizen and Wette (2008) have suggested that using techniques of 'narrative inquiry' to explore teachers' experiences via their own written or verbal accounts is a helpful way of both researching teaching practices and contexts and raising teachers' awareness of the influences and experiences that have shaped their current approach.

Affective factors, an integral aspect of experience, are known to play a significant role in teacher growth (Golombek and Johnson, 2004). This chapter will therefore pay specific attention to the environment within which development takes place, since the need to change practice or develop new skills may be seen by some as threatening or unsettling, while others find change inspiring. Motivation is a powerful affective factor affecting the way teachers engage (or not) with the development process. Kubanyiova (2009) suggests that teachers do recognise how they practise and are usually motivated to reduce the gap between their current practice and their ideal teaching self, their personal vision of how they would ideally like their practice to be. However, teacher developers may recognise that some teachers are motivated more by a feeling of what they think they *ought* to be doing, looking to standards and practice determined by others, rather than working towards such a personal vision, what Kubanyiova (ibid., p.316) terms their 'ought-to teacher self'. She draws on the framework and psychological research presented in Dörnyei's (2005) elaboration of an L2 motivational self-system. According to Kubanyiova (2009) this suggests a third category, that of the 'feared teacher self', a negative view of how their practice may develop if they do not take steps to avoid this scenario. Conversations between the teacher and the teacher developer will be very helpful in identifying individual perspectives and working out appropriate development plans in response.

This chapter should be read in conjunction with Chapter 16, which offers specific practical suggestions for teacher development in the blended context. Neither of these chapters claims to be all-encompassing or to take account of all possible blended teaching contexts. It is acknowledged that some teachers may work in an environment where formal development of their professional skills is not offered, but it is hoped that the discussion will nonetheless be relevant to them.

The development context

As in any developmental context, teacher developers working with practitioners in blended provision will need to construct a supportive environment for that development to happen successfully. They will need to ensure that needs are met. Needs and possible ways of identifying them (for example, via recruitment procedures, skills audits, teaching observation, teacher reflection and self-evaluation, or institutional processes such as appraisal) will vary tremendously. However, a number of key issues are important.

First, teachers themselves will need to be encouraged to identify differences between their previous experience and the knowledge and skills they require to develop in the new context, part of the process of developing their vision of the ideal teaching self in a blended context. This will begin as early as the recruitment process, but optimally will continue as part of career-long professional enhancement, perhaps with the help of techniques such as narrative inquiry mentioned above. In planning programmes of development, teacher developers will have to take account of diversity in individual teachers' experience and skills, as this may dictate how and when input is needed, as well as determining content. Teachers' provenance will be a key factor in all of this, because, as Chapter 3 has noted, the teacher's educational, professional or cultural background may not only result in differences in practice values, approaches to standards and objectives, to learner support and to cultural issues but may also lead to different understanding and expectations of the development process, all of which will need to be recognised by both the teacher developer and the teachers themselves.

Second, and where relevant, teacher developers will also consider broader team needs, which may coincide with the needs of the majority in some cases or sometimes be separate from this, depending on the ethos the teacher developer wishes to encourage. For example, although individuals in the team may have low expertise levels in technology, this should not prevent the team from discussing higher level pedagogic issues surrounding the use of technology in language teaching. In many contexts, the fostering of shared team understandings as part of a broader and dynamic development programme is equally important in ensuring both learner support and teacher enhancement.

Third, the teacher developer will want to harness teachers' experience in such a way that their 'classroom' itself in all its blended forms becomes a 'site of professional learning' (Johnson, 2006, p. 243) which feeds into the development process, perhaps through the use of practitioner research or through 'exploratory practice' (Allwright, 2005), an approach that focuses on better understanding of 'classroom' life and on an improvement of the 'quality of life' for all participants in the teaching context. The reflection that happens here and the knowledge gained will sit alongside learner feedback, scholarship and a broader research base in guiding development programmes and in providing a useful link to deeper understanding of concepts and arguments in the fields of methodology and learner support.

Finally, teacher developers may also have to consider development needs arising from institutional changes relating to new laws: for example, the requirement to make 'reasonable adjustments' to support learners in compliance with the 2001 Special Educational Needs and Disability Act. Other teacher needs may emerge through formal arrangements such as probationary reviews or appraisal meetings. These may be viewed by some as belonging more to a vision of an ought-to teacher self (Kubanyiova, 2009, p. 316). The teacher developer has an important role to play in helping teachers to understand and integrate such requirements into their ideal practice.

Crucial in how and when development takes place are the external factors that constrain teachers' scope for engagement in professional development and what teacher developers can reasonably expect from them. Working patterns, geography and institutional demands will play their part in the overall picture and will affect motivation. Part-time language teachers may combine two or more jobs in different institutions and have to fulfil different demands in each. Some may have little time or opportunity for development compared with full-time staff in a single institution. Geographical location and dispersal of a teaching team can have an important impact on the choice of modes of delivery and on feelings of isolation, unless technology is harnessed to break this down. Isolation may also occur where a teacher is the only specialist in their language in the institution or indeed the only language teacher in their broader context. As in the teaching process itself, the variety and flexibility of modes and tools available in blended contexts provide many options for supporting development. They enable development to be tailored to specific teacher needs, goals and situations and facilitate greater sharing of ideas and good practice with peers in the team.

This chapter therefore will focus primarily on some significant issues that may be useful and relevant in teacher development in a variety of blended contexts.

Developing teacher knowledge and skills

In reality, a pragmatic approach to teacher development for blended teaching is likely to encompass the areas suggested in Figure 15.1, depending on the experience of the participants involved and the blend in which they are working:

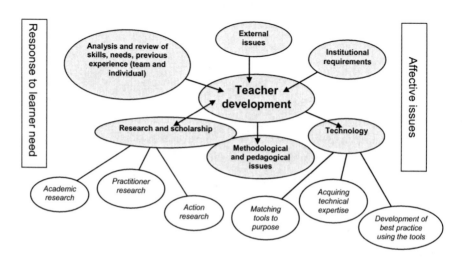

Figure 15.1: An approach to staff development for blended teaching.

Before exploring specific areas relating to teacher development, two aspects are considered which are over-arching and impact on all areas. The first is the affective dimension which may be just as strong for teachers in the process of their own professional development as it is for learners in their language learning trajectory. The second is the greater versatility and flexibility of response to learners which is demanded of teachers in blended provision, both as a result of the multi-modality of the blend and because, as Chapter 3 has shown, diversity is more prevalent in the world of adult blended learning than it may previously have been.

The affective dimension

The affective side of learning will permeate the planning and implementation of teacher development if this is to be carried out sensitively and effectively. In blended environments, a range of affective factors can impact on teacher practice, motivation and readiness to develop. Some of these may be no different from those encountered in more conventional single-mode teaching, such as how to deal with specific learner support issues (for example, motivation, participation levels, skill development, differentiation and anxiety). However, in the blended context a number of additional issues may come into play, resulting in teachers experiencing new anxieties or their confidence being shaken. These may arise from:

- encountering technical difficulties beyond their control related to software, hardware, system and/or network failure or to internet access problems that they feel powerless to resolve and that interrupts the teaching process for them;
- being unfamiliar with teaching modes or tools in the blend, which causes anxiety about their knowledge base and capabilities, and undermines their confidence with learners and peers;
- being expected to use methods or assume a teacher role previously unfamiliar to them and challenging to their way of working;
- experiencing difficulties in responding to certain types of learner need;
- experiencing feelings of inadequacy with peers, managers or even learners who, for example, may be more experienced than they are in use of technology, in the teacher's role as facilitator or in blended contexts.

Any of these might influence the way teachers approach the different teaching modes, their decisions about using a particular tool, their response to particular learner circumstances, their motivation for the job and indeed their own development. Teacher developers therefore have to create a working relationship where teachers can feel free to express these concerns without fear of judgement and with the knowledge that support and practical advice will be forthcoming. Some examples of possible approaches might include peer mentoring and observation, team and tandem teaching or review meetings, and these are covered in greater detail in Chapter 16.

Flexibility of response to learner need

More than ever before, understanding and responding to the diversity of learner needs (see Chapter 3) is an essential part of any development programme for teachers working with adult learners in blended contexts. As Nicolson and Adams (2008, p. 114) have pointed out, as a result of '[s]ocietal changes and the resulting diversity of expectations and needs', those teaching adult learners need to be 'creative and responsive'. They also suggest that it is the responsibility of an institution 'to foster creativity and responsiveness among its staff' (ibid.). Learner diversity, in conjunction with the multi-modal nature of the blended environment, certainly calls for more flexible and diverse teacher practice. This encompasses consideration of and sensitivity to individual learners' needs and motivations, including taking account of learner choice (for example, what topics interest them, what task roles they wish to assume, what their desired outcomes are and at what level and with whom they are comfortable working). This may be challenging for those who come from teaching environments that are less learner-centred or where learner groups are more homogeneous. The most effective way to achieve teacher development in these areas is to model the development programme in a way that mirrors the nature of the teaching programme. This will mean that the teacher developer similarly adopts a facilitative role with regard to the professionals with whom s/he is working and that the diversity of teacher needs and responses to these is made explicit both in individual and in group teacher development.

As well as these over-arching issues, Figure 15.1 shows three main areas of development for blended teaching which teachers and teacher developers will want to consider. These are technology, methodology and research and scholarship. They are now examined in turn.

Technology

Teachers and teacher developers may need to explore three aspects related to technology. First is the specific level of technical expertise required in the range of tools and modes to be used. Second is the awareness of how to select and match the best mode or tool for a specific purpose, such as the enhancement of a specific language skill. Third is the development of best teaching practice for the tool/mode in question with an understanding of the affordances of each (see Chapters 8–12).

Technical knowledge in use of tools /modes

Teachers, and teacher developers for that matter, bring with them a range of technological expertise and experience of applying it in teaching contexts. Some teachers may have made little use of ICT, either in their personal lives or in teaching, and therefore have little technical expertise. Others may have acquired high levels of familiarity with, for example, voice-over-internet telephony (for example, Skype), instant messaging, mobile blogging (for example, Twitter), social networking and internet-based information searching, and may view the technical knowledge used in different teaching modes as a natural extension of their existing expertise. Yet others may already be familiar with teaching using online voice conferencing, asynchronous forums, wikis, blogs and/or telephone conferencing, and therefore already possess the technical expertise needed in teaching via a wide variety of tools and modes. Indeed the addition of other modes or tools may be technically unproblematic for them.

The result can be a multiplicity of expectations and skills. A variety of technical skills within a team can be a positive asset in development, provided the teacher developer creates opportunities to share technical knowledge and explore the affordances of any tool or mode. Teacher developers will also be aware that a full audit of skills is helpful, as there can be dangers in making assumptions regarding technical expertise based on age, gender, geography, previous teaching background and so on. They will also want to avoid undermining the professional identity and confidence of teachers who come to this context having had fewer opportunities to develop technical skills in their past teaching. They will want to look for ways of enabling teachers to gain familiarity with the new technology *per se* before embarking fully on the pedagogic use of any mode or tool. This might involve taking part in development using less familiar tools or modes such as asynchronous forums or telephone conferences.

Matching mode or tool to purpose

The central focus for teacher development where teachers are responsible for choosing modes or tools is developing teacher understanding of their pedagogic usefulness and their value in relation to specific language skill development. For example, an asynchronous forum is better suited to the development of spontaneous writing skills than to pronunciation. An understanding of the affordances of modes and tools within the particular blend goes hand-in-hand with learning how to use them. Learning by doing is a powerful mechanism for encouraging not only a deeper understanding of the potential but also the challenges inherent in using a particular tool to develop a particular skill. It also helps to develop more understanding of pedagogic practice in that tool. An example is presented in Chapter 16 where a group of teachers from the OU and the Universitat Oberta de Catalunya engaged in a collaborative learning project to understand how best to support learners in such situations (see pp. 243–4).

Pedagogy and technology

Teacher development and teacher reflection will need to take into account the fact that some tried-and-trusted techniques may be completely transferable to new tools and modes, some may be transferable with modification and some may not work at all. For example, a teacher who is used to aiding learner understanding with the help of gesture, mime and drawing may need to explore different ways of convey-ing meaning in an online environment, such as via the text chat or creative repeti-tion. However, groupwork and pairwork, which are common features of face-to-face teaching, can easily be replicated in a synchronous conference where virtual break-out rooms are available or in a telephone conference where bridging facilities are possible. Modification of practice may also be necessary not because of the require-ments of the tool or mode, but because of teacher reactions to change. For example, teachers who are highly learner-centred and facilitative in face-to-face work may, through technical anxiety, become more and arguably unnecessarily teacher-centred in online synchronous environments until they feel more at ease with them. Again, peer observation and tandem teaching (see Chapter 16) can be of immense help here.

Levy *et al.* present an example from an Australian project of 'understanding and supporting the processes that experienced face-to-face language teachers undergo in order to become confident and competent online tutors' (Levy *et al.*, 2009, p. 18). In this project a reflective cycle was used by teacher developers with a group of expe-rienced campus-based Chinese teachers. The first phase not only developed their computing skills but also rehearsed the techniques and strategies they might use with learners. The second phase involved the teacher using the tools over a period of time with a group of volunteer learners, while being observed by peers and the teacher developer. The process was supported by both synchronous and asynchro-nous tools, which enabled reflection on and discussion of the teaching by the group of teachers who were developing their online teaching skills.

An important pedagogic/methodological point to be discussed with teachers will be the interconnectedness of the different elements of the blend so that teach-ers see all modes as part of an overall picture, rather than a series of discrete ele-ments in isolation, and present them as such to learners. In synchronous teaching sessions, for example, clear links to work carried out in self-study materials, assess-ments and asynchronous conferences can be explicitly made by the teacher. If the teacher development programme models itself in a similar way, so that the parts of the developmental jigsaw link into each other, then this is better understood by teachers in terms also of their teaching process. The collaborative project referred to above and described in Chapter 16 also illustrates how different modes can be com-bined, and the understanding that can be derived by teachers from experimenting with combinations.

In constructing an overview of possible stages in teacher development related to technology in blended language teaching, Hampel and Stickler's 'Pyramid of skills for online teaching' (Hampel and Stickler, 2005) is useful in illustrating how a tiered and incremental approach is needed. They offer the possible stages of devel-opment shown in Figure 15.2. Whether or not the teacher or teacher developer finds diagrammatic representation useful, they will certainly wish to consider the stages

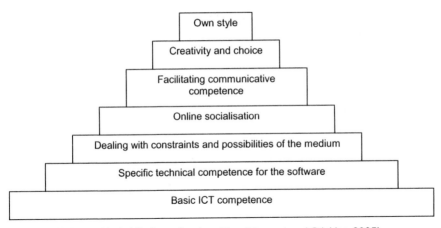

Figure 15.2: Pyramid of skills for online teaching (Hampel and Stickler, 2005).

needed in their own context, in terms of the overview of the growth in knowledge, vertical and perhaps lateral, required at different times.

Methodological and pedagogical issues

As mentioned earlier, the blended context will inevitably focus attention on how the use of technology impacts on pedagogy. However, it will also raise general awareness of the increased flexibility in the teacher role and in approaches to methods generally.

The language teacher's role has changed considerably over the last century and teaching teams may include individuals whose practice is still influenced by any one or more of a variety of methods and approaches, such as the grammar-translation method, audiolingual and audiovisual methods, communicative language teaching (CLT), total physical response (TPR) or total immersion. Teachers and teacher developers will be aware that teaching in the blended context may combine a number of these methods or move into new territories. Indeed, where historically there was 'a method', the way forward may actually be best charted through the teacher, as informed practitioner, determining best practice for their particular teaching environment, in discussion with learners, peers and line managers, team leaders or developers. A dynamic approach to teaching methods and approaches that best responds to the individual context is increasingly important rather than rigid adherence to a method. Based on a pragmatic vision that seeks to bridge the divide between theory and practice, this relies both on Kumaravadivelu's idea of particularity, outlined in Chapter 3, and his 'post-method condition' (Kumaravadivelu, 2003) sometimes known as 'principled pragmatism'. This proposes that those embarking on a teaching career are imbued with an understanding of a set of 'macrostrategies' for language teaching. The individual teacher can then use these as appropriate to develop suitable techniques or 'microstrategies' in their particular teaching context.

Kumaravadivelu (ibid.) draws on the philosophy of Freire (1970) in arguing that teachers and learners should be empowered and prepared to challenge the *status quo* as opposed to perpetuating set social relations.

The teacher and the teacher developer may find Kumaravadivelu's analysis of three teacher roles a useful framework. These may be: pure technician (limited to passing on knowledge), reflective practitioner, or transformative intellectual (Kumaravadivelu, 2003). A key strength of this analysis is that it invites reflection on the specific teaching context and encourages an evolution in the development of relevant strategies. A reflective practitioner, as in Kolb's cycle (Kolb, 1984) of experiential learning, develops through a succession of action and reflection. Teachers who perform as transformative intellectuals take control of their own teaching philosophy and generate informed strategies appropriate to the particular teaching context, 'to theorise from their practice and practise what they theorise' (Kumaravadivelu, 2003, p. 43), and in the blended context this may be the most appropriate approach to teacher development (see Chapter 16).

In his strategic framework Kumaravadivelu (1994, p. 32) suggests that teachers should be encouraged to:
- maximise learning opportunities;
- facilitate negotiated interaction [between learners and teachers, and learners and learners];
- minimise perceptual mismatches [between the intention of the teacher and interpretation of the learner];
- activate intuitive heuristics [i.e. provide material that enables inference of rules of grammar and communication];
- foster language awareness;
- contextualise linguistic input;
- integrate language skills [rather than a rigid separation of reading, writing, listening and speaking skills];
- promote learner autonomy;
- raise cultural consciousness [in which the learner's culture is valued];
- ensure social relevance [to develop awareness of the society, and economic and political contexts in which the teaching and learning takes place] (Kumaravadivelu, 1994, p 42).

These ten macrostrategies can be equally well tailored to apply to teacher development activity and can form useful criteria for the evaluation of development events and activities. Where Kumaravadivelu uses 'learner', then 'teacher' can be substituted. Where he uses 'teachers', then 'teacher developers' may be inserted. Where he refers to language input, appropriate developmental concepts can be entered. A new list of macrostrategies for teacher development might look like this:
- maximise development opportunities using the variety of modes in the blend;

- facilitate negotiated interaction between teachers and teacher developers;
- minimise perceptual mismatches between the intention of the teacher developer and interpretation of the teacher;
- activate intuitive heuristics (i.e. provide development that enables inference of rules of engagement in teaching modes);
- foster development awareness;
- contextualise development input;
- integrate teaching skills rather than a rigid separation of presentation and practice or induction and deduction, for example;
- promote teacher autonomy;
- raise cultural consciousness in which the teacher's culture is valued;
- ensure social relevance to develop awareness of the society, and economic and political contexts in which the teaching and learning take place.

Teacher developers have to practise what they preach for their leadership to be credible.

Research and scholarship

As Ellis (2010) points out, it is valid in all teacher development to link practice to theoretical frameworks. However, in blended teaching, where knowledge is constantly evolving about new modes and their affordances, about new teacher roles and learner–teacher relationships, it will be crucial to widen horizons, grasp what knowledge is documented and well founded from reliable sources and gain better understanding of the rationale behind and options for practice. As new teaching and learning scenarios develop, so they provide the opportunity for key concepts to be explored in an interconnected way, which feeds research into dynamic practice and practice back into research. For many teachers, good practice and choice of technology may have been a question of following accepted norms or trends rather than being based on an understanding of theoretical principles or an informed choice of pedagogical approaches. The variety of blended learning contexts can fruitfully unite teacher and researcher roles in what Ellis defines as 'an academe capable of conducting research and building espoused theories of language learning' (ibid., p. 186), with the teacher developer as facilitator of the transmission of knowledge between researchers and teachers. It is useful to examine the three main types of research available in the development context and on which teacher developers and teachers themselves will want to draw:

Academic research

Such research can often be the source of explanation about methodological givens. For a long time, as in other professional areas as Ellis points out, there was an acknowledged gap 'between academic research and theory on the one hand and practice on the other' (Ellis, 2010, p. 184). Research was deemed to be less useful to teaching practitioners, sometimes too esoteric and removed from the reality of the teaching context in which they found themselves. However, if harnessed and used with practical application, then such research can develop the teacher's repertoire in blended contexts as in others. Indeed teachers' own action research (see below) may draw on and feed into academic research. Research into an aspect of teaching in a relatively unfamiliar mode or tool in use, or into the relationships between two or more modes or tools, could help the teacher to identify underlying principles and become more confident in the blended context.

Practitioner/insider research

This refers to academic research carried out by those involved in teaching or teacher development. Such research often has the benefit of both perspectives, in that it draws on academic research while also making links to how this translates in broad practice terms. It can link to teacher development programmes and draw themes and practice discussions from its findings: for example, Murphy's research on auton-omy (Murphy, 2005), or Nicolson and Adams' (2008; 2010) research on diversity, all in blended contexts at the OU, have underpinned work in their own and other teaching teams and in course production in the OU's blended language provision.

Action research

The term 'action research' describes work carried out by the teacher in conjunction with their learners, and sometimes with peers and line managers or teacher develop-ers. In the 1990s and early 2000s, Schön (1987), Kemmis and McTaggart (1992) and Burnaford, Fischer and Hobson (2000) among others highlighted the importance of teachers engaging in reflection and by extension in action research. As explained by Burns (2003), they did so because 'researching one's own classrooms and teaching contexts is something that should be considered by language teachers as a realistic extension of professional practice' (ibid., p. 12) and it is no less relevant in blended teaching contexts. Alternatively Allwright (2005) argues for what he terms 'explora-tory practice' where the emphasis is on *understanding* rather than *problem-solving* which he sees as the focus of action research.

In their development programmes in blended contexts, teacher developers will want to underpin their discussions with the views of all research types. They may use research itself as a development tool for teachers, encouraging them to conduct their own action research or explore their practice in groups or as individuals, bringing this back to the development forum for discussion.

Conclusion

This chapter has reinforced the fact that the role of the teacher, and therefore of the teacher developer, changes within a blended context. The variety of skills and knowledge required of teachers will need to be addressed, as will the accrual of technological, pedagogical and research expertise which will help teachers to develop them, together with their motivation to do so. The chapter has shown that achieving a sound understanding of what the different modes can offer, and how the learning resources and tools may impact on teachers' teaching styles and practice, are crucial in development. In recognising teachers' needs, teacher developers will be aware of differing motivations, and encourage teacher autonomy by providing development opportunities through the range of modes available. With a principled framework, teachers in blended contexts can adapt strategies and approaches throughout their careers, as conditions change. Action research or exploratory practice and mutual support within a community of practice enrich the teacher repertoire and the learner experience. Chapter 16 will look at how aspects of development, both in and for blended teaching, can be tackled within the parameters of development options, teaching modes and individual circumstances so that practitioners can make their ideal teaching selves a reality.

Chapter 16: **Practical Approaches for Teacher Development**

Matilde Gallardo, Sarah Heiser
and Margaret Nicolson

Introduction

This chapter builds on the overview of key aspects in Chapter 15 by offering practical suggestions for teacher development in blended contexts. It examines a variety of techniques and resources that rely on the modes and tools that teachers may themselves have to use in their blended teaching. It also specifies aspects of development that can be tailored to the experience, needs, approaches, working patterns and locations of individual teachers and of the group in which they work. Since the institutional and formal settings in which teachers work will vary, as will the teaching blend, the ideas and suggestions presented here should be used as appropriate and tailored to fit the circumstances of the individuals and teams concerned.

The blended development context

In the blended context, as Figure 16.1 illustrates, a variety of techniques and resources may be available to support teacher development. Many of these techniques and resources will be familiar, but their exploitation and use in the blended context may differ. They may also be used in combination with each other to support a blended approach to teacher development which mirrors their learners' experience of the blend as a whole. In the sections that follow, the techniques and resources in Figure 16.1 will be examined in turn. A brief discussion of collaborative learning and a project involving collaborative teacher development will then be offered to demonstrate one example of a blended development approach in practice.

Teacher development techniques

Peer support techniques

Peer support may be informal or formal, unstructured or structured, and may take a number of forms. A line manager, team leader or teacher developer is more likely to be involved in setting up peer arrangements that are formal, such as mentoring or peer teaching support, outlined below. However, s/he will also want to create a climate in which teachers themselves seek to build on formal input through informal co-operation, sharing and collaboration with peers without the intervention of the teacher developer or line manager. This is best fostered by encouraging communication among team members and creating a sense of team spirit, where everyone,

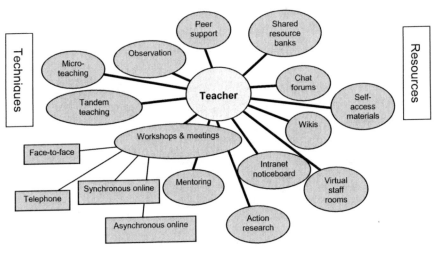

Figure 16.1: Techniques and resources for teacher development.

including the team leader or teacher developer, works towards common goals in a supportive environment without fear of judgement or criticism.

The nature of peer support can vary. It may take the form of a link between an experienced practitioner and a teacher with less experience: for example, where new tools are being integrated into an existing blend, peers who have gained experience at an early stage, perhaps in a pilot, can support colleagues in mastering these new tools and developing good practice. Alternatively, it may involve a link between teachers who have a common interest and work together: for example, in developing best practice in the management of online asynchronous forums, and then sharing this with the rest of the team. Peer support does not need to be confined to subject specialists. It may work not only across different languages but also across other subject areas: for example, teachers from other disciplines who have particular expertise in the use of specific online teaching and learning technologies may provide collegial support that is a useful adjunct to the language-specific perspective.

Mentoring
This is a formal peer support arrangement whereby a teacher or group of teachers new to the blended context are supported by an experienced colleague or colleagues either via one-to-one or group mentoring. Group mentoring has the advantage of pre-empting some of the challenges of one-to-one mentoring when the two professionals do not 'gel'. The mentor(s) may teach the same or a similar course, but this need not always be the case or may not indeed be possible. It is reassuring for teachers new to a context to know they can call on an experienced colleague to help in an informal way. As well as reaping the benefits of that person's experience, it also prevents the new teacher having to refer constantly to the line manager for support when they may prefer not to do so.

To maximise the benefits of this type of support, line managers and those responsible for teacher development will want to consider appointing mentors who have similar teaching patterns, are in the same location where this is relevant, or who can be anticipated to work well with the mentee(s). The mentors and the mentees should be briefed about the aims of this practice. Figure 16.2 provides an extract from an OU online briefing document for mentors and mentees.

The job of a mentor in the OU

- to be proactive in making early contact with a new member of staff. In some instances the [line manager] may ask a mentor to brief the mentee on the content and delivery of the course;
- to be available on the telephone, particularly in the early weeks of the mentee's employment, to advise and encourage on all aspects of the job;
- to make contact before and after the first tutorial;
- to make contact around the time of the first [assessement submission] cut-off date;
- to be a continuing resource for the mentee during their first year.

What new members of staff want from their mentor

The following are some of the things that newly appointed OU teaching staff have said they valued from their mentors (in no particular order).
- mentor being proactive at the beginning;
- vital back-up for unusual situations (e.g. student challenging mark; needs of a disabled student);
- meeting to mark scripts and to discuss standardisation of criteria for marking;
- exchange of ideas on tutorial input and perhaps arranging for the mentee to visit one of the mentor's tutorials;
- providing information on tutorial accommodation;
- advice on introductory letter to students;
- offers of past [assessment] scripts, activities for tutorials, exam questions and suggestions for exam preparation sessions;
- reassurance and a sense of security — 'knowing there is somebody there'.

(taken from evaluation reports from North West and East of England regions)

What kind of mentoring has been found to be helpful?

Opinion varies as to whether mentoring should be formal or informal but generally it has been found most useful when the mentor is proactive at the beginning, offering a clear structure. The relationship can become more flexible as it progresses. The relationship will be most useful when the mentor"
- contacts the tutor as soon as possible after their appointment;
- offers specific and practical forms of help as well as being available to answer questions and discuss problems;
- is interested in the new member of staff's previous experience and does not assume that 'being new means knowing nothing' ;
- is generally enthusiastic about the job and the OU;
- shares experience of their own difficulties and where there is no immediate answer is prepared to have a discussion with the mentee;
- knows who to contact to find out answers to questions they cannot answer themselves.

Figure 16.2: Extract from The Open University's 'Briefing notes for mentors' (internal website).

The communication between mentors and mentees can take place via any of the modes, telephone, online, face-to-face, available in the blend in which teachers work, depending on what is suitable for teachers' circumstances.

Tandem teaching
andem teaching refers to the situation where two or more teachers work together in planning, delivering and evaluating a teaching session. This can be done in any mode within the blend. Ideally, it capitalises on the strengths of each practitioner. For example, one teacher, who has much experience in online teaching, may take the lead in determining the use of resources and online affordances in a synchronous conference, while the other, who has extensive experience of language teaching in face-to-face contexts, determines the best content for the session. The former then manipulates online resources during the session, while the latter presents the material and interacts with the learners. As well as fostering team-working skills, it allows for experimentation and development in a supportive, collegial context. Teacher developers will want to take account of timetabling restrictions and resource constraints as well as the willingness of team members to engage. There also has to be a clear understanding of relationships and roles at the planning stage, including decisions about whether roles and input are to be equal or not.

Peer observation
This technique involves a mutual arrangement between two or more colleagues who observe each other's teaching and provide feedback. Optimally this requires clear guidelines about what will be observed, when and how, how the feedback will be given and what issues will be in focus. An example of guidance developed for an OU peer observation project (Harper and Nicolson, 2010), based on an original list by Rowntree (unpublished internal document), is shown in Figure 16.3.

The focus of the observation will also need to be negotiated. In an asynchronous situation, such as a forum, the observation may concentrate on the management of activities and responses, the frequency and relevance of these, the tone and style used, the encouragement given to learners and the focus of the activities. In a synchronous situation, the observer might note, among other aspects, the teacher–learner interaction, timing, relevance and sequencing of the activities, group management and attention to the competence and confidence levels of learners. In any mode, peer observation may be set in train because teachers want feedback on *specific* aspects of their practice for a particular reason, perhaps because they want to improve in that area or because they are carrying out action research in it.

In addition to observing teaching sessions, teachers can also engage in peer observation of assessment feedback. Again, clear guidelines need to be provided so that the participants can agree from the outset the terms on which they will co-operate. Some guidelines produced at the OU and shown in Figure 16.4 may be helpful in this regard.

Tips for providing feedback

Please treat these points below simply as helpful suggestions. Your group may have others they wish to add.

The purpose of your visit is to enable you and your colleague to reflect critically on the session, with a view to enhancing both your own and your colleague's future sessions. You can learn from what you see as much as your colleague can learn from what you say. Remember that your comments should lead to a reflective discussion rather than it being a one-sided 'report' of your impressions. To this end, try to observe the following pointers in providing feedback:

- Bear in mind that your colleague may have been nervous about your observation.

- Comment on your colleague's session as you would wish her/him to comment on yours — as a supportive colleague, exploring ideas together, rather than as an 'inspector' making judgements.

- Decide 'where you are coming from' as an observer: e.g. are you a fellow subject expert; an experienced tutor of the same level in another language; someone with considerable experience of online tutorials; someone trying to feel what it would be like to learn from the session (a learner by proxy); someone relatively new to the technology; or someone who has sometimes had difficulty in delivering an effective session.

- Always begin by commenting on something you were impressed by or that you liked or found interesting before you draw attention to things that seemed less successful.

- Tell your colleague if there are aspects of her/his session that have inspired you or that you would like to incorporate in your own teaching.

- Where you felt there were aspects that could be further developed or improved, be ready to discuss with your colleague how improvements might be achieved. Note that you are not expected to have 'the answer' — it is a forum for sharing ideas – but it might be helpful to have at least one suggestion.

- Remember that you are helping your colleague to improve what s/he is doing, not to do what you do. It may be more helpful to think through issues and come up with various possibilities through reflection — and not necessarily immediately — than for you to come up with a quick solution.

- If there seem to be a number of areas that could be developed or in some way improved, focus on the main ones — don't overwhelm your colleague with criticisms or suggestions, even if you are trying to be helpful, as this will be discouraging.

- Avoid judgemental language, such as 'I think you should', 'It would be better to'. Phrase your suggestions as possibilities to promote discussion, e.g. 'I wonder whether ...', 'What about ...'

- Make sure your colleague knows that you will welcome and value her/his comments on your session when the time comes or, if you have already been observed, acknowledge how you felt about it.

- Aim to leave your colleague feeling understood, valued and invigorated by the attention you've given to the session.

Figure 16.3: Example of peer observation guidelines

Outline for tandem observation

1 Starting out

Observee

- Think about what aspect of your assessment feedback you would like a colleague to look at. It might be the way you explain errors, your marking system, how you categorise errors, the tone of your feedback, the way you comment on positive features as opposed to negative points, how you handle pronunciation problems, how you stretch able students or how you support weaker students.
- Consider any possible pitfalls. What might make you feel uncomfortable? Do you have any concerns about someone else reading or listening to your feedback?

2 Briefing

Observee

- Make a copy of an assignment, deleting personal information (student's name) etc.
- Decide what aspects you would like your colleague to look at.

Observer and observee

- Agree whether you want to exchange unmarked as well as marked versions.
- Make sure both parties are absolutely clear about what is going to be examined.
- Agree confidentiality.
- Agree a timescale.
- If either of you sees any pitfalls, bring them up with your partner.
- Exchange the scripts/or and audio file by email with your colleague.

3 Examine the assignment within the timescale agreed

4 Feedback

- Agree a mutually convenient time and way to meet (e.g. in person, by phone, online).
- Observee to give their view of the aspects under consideration.
- Observer to offer information/comment on aspect requested.
- Notes written up if desired and kept by observee (decide format, e.g. electronic copy).
- Discuss the process and any changes made which can then be implemented in the reverse process.

5 Exchange roles

- Repeat the above process with the roles reversed if you haven't already worked in parallel.

6 Review

Consider what you have learned from the process and how you will apply it in your assignment feedback in future.

Figure 16.4: Peer observation of assignment feedback

Asynchronous forums and conferences

This is an appropriate technique for developing teacher use of asynchronous communication tools both for teaching and for their own developmental use. The forum moderator, who might be the developer or a peer experienced in this mode, could set up a clear sequence of tasks and encourage participants to post their messages. The forum might run for a specific period of time, or be an open space for teachers to engage in discussion during the academic year. This discussion might focus on examples of good forum practice in relation to content, style of messages, accuracy or periodicity (how often a forum moderator plans to check the forum and respond to postings), and the application of the code of conduct to ethical issues. This tool can be particularly useful for development work in departments or teams with dispersed or part-time colleagues, as teachers themselves can set up their own peer-support groups to exchange ideas and concerns with colleagues while not being tied down to set times or locations.

Forums can also be used to support and extend teacher development in other modes: for example, discussion in a synchronous workshop can be extended after the event via an asynchronous forum. Presentation materials or discussion points can also be posted here. This not only allows for an ongoing development of ideas but also enables members of the team who could not participate in the synchronous workshop to contribute. More long-term development projects (such as perhaps a teaching and learning or research topic) can usefully be returned to regularly, as evolving practice over the year helps to inform and enhance discussion. In all these ways, teacher development can usefully model the integration of components in the teaching blend.

Workshops and meetings

Synchronous telephone and online development workshops and meetings
These are particularly useful in bringing together dispersed or part-time teams for development purposes and can be more easily fitted into busy schedules than face-to-face meetings when time may be at a premium for those participating. A particular benefit of this approach is that it enables teachers to experience the protocols and practicalities of the mode at first hand. Important discussion points in relation to using the mode or tool itself might include aspects such as group management, tone of voice, timing of activities and use of available communication tools (for example, online emoticons, online chat boxes or telephone bridging mechanisms). A particular teaching issue that affects a specific mode or tool could be designated the focus of the workshop: for example, as participants experience the absence of body language and facial expression for themselves, they can more easily reflect on how to deal with pronunciation issues in the teaching context.

Online and telephone meetings can also give teachers the opportunity to clarify doubts, ask questions and seek advice on assessment issues, learners' progress and teaching strategies through informal discussions at key times during the year. They may be held among peers or with a teacher developer or line manager.

Face-to-face workshops and meetings
Where this is a practical option, face-to-face workshops or meetings are valuable in building up and maintaining social interaction and team spirit and also help teachers understand the issues that surround face-to-face group dynamics, which they may usefully transfer to their own face-to-face teaching. For teachers working in blended programmes in distance contexts, face-to-face events may provide rare, valuable opportunities to meet colleagues in person. To ensure they are well attended and

successful, a variety of factors should be taken into account, such as timing, location, content, choice of themes and range of activities. The focus may be on sharing expertise, a specific development issue, teaching practice, or research and scholarship whether pure or applied. Often the opportunity provided by these meetings for off-the-record chats and networking can be as valuable as the formal content itself. Face-to-face workshop discussion, implementation of ideas developed there, or the sharing of resources created, can be extended, once again, after the meeting through the use of other tools/modes in the blend.

Formal support

Induction

Induction programmes provide opportunities for teachers to learn more about the institution or context in which they have come to work as new employees or as new to a role. Induction may vary from large events for many staff to smaller team sessions or one-to-one sessions with line managers. As part of induction it is likely that presenters will explore processes of familiarisation with the *modus operandi* of the institution, department and/or teaching team, its teaching and learning philosophy, the objectives and learning outcomes of the programmes, and also the range of blended teaching tools in place at that particular institution. Smaller group sessions at induction may focus on shared understanding of practice and learner support. One-to-one induction may also be an opportunity to address individual training needs and the variety of ways in which these may reasonably be met by the institution or line manager. To ensure that induction is welcoming and not a daunting experience for new teachers, line managers or teacher developers will want explicitly to value the new teacher's personal experience, and acknowledge any uncertainties or anxieties that may arise because of lack of experience or expertise in parts of the blend. They will also want to limit what they can reasonably expect new teachers to take on board. Too much information can lead to little being processed and the need for more input at a later juncture. For induction events it can be useful to invite mentors or experienced team members as they can give the practitioners' view on the reality of the experience, which can be reassuring for new staff.

Teaching observation

Observation may be a familiar element to many teacher developers and teachers. However, in the blended context, observation visits will have to take place in the relevant teaching mode. As in traditional contexts, these visits will be based on criteria shared in advance and followed by discussion and feedback after the visit. Areas for observation at a face-to-face session may include:

- teaching session preparation and organisation (e.g. tutorial plan, materials, evaluation methods);
- teaching session atmosphere;
- use of physical space;

- explanation of aims and objectives;
- general sequencing and gradation of activities;
- use of materials and resources;
- individual activity choice;
- balance of activities (e.g. teacher-centred, learner-centred, plenary, pair, group);
- differentiation in activities;
- use of L1 and L2;
- group management;
- activity management;
- integration of study/learning skills;
- responses to specific individual or group issues;
- issues with specific activities;
- handling of learner feedback;
- overall areas of success;
- overall areas that need further discussion.

In many scenarios the list will be negotiated by teams and individuals to reflect the type of feedback they will find most useful.

Probationary periods and review meetings

In larger institutions, probationary periods for new staff may be a prerequisite, even for teachers who have come with much experience in other teaching domains. Probationary periods may result in more observation and more monitoring of work than experienced by those who have completed a longer period with the institution in question. As part of the probationary process, review meetings may be built in to discuss progress, assess strengths and address challenges. Where there are specific challenges, tailored and individual teacher development with peers or the teacher developer may be put in place to help teachers satisfactorily complete their probation.

Appraisal

Employers may offer appraisal procedures as part of their structure to ensure good performance and appropriate career development and training. These will usually take place with a line manager and will involve a preparation stage before the meeting, the actual meeting, and production of a negotiated report after the meeting. Reflection may focus on how objectives have been fulfilled in the previous working year, what challenges and successes have arisen and objective-setting for the next period along with training and development needs and how they may be met.

Monitoring/moderating of marking and feedback

More formal monitoring or moderation of marking and feedback will take place within set parameters, usually involving a sample of written or recorded assessments being scrutinised by another marker to assess whether numerical marks are in order and whether the teaching offered via feedback is appropriate in content and organisation (see also Chapter 6). This feedback can serve as a prompt to reflection and further development on the teacher's part and can entail a useful developmental dialogue between the teacher and the monitor/moderator, usefully overseen by the teacher developer where possible to make sure that common aims are followed.

Other techniques

Action research

Coats *et al.* (2009, p. 36) describe action research as 'a process of enquiry by [the teacher] as a practitioner … into the effectiveness of [her/his] own teaching and [her/his] students' learning …' The process of pausing and reflecting is formalised in an action research cycle. This involves:

- planning a change in practice to address an issue which has come to light, usually in partnership with learners and sometimes as a result of discussions with a line manager or teacher developer;
- implementing the plan;
- observing the impact;
- reflecting and evaluating the outcomes ready to follow these up in the next teaching session.

Where teachers are working in a team ethos, they may be invited to present their action research to colleagues using any of the modes or tools in the blend and this may widen the impact. Teachers can be encouraged to collaborate with others on such projects as part of their continuing professional development (see, for example, Coats *et al.*, 2009, p 39). They may choose as the focus of their research something that they have noticed does not work for certain learners and that needs further investigation. Alternatively, they may want to investigate an aspect of teaching that is new to them and that they wish to develop.

Micro-teaching

This is a well-tried technique which adapts well to blended teaching contexts. It involves the presentation of a teaching session to peers who take on the role of learners. Following the teaching session, the presenter and 'learners' reflect, from their own perspectives, on how the session went. Micro-teaching is useful in allowing the 'teacher' to try out new methods or in reminding teachers what it is like to be a learner (for example, in a new language). Ellis (2010) suggests that the discussion around pedagogical practices used in such micro-teaching or 'mini-lessons' (for example, in an unfamiliar language) can usefully be linked to research on related topics and therefore contribute to making clearer connections between research and practice (ibid., p. 196).

Teacher development resources

Also important, as part of any successful development programme, are the resources that teachers can turn to when they need them. A few of the most useful ones are suggested here.

Shared resource banks

This has been an established pedagogical practice for teachers over many years, which originated in the sharing of paper copies of ideas and materials related both to teaching and to the teacher's own development. It is fair to say that technology has generally made resource banks more accessible as well as easier to put together, systematise, access and update. For example, sharing materials can be facilitated by online repositories such as the Faroes Project Languages Box (Subject Centre for Languages, Linguistics and Area Studies, Southampton), which enables the storage of teaching materials in a variety of modes and allows items placed in the repository to be tagged and given a brief description to facilitate searching. This would also be an accessible way of storing teacher development materials, although some institutions do already make certain materials available via websites.

Virtual staff rooms

Setting up a shared area within a network, an intranet or VLE can serve as a useful single access point with multiple uses. It can be a communication base for notices and information, can allow for the posting and sharing of materials, or can act as a navigation point for redirection to linked websites, online teaching rooms, wikis and the like. In developing such shared areas online, institutions and/or teacher developers will want to consider format, content and accessibility.

Many university intranets can now provide links to recorded synchronous development sessions, research events and presentations, accompanied by pdf or PowerPoint documents and handouts. In addition, video clips placed on YouTube may be a resource for teachers and learners. Facebook and other social networks are also gaining popularity as spaces for group discussion on shared interests, language teaching included.

Forums

Forums may be used as a peer support mechanism, as a channel for information or as a place to discuss issues related to a specific course (for example, the interpretation of assessment guidelines and criteria, teaching strategies, course content and resources). Participation may depend on individual needs, available time and willingness to share ideas. Such forums can facilitate peer guidance and support across different languages and around issues of broad common interest as well as within specific courses or languages. The advantage of an asynchronous forum is that teachers can read content and post their comments when it suits them. However, one challenge is that, if a particular time is not set aside, it can be difficult for busy teachers to fit participation into their schedules.

Wikis

A wiki (see Chapters 5 and 12) can be used to store ideas on a particular topic and to facilitate ongoing discussion. The wiki allows new additions to be tracked and made visible and for changes to previous entries to be modified *in situ*. It can be used for gathering troubleshooting ideas and sharing solutions to technical difficulties, as well as for jointly compiling and modifying a single document of ideas on any one topic.

Collaborative learning and teacher development

As the ability to work with others has entered the learning objectives of many learning programmes as a core skill, teachers need to understand how to promote learner collaboration using the different modes and tools available in a blend. They may also have to guide learners through the more complex environment of defining what constitutes their own work for assessment (see Chapters 5 and 6). Teacher developers will therefore want to devise ways to establish and define with teachers the likely changes in their role resulting from adoption of collaborative learning. At the same time, this will support development of techniques for enhancing learners' collaborative skills and allow for the preparation of guidance for learners on how to present their own part of the work for assessment, if it is to be assessed individually. For example, as part of a development programme, teachers could be asked to present for discussion with colleagues some (anonymous) examples of learner interaction from an asynchronous forum. Alternatively, pre-selected or made-up scenarios could be used. This discussion could take place at a synchronous meeting or workshop or over a longer period of time in an asynchronous forum or in linked formats using both meetings and forums. A useful format is group discussion followed by a final plenary that is later written up and distributed to participants. Experience shows this works both face-to-face on a particular day and over a longer period in an asynchronous format.

Apart from the impetus for collaboration provided by the core skills referred to above, both socio-cultural learning theory and technological developments support a focus on the development in language learning of spoken interaction through collaborative tasks. However, many teachers lack experience in facilitating collaborative learning of this kind. In response, the project described below was set up to understand teacher needs and how to meet them through practical experience of collaborative learning. It illustrates the power of teacher development through experiential learning.

Informed by Vygotsky's social constructivist view of learning (Vygotsky, 1986) and Hoven's experiential modelling approach (Hoven, 2006), colleagues at the OU and the Universitat Oberta de Catalunya set up an online collaborative teacher development project in 2008. For six weeks, twenty teachers from the two universities were brought together online to work collaboratively, with a brief to produce a task for intermediate learners of English. Through the structured project, participating teachers learned how to use or further their skills with online tools. This included the use of forums and wikis for asynchronous group communication and to support the collaborative production of teaching materials, together with synchronous web conferencing for occasional meetings.

Access to the tools and tasks was provided via a dedicated Moodle website. Teachers were first invited to introduce themselves by uploading a photo and an individual profile along with a message and to comment on each other's initial messages. In an asynchronous forum they were then invited to discuss an online collaborative case study as well as recommended theoretical reading on collaborative learning. The next phase required them to break into groups and design a task on a theme of family and home life. Finally, they presented their task via a wiki, and commented on the tasks produced by other groups. The project both furthered their understanding of how individuals interact online when working together with common purpose, and served to illustrate a development model. The participating teachers, by actually experiencing new ways of online learning rather than just learning about them, were left feeling more confident about teaching with these tools themselves. Some reported a strong feeling of social presence and surprise at how quickly a sense of community established itself.

Involvement in a project of this type with staff from another institution is an experience that opens teachers' eyes to different ways of interacting. By developing comparative awareness, teachers may become more open to the diverse possibilities for supporting their learners using new modes and tools. Teachers may gain insight into the social and psychological experience of online interaction, and use this insight in the future to support their learners. One participant commented that this kind of experience was essential for anyone facilitating collaborative learning.

Conclusion

This chapter has shown that there are many ways of supporting teacher development in the blended context, using a variety of techniques and resources. The combination of these techniques and resources in any teacher development programme should reflect the blend in which the teachers themselves are working and use the tools and modes most appropriate to delivering what teachers need to enhance their practice and professional well-being. Over time, teachers are supported to develop their own distinctive teaching style and their own creative use of the teaching environment, the teaching modes, tools and resources available. With the increased use of the internet and the expansion of the range of online tools available, the opportunities for teacher development may also increase as rapidly as those for learner development. Quality of access and content is crucial. As the language teaching world gets to grips with the age of diversity and increased digital literacy, where blends are likely to become more rather than less complex, it is certainly the case that teachers in blended contexts will be required to become resourceful professionals, with an increasing number of skills needed at their fingertips, both literally and metaphorically.

Chapter 17: **Present and Future Contexts**

*Margaret Nicolson, Linda Murphy
and Margaret Southgate*

Introduction

It would seem that blended teaching and learning are not only here to stay but are likely to become the predominant approach in adult learning as educational needs evolve in a world of continual technological, social and economic change. A greater number and variety of blends are already emerging as technology becomes more sophisticated and will undoubtedly increase as further developments occur. Blended programmes will continue to offer the most flexible option for delivery of education in a context where individuals lead ever more complex and itinerant lives and where global and local resource constraints influence educational choices. As Sharma (2010, p. 458) argues, even if the term 'blended learning' itself becomes redundant because of its many and varied definitions, the concept is likely to remain important for language teachers as they seek 'the optimum mix of course delivery in order to provide the most effective language learning experience'. Blended learning is therefore an educational scenario that all those teaching languages to adults are likely to face in their careers. While future generations may come to view blended teaching and learning as the norm, those who represent transitional generations have to pave the way in developing and cataloguing good practice and pragmatic advice. The chapters in this book have aimed to support this process. They have also sought to demonstrate that the strength of any blended programme lies in its ability to offer a variety of integrated learning opportunities which teacher and learner can exploit in the way that best suits need.

Emerging principles for blended teaching practice

Although throughout this book authors have stressed the existence of different types of blended teaching, and the importance of adapting the ideas offered to suit local and particular needs, the nature of this adaptation will depend on the time available to teachers, the relative balance between teaching modes within the blend, the intended outcomes of the learning programme and the learning needs and goals of the participants. As many of the preceding chapters have demonstrated, this calls for a high degree of critical awareness and reflection on the part of the teacher.

It is also clear that the thinking in chapters on varying aspects of blended teaching and learning is linked through a number of key principles that are important irrespective of the specific institutional or teaching context under discussion, the mix of modes within the blend, their relative complexity or simplicity, the learner population or the level and language taught. These principles underpin effective teaching in blended contexts and could be compared to maxims, described by Richards (1998, pp. 53–4) as principles that guide teachers' behaviour and interpretation of their responsibilities. It could be argued that these are core principles for good language teaching in any context, but that they assume enhanced significance in blended language teaching. Those maxims that have emerged throughout the book are as follows.

Responsiveness

In the broader institutional or departmental setting, responsiveness relates to the need to develop a language teaching and assessment blend that best suits the needs of the target population it serves. The earlier chapters of *Language Teaching in Blended Contexts* have stressed this in relation to decisions about the choice of components in the blend and their suitability for their intended purpose, the needs linked to the diversity inherent in most adult learning groups and the way assessment strategies and tests are developed to dovetail with teaching and learning. For example, it is unlikely that a synchronous voice conferencing element would be introduced where a substantial number of learners cannot access computers or have poor broadband connectivity. It may be necessary to adapt materials and tasks to suit a wide variety of specific learner needs or to examine the assessment strategy to ensure it reflects when and how learners are undertaking the learning that is to be assessed.

In the specific individual or group teaching situation, responsiveness means that the language teacher has to develop the ability to:

- understand the context in which she/he is teaching and supporting learners;
- understand learner needs and behaviour (as language learners and as human beings) in a teaching and learning context;
- notice and analyse particular situations that arise and act on them to modify or change where these are unhelpful;
- be aware of the differing affordances of different modes and the way these interact with each other;
- make choices, in conjunction with learners, which reflect responsiveness to these circumstances.

The time that teachers have to respond will of course vary. In some situations a longer-term response will be appropriate: for example, when modifying tasks to suit a different teaching mode. In other situations there may be no time to plan the response. Schön (1983), in his seminal work on the reflective practitioner, identifies what he termed 'reflection-on-action' and 'reflection-in-action'. The former relates to those situations where it is possible to review and plan a longer-term response as opposed to latter, which relates to those occasions where it is necessary to make quick decisions as events unfold. As well as developing the habit of reflecting on teaching in order to inform future plans and respond to the affordances of new modes, teachers will need to develop strategies that enable them to react on the spot and to think on their feet, as many of the chapter authors have indicated. Some situations can be anticipated and prepared for in advance: for example, by having task modifications to hand or a bank of supplementary tasks in reserve. Others may need quick thinking on the spot, as no amount of forward planning could have anticipated they would arise: for example, having to move learners to a different pair or group because they clearly do not get on. It is important for teachers to cultivate good observation skills as they can be a great help in identifying potentially problematic issues and responding before they come to a head.

Teacher developers have to be responsive too, both to individual teacher need and the needs of teacher groups. As highlighted elsewhere in this book, not all teachers will be familiar with blended teaching or with the diversity of learners they may face in some contexts, and some groups of teachers (such as those teaching community and indigenous languages) may have to tackle additional issues for which they need specific preparation and support, as outlined in Chapters 13 and 14.

Creativity

The principle of creativity refers to how teachers choose to develop the use of tools, resources and methods available, rather than constantly to develop new resources, tools or methods. This is not to deny that some aspects of that creativity may also overlap with innovative practice. Creativity in blended teaching will come into play on various levels. For an institution, the best response to the needs of language learners will involve creativity in determining what blend best combines what the institution can offer and what best suits the learner population in question. For the teacher, creativity may have always been a hallmark of her/his good teaching irrespective of the teaching mode in operation, and the blended context should be viewed no differently, as Chapters 7–12 have pointed out. There is still the need to offer learners the most interesting set of tasks/activities and/or ways of doing them. Teachers have to think creatively around needs, contexts, modes and language use, for example, and to encourage their learners to do so as well. This might involve making tasks relevant to learners' particular needs, and also allowing space for learners' creativity by making the most creative yet relevant use of internal and external resources (for example, websites, broadcast media and social networking) and sometimes by pushing boundaries in terms of teaching tasks where the group in question can cope with this. Teachers will encourage learners to see that creativity in how learners approach their own learning needs and how they work with the teacher and the materials is a key factor in successful language learning.

For teachers who have very little or no formal support available, it will also be important to be creative in seeking out colleagues and building up networks for the purpose of collaboration, mutual support and teaching skills enhancement, since peer co-operation can break down any sense of isolation. For teacher developers, creativity will be essential in working with teachers delivering blended programmes, particularly where teams are dispersed and where the needs and motivations of individuals within any one team differ. They will also have to apply creative thought on how to deal with differences in cultural backgrounds and educational experiences which teachers bring with them to the development context.

Openness

Implicit in much of what has gone before in this book is the view that practitioners have to be open to many things. In blended teaching they may have to embrace new technologies, new teaching methods and new ways of developing themselves as professionals, both independently and in conjunction with other teachers, with managers, teacher developers and learners. At all times they will need to:

- be clear about the teaching purpose and how that can best be achieved;
- have a sense of the place of the individual components within the whole blend and their links to each other.

This calls for openness to what Kumaravadivelu (1994, p.31) suggests is a method that is 'active, alive or operational enough to create a sense of involvement for both the teacher and the student'. In that spirit, teacher developers and managers also have to be open to a relationship of trust with their teachers and accept every teacher's prerogative to take an independent view as long as it emerges from 'informed teaching and critical appraisal' (ibid.).

Pragmatism

At regular intervals throughout *Language Teaching in Blended Contexts* there is evidence of the principle of pragmatism. Teachers need to retain a sense of proportion. They will naturally want to do the best possible job, but have to take account of circumstances. Although authors have suggested optimal ways of working and modes of operation, they have acknowledged possible practical limitations and repeatedly emphasised the need to keep learners, outcomes and circumstances firmly in view. In implementing their suggestions, teachers and teacher developers will want to ensure that they are not achieved at the expense of being reasonable. It may not always be possible to cater for all of the people all of the time. In some situations a working norm may have to be established. This does not mean that the effort should not be made, but that it should be tempered with common sense and sometimes acceptance that there is no single way which will suit all or meet all needs.

For institutions this means not adopting a particular technology without evaluating its fitness for purpose, or expecting learners to work independently without first considering their ability to do so. Institutions need to ensure that learners are given appropriate guidance in how to use any resource provided to them for their language learning. Without such guidance and support, as Benson (2007b, p. 27) points out, neither learners nor teachers will gain the confidence to use them independently so as to function autonomously, using the tools and resources to achieve their individual goals and continuing to learn and develop whether as language users or teachers.

For teachers this means recognising the need for compromise: for example, in the range of tools that are used for teaching. Enthusiasm for new methods and technologies may have to be tempered to avoid overwhelming learners. It may be more appropriate to introduce one or two tools so that learners become thoroughly familiar with them and feel comfortable using them. Otherwise, if learners are expected to engage in too many different components it can lead to a serious sense of overload. Similarly when using a particular mode, it is better to focus on a specific skill. For example, in synchronous online conferencing it will be more appropriate to focus on the spoken word rather than trying to exploit all potential tools and incorporating lengthy spells of on-screen reading and writing, even though many conferencing systems allow presentation of texts and the option for learners to co-produce their own text alongside speaking functions.

For teacher developers pragmatism means recognising teachers' life contexts, their motivations, their place and relative comfort in any teams within which they work, and the way in which these influence their motivation and readiness to develop aspects of blended teaching. Teacher developers will then need to work with teachers accordingly. For example, if a teacher forum is set up to exchange ideas on how this tool can enhance writing skills, the developer needs to consider a realistic level of engagement that can be expected and ensure that teachers can see immediate benefits from participation, both in terms of application to their teaching and in relation to their personal skill development.

Next steps

Teachers who want to develop their knowledge and skills beyond the contents of this book have a number of avenues at their disposal. The suggestions here offer just a glimpse of the possibilities.

Blended language study

A good way to gain insight into blended language teaching and learning is for a teacher to take a course as a learner in a language that is unfamiliar to her/him. This can be a way of increasing familiarity with tools and gaining awareness of the issues from a learner perspective. Some of the suggestions in Chapter 16 (particularly peer observation and tandem teaching) can also provide a similar insight if signing up for a whole programme of study is not practical.

Organisations

A range of practitioner and research communities exist in the UK which can offer peer support and information. Involvement can offer the opportunity to take part in conferences or online discussion forums, or to access resources. Examples include:

- Association for Language Learning (ALL) and Scottish Association for Language Teaching (SALT) are primarily practitioner organisations which organise conferences and host websites with access to news, events and publications for language teachers across sectors;
- British Association for Applied Linguistics (BAAL) is primarily a researcher organisation which hosts a website with news, information on special interest groups, research conferences and journals;
- Languages, Linguistics and Area Studies (LLAS) Subject Centre for Languages and Higher Education Academy (HEA) organise conferences and workshops with a focus on both research and practice in higher education. They also host websites with access to a teaching resources, information about events and funding sources for small-scale projects;
- The National Centre for Languages (CILT), the Scottish Centre (SCILT) and the Centre for Wales (CILT Cymru) provide news and information about events and resources for language teachers in all sectors via their websites and publications;
- Language-specific organisations, local and national (such as the Goethe-Institut for German, Instituto Cervantes for Spanish, Alliance Française and Institut Français for French), are a source of courses and news relevant to language learning and teaching or there may be associations for language teachers in a specific locality.

The web addresses of these and many more organisations mentioned in this book are listed on pp. 264–5.

Research

The bibliography contains a range of references to research in the area of blended language teaching and learning, which can be followed up and which will lead to further reading. Researchers generally welcome contact from readers who are interested in their ideas and want to engage in dialogue about them. As suggested in Chapter 16, action research can also be a good way to develop understanding of a particular aspect of blended teaching in the context of a specific group or programme.

Further study

Becoming a learner in a blended language programme, as suggested above, is one option, but another is to register for a qualification with a focus on developing knowledge and skills specifically for blended teaching or on developing teaching skills through the medium of blended learning. Examples include the Open

University Postgraduate Diploma in Online and Distance Education, or the International House Certificate in Teaching Languages with Technology (Blended CertICT validated by Trinity College and the Departament d'Educació of the Generalitat de Catalunya). Teaching qualifications and development programmes are increasingly offered in blended formats combining some face-to-face delivery with online components.

Concluding thoughts

Language teachers cannot be sure what lies ahead, but adoption of the principles outlined in this chapter, combined with the practical advice offered in all the chapters in *Language Teaching in Blended Contexts*, should enable them to meet the challenges and provide effective teaching in blended contexts. Technology will open up further as yet unimagined and ever-changing possibilities, but the principles in themselves are timeless, and, as mentioned in this chapter, can arguably be applied to any teaching context, not just blended programmes. However the blends evolve, the editors and authors of this book believe that these principles should remain at the forefront and will assure good practice in promoting the very best in blended language teaching and learning in the future. They will enable appropriate choices and decisions to be made so that language learners can achieve their goals and teachers can experience the satisfaction of fulfilling their roles and responsibilities with confidence.

Bibliography

Adams, A., Coughlan, T., Lea, J., Rogers, Y., Collins, T., Davies, S., Swithenby, S., Sellen, A. and Medicoff, D. (2010) 'Out there and in here: connected to place, task and others through innovative technologies', Computers and Learning Research Group (CALRG) conference paper, Milton Keynes, 24–25 May 2010, The Open University, available from http://kn.open.ac.uk/public/workspace.cfm?wpid=9385 (accessed 10 May 2010)

Adams, H. and Nicolson, M. (2010) 'Biting the bullet: getting the best out of speaking practice in languages tutorials', *Classroom Discourse*, Vol. 1, No. 2, pp. 104–20

Agostini, A., Giannella, V., Grasso, A., Snowdon, D. and Koch, M. (2000) 'Reinforcing and opening communities through innovative technologies', in Gurstein, M. (ed.) (2000) *Community Informatics: Enabling Communities With Information and Communications Technologies*, London: Idea Group Publishing, pp. 380–403

Aitchison, J. and Carter, H. (2000) *Language, Economy and Society*, Cardiff: University of Wales Press

Aitchison, J. and Carter, H. (2004) *Spreading the Word*, Talybont: Y Lolfa

Alderson, J. C. and Wall, D. (1993) 'Does washback exist?', *Applied Linguistics*, Vol. 14, No. 2, pp. 115–29

Aljaafreh, A. and Lantolf, J. P. (1994) 'Negative feedback as regulation and second language learning in the zone of proximal development', *The Modern Language Journal*, Vol. 78, No. 4, pp. 465–83

Allen, M. (2009) 'Authentic assessment and the internet: contributions within knowledge networks', EdLearn 2009, Association for the Advancement of Computing in Education (AACE) conference paper, Vancouver, Canada, October 2009, available from http://netcrit.net/content/aaceauthenticassessment2009.pdf (accessed 24 May 2010)

Allwright, R. (2005) 'Developing principles for practitioner research: the case of exploratory practice', *The Modern Language Journal*, Vol. 89, No. 3, pp. 353–66

Anderson, J. (2008) 'Pre- and in-service professional development of teachers of community/heritage languages in the UK: insider perspectives', *Language and Education*, Vol. 22, No. 4, pp. 283–97

Arnold, J. and Brown, H. D. (1999) 'A map of the terrain', in Arnold, J. (ed.) (1999) *Affect in Language Learning*, Cambridge: Cambridge University Press

Asher, J. (1988) *Learning Another Language Through Actions: The Complete Teacher's Guidebook*, Los Gatos, CA: Sky Oaks

Auerbach, E. (2007) 'Autonomy and democracy in language education', *Language Issues*, Vol. 19, No. 1, pp. 50–7

Barfield, A., Ashwell, T., Carroll, M., Cowie, N., Critchley, M., Head, E., Nix, M., Obermeier, A. and Robertson, M. C. (2001) 'Exploring and defining teacher autonomy: a collaborative discussion', proceedings of the College and University Educators, *Developing Autonomy*, Shizuoka, Japan, The Japan Association for Language Teaching, available from www.encounters.jp/mike/professional/publications/tchauto.html (accessed 30 March 2010)

Barkhuizen, G. and Wette, R. (2008) 'Narrative frames for investigating the experiences of language teachers', *System*, Vol. 36, pp. 372–87

Baxter, J., Daniels, H., Haughton, J., Gaskell, A., MacDonald, J., McDonnell, E., McQueen, B., Pagis, Z., Parsons, R. and Rasheed, L. (2009) *Teaching and Learning with The Open University*, a guide for associate lecturers, booklet 2, Milton Keynes: The Open University

Beatty, K. (2003) *Teaching and Researching Computer-assisted Language Learning*, Essex: Pearson Education

Bennet, S., Kervin, L. and Maton, K. (2008) 'The 'digital natives' debate: a critical review of the evidence',

British Journal of Educational Technology, Vol. 39, No. 5, pp. 775–86

Benson, P. (2001) *Teaching and Researching Autonomy in Language Learning*, London: Longman

Benson, P. (2007a) 'Autonomy and its role in learning', in Cummins, J. and Davison, C. (eds) (2007) *The International Handbook of English Language Teaching*, Norwell, MA: Springer, pp. 733–46

Benson, P. (2007b) 'Autonomy in language teaching and learning', *Language Teaching*, Vol. 40, No. 1, pp. 21–40

Benson, P. (2007c) *Learner Autonomy 8: Teacher and Learner Perspectives*, Dublin: Authentik

Bentley, E. (1965) *The Life of the Drama*, London: Methuen

Biggs, J. (1999, 2nd edn 2003) *Teaching for Quality Learning at University: What the Student Does*, Buckingham: Society for Research into Higher Education and The Open University Press

Bishop, G. and Thorpe, K. (2004) 'Lessons from the SOLO approach to language teaching: an adaptable, low resource approach for day schools and short courses', available from http://kn.open.ac.uk/ public/document.cfm?docid=5414 (accessed 24 September 2010)

Black, P. and Wiliam, D. (1998) 'Assessment and classroom learning', *Assessment in Education*, Vol. 5, No. 1, pp. 7–74

Block, D. (2003) *The Social Turn in Second Language Acquisition*, Edinburgh: Edinburgh University Press

Block, D. (2007) *Second Language Identities*, London: Continuum

Blommaert, J. (2005) *Discourse: A Critical Introduction*, Cambridge: Cambridge University Press

Borg, S. (2006) 'The distinctive characteristics of foreign language teachers', *Language Teaching Research*, Vol. 10, No. 1, pp. 3–31

Boud, D., Keogh, R. and Walker, D. (1985) 'Promoting reflection in learning: a model', in Boud, D., Keogh, R. and Walker, D. (eds) (1985) *Reflection, Turning Experience into Learning*, London: Kogan Page, pp. 18–40

Boud, D. and Walker, D. (1993) 'Barriers to reflection on experience', in Boud, D., Cohen, R. and Walker, D. (eds) (1993) *Using Experience for Learning*, Buckingham: The Open University Press, pp. 73–86

Brash, B. and Warnecke, S. (2009) 'Shedding the ego: drama-based role-play and identity in distance language tuition', *Language Learning Journal*, Vol. 37, No. 1, pp. 99–109

Bronson, M. (2000) *Self-Regulation in Early Childhood: Nature and Nurture*, New York, NY: Guildford Press

Brown, E. (ed.) (2001) *Mobile Learning Explorations at the Stanford Learning Lab*, Speaking of Computers, 55, Stanford, CA: Board of Trustees of the Leland Stanford Junior University

Brown, E. and Glover, C. (2006) 'Evaluating written feedback', in Bryan, C. and Clegg, K. (eds) (2006) *Innovative Assessment in Higher Education*, Abingdon: Routledge, pp. 81–91

Brown, H. D. (5th edn 2006) *Principles of Language Learning and Teaching*, Englewood Cliffs, NJ: Prentice-Hall

Burnaford, G., Fischer, J. and Hobson, D. (2000) *Teachers Doing Research: The Power of Action Through Inquiry*, London: Lawrence Erlbaum Associates

Burns, A. (2003) *Collaborative Action Research for English Language Teachers*, Cambridge Language Library, Cambridge: Cambridge University Press

Chamot, A. U. (2001) 'The role of learning strategies in second language acquisition', in Breen, M.P. (ed.) (2001) *Learner Contributions to Language Learning*, Harlow: Pearson Education, pp. 25–43

Chinnery, G. (2006) 'Emerging technologies: going to the MALL: mobile assisted language learning', *Language Learning and Technology*, Vol. 10, No. 1, pp. 9–16

Clandinin, D. J. and Connelly, F. M. (2000) *Narrative Inquiry: Experience and Story in Qualitative Research*, San Francisco, CA: Jossey Bass

Coats, M., Gaskell, A. and Wiltsher, C. (2009) 'Your professional development', a guide for associate lecturers, Booklet 3 (internal document), Milton Keynes: The Open University

Cockett, S. (2000) 'Role-play in the post-16 language class: a drama teacher's perspective', *Language Learning Journal*, Vol. 22, No. 1, pp. 17–22

Comanaru, R. and Noels, K.A. (2009) 'Self-determination, motivation, and the learning of Chinese as a heritage language', *Canadian Modern Language Review*, Vol. 66, No. 1, pp. 131–58

Cooney, C. (2010) *Mobile phones: Dialing for Success in Spoken Learning and Assessment*, M-Learn 2010 conference paper, Valletta, Malta, available from www.mlearn2010.org (accessed dd mm yyyy)

CSO (2007) *2006 Census of Population, Vol. 9 Irish Language*, Dublin: Central Statistics Office (press statement 4 October 2007)

Coughlan, P. and Duff, P. A. (1994) 'Same task, different activities: analysis of SLA task from an activity theory perspective', in Lantolf, J. P. and Appel, G. (eds) (1994) *Vygotskian Approaches to Second Language Research*, Westport, CT: Ablex Publishing, pp. 173–94

Daly, J. (1991) 'Understanding communication apprehension: an introduction for language educators', in Horwitz, E. and Young, D. (eds) (1991) *Language Anxiety: From Theory and Research to Tutorial Implications*, Englewood Cliffs, NJ: Prentice Hall

Dam, L. (1995) *Learner Autonomy 3: From Theory to Classroom Practice*, Dublin: Authentik

Dam, L. (2003) 'Developing learner autonomy: the teacher's responsibility', in Little, D., Ridley, J. and Ushioda, E. (eds) (2003) *Learner Autonomy in the Foreign Language Classroom: Teacher, Learner, Curriculum and Assessment*, Dublin: Authentik, pp. 135–46

Davies, N. F. (1976) *The Use of the Telephone in Distance Teaching*, Linköping, Sweden: Department of English, University of Linköping

De Los Arcos, B., Coleman, J. A. and Hampel, R. (2009) 'Learners' anxiety in audiographic conferences: a discursive psychology approach to emotion talk', *ReCALL*, Vol. 21, No. 1, pp. 3–17

De Los Arcos, B., 'Emotion in online distance language learning: learners' appraisal of regret and pride in synchronous audiographic conferencing' (unpublished PhD), Milton Keynes: The Open University

Deci, E. L. and Ryan, R. M. (1985) *Intrinsic Motivation and Self Determination in Human Behaviour*, New York, NY: Plenum Press

Demouy, V. and Kukulska-Hulme, A. (2010) 'On the spot: using mobile devices for listening and speaking practice on a French language programme', *Open Learning*, Vol. 25, No. 3, pp. 217–32

DfEE (1999) *Learning to Succeed: A New Framework for Post-16 Learning*, Cm 4392, London: Department for Education and Employment, HMSO

Dickinson, L. (1992) *Learner Training for Language Learning*, Dublin: Authentik

Dixon, S. (2009) 'Now I'm a person: feedback by audio and text annotation', A Word in your Ear 2009: audio feedback conference paper, December 2009, Sheffield Hallam University, available from http://research.shu.ac.uk/lti/awordinyourear2009/docs/Dixon-Now-Im-a-person_.pdf (accessed 21 January 2010)

Dlaska, A. (2009) 'Language learning in the university: creating content and community in non-specialist programmes', *Teaching in Higher Education*, Vol. 8, No. 1, pp. 103–16

Donahue, S. (2005a) *RXNET WRITER™ Essays: Telephone Learner*, United States, Steven Donahue, available from: http://www.lulu.com/donahuesteven (accessed 19 January 2011)

Donahue, S. (2005b) 'Telephone language learning', *www.languagemagazine.com*, Vol. 5, pp. 29–31

Dörnyei, Z. (2001) *Teaching and Researching Motivation*, Harlow: Pearson Education

Dörnyei, Z. (2005) *The Psychology of the Language Learner*, Mahwah, NJ: Lawrence Erlbaum Associates

Dörnyei, Z. and Ushioda, E. (eds) (2009) *Motivation, Language Identity and the L2 Self*, Second Language Acquisition, Bristol: Multilingual Matters

Duensing, A., Stickler, U., Batstone, C. and Heins, B. (2006) 'Face-to-face and online interactions: is a task a task?' *Journal of Learning Design*, Vol. 1, No. 2, pp. 35–45

Dyke, J. E. (2008) '*Incorporating formative, feed-forward feedback into summative tutor marked assignments*', Centre for Open Learning of Mathematics, Science, Computing and Technology (COLMSCT) Final Report, Milton Keynes, UK: The Open University, The Open Centre for Excellence in Teaching and Learning (CETL), available from www.open.ac.uk/opencetl/resources/details/detail.php?itemId=48abf7ade87df (accessed 1 February 2010)

Eccles, J. S., Adler, T. F., Futterman, T., Goff, S. B., Kaczaln, C. M., Meece, J. L. and Midgely, C. (1983) 'Expectancies, values and academic behaviors', in Spence, J.T. (ed.) (1983) *Achievement and Achievement Motivation*, San Francisco, CA: W. H. Freeman, pp. 75–146

Edge, J. (ed.) (2001) *Action Research*, Alexandria, VA: Teachers of English to Speakers of Other Languages (TESOL) Inc.

Ehrman, M. E. (1996) *Understanding Second Language Learning Difficulties*, Thousand Oaks, CA: Sage

Publications

Ehrman, M. E., Leaver, B. L. and Oxford, R. L. (2003) 'A brief overview of individual differences in second language learning', *System*, Vol. 31, pp. 313–30

Ellis, R. (1985) *Understanding Second Language Acquisition*, Oxford: Oxford University Press

Ellis, R. (2010) 'Second language acquisition, teacher education and language pedagogy', *Language Teaching*, Vol. 43, No. 2, pp. 182–201

Fell, P. (2009) 'Sounding out audio feedback: does a more personalised approach tune students in or switch them off?' A Word in your Ear 2009: audio feedback conference paper, Sheffield Hallam University, available from http://research.shu.ac.uk/lti/awordinyourear2009/docs/Fell-short-paper.pdf (accessed 3 June 2010)

Fenner, A. B. and Newby, D. (eds) (2000) *Approaches to Materials Design in European Textbooks: Implementing Principles of Authenticity, Learner Autonomy and Cultural Awareness*, Graz/Strasbourg: European Centre for Modern Languages/Council of Europe Press

Field, J. (1996) 'Open learning and consumer culture', in Raggatt, P., Edwards, R. and Small, N. (eds) (1996) *The Learning Society: Challenges and Trends*, London: Routledge

Field, J. (2003) *Researching Lifelong Learning: Trends and Prospects in the English-speaking World* (online) Stirling: University of Stirling, available from www.ioe.stir.ac.uk/staff/docs/field-researchinglifelong.pdf (accessed 20 January 2010)

Field, J. (2006) *Lifelong Learning and the New Educational Order*, Stoke on Trent: Trentham

Field, J. and Malcolm, I. (2006) *Learning, Identity and Agency in the New Economy: Social and Cultural Change and the Long Arm of the Job* (online) Economic and Social Research Council (ESRC)-funded Learning Lives research project working paper, Universities of Stirling, Leeds, Exeter and Brighton, available from www.ioe.stir.ac.uk/staff/docs/fieldmalcolm-learning.pdf (accessed 20 January 2010)

Fiontar (2009) *20-Year Strategy for the Irish Language*, Dublin: Fiontar, prepared for the Department of Community, Rural and Gaeltacht Affairs

Fishman, J. (2001) '300-plus years of heritage language education in the United States', in Kreeft Peyton, J., Ranard, D. and McGinnis, S. (eds) (2001) *Heritage Languages in America: Preserving a National Resource*, Washington DC: Center for Applied Linguistics and Delta Systems, pp. 103–16

Freire, P. (1970) *Pedagogy of the Oppressed*, New York: Continuum

Furnborough, C. and Truman, M. (2009) 'Adult beginner distance language learner perceptions and use of assignment feedback', *Distance Education*, Vol. 30, No. 3, pp. 399–418

García-Carbonell, A. (2001) 'Simulation/gaming and the acquisition of communicative competence in another language', *Simulation & Gaming*, Vol. 32, No. 4, pp. 481–91

Gardner, H. (2008) 'Five minds for the future', available from http://jenleehongkong.blogspot.com/2007/05/mind-for-future.html (accessed 24 January 2008)

Gardner, R. C. (1985) *Social Psychology and Second Language Learning: The Role of Attitudes and Motivation*, London: Edward Arnold

Gardner, R. C. and Lambert, W. (1972) *Attitudes and Motivation in Second Language Learning*, Rowley, MA: Newbury House

Garrison, D. R. and Kanuka, H. (2004) 'Blended learning: uncovering its transformative potential in higher education', *The Internet and Higher Education*, Vol. 7, No. 2, pp. 95–105

Garrison, D. R. and Vaughan, N. D. (2008) *Blended Learning in Higher Education*, San Francisco, CA: Jossey-Bass

Gaskell, A. and Mills, R. (2004) 'Supporting students by telephone: a technology for the future of student support', *European Journal of Open, Distance and E-Learning (EURODL)*, Vol. 1 (online)

Gibbs, G. and Simpson, C. (2004–5) 'Conditions under which assessment supports students' learning', *Learning and Teaching in Higher Education (LATHE)*, Vol. 1, pp. 3–31

Golombek, P. R. and Johnson, K. E. (2004) 'Narrative inquiry as a mediational space: examining emotional and cognitive dissonance in second-language teachers' development.' *Teachers and Teaching: Theory and Practice*, Vol. 10, No. 3, pp. 307–27

Grannd, D. (2010) *Presentation of Gaelic Ùlpan*, Cardiff University, 7 September 2010

Hall, S. (1990) 'Cultural identity and diaspora', in Rutherford, J. (ed.) (1990) *Identity: Community, Culture,*

Difference, London: Lawrence and Wishart

Hampel, R. and Hauck, M. (2006) 'Computer-mediated language learning: making meaning in multimodal virtual learning spaces', *JALT CALL Journal*, Vol. 2, pp. 3–18

Hampel, R. and Stickler, U. (2005) 'New skills for new classrooms: training tutors to teach languages online', *Computer Assisted Language Learning (CALL)*, Vol. 18, No. 4, pp. 311–26

Harper, F. and Nicolson, M. (2010), 'Peer observation project guidelines' (internal document), Milton Keynes: The Open University

Harrison, R. and Thomas, M. (2009) 'Identity in online communities: social networking sites and language learning', *International Journal of Emerging Technologies and Society*, Vol. 7, No. 2, pp. 109–24

Hattie, J. A. (1987) 'Identifying the salient facets of a model of student learning: a synthesis of meta-analyses', *International Journal of Educational Research*, Vol. 11, pp. 187–212

Hauck, M. and Hampel, R. (2008) 'Strategies for online environments', in Hurd, S. and Lewis, T. (eds) (2008) *Language Learning Strategies in Independent Settings*, Clevedon: Multilingual Matters, pp. 283–302

Hauck, M. and Youngs, B. L. (2008) 'Telecollaboration in multimodal environments: the impact on task design and learner interaction', *Computer Assisted Language Learning (CALL)*, Vol. 21, No. 2, pp. 87–124

Heinze, A. and Procter, C. (2004) 'Reflections on the use of blended learning', proceedings of the conference 'Education in a changing environment', Salford, 13–14 September 2004, The University of Salford, available from www.edu.salford.ac.uk/her (accessed 22 January 2010)

Henderson, J. (ed.) (2010) *Open House*, Issue No. 426, Feb–March 2010, Milton Keynes: The Open University (internal publication)

Hewer, S., Nicolson, M. and Stevens (1997), A., 'Telephone tuition for language learning' (internal staff development pack), Milton Keynes: The Open University

Holec, H. (1981) *Autonomy and Foreign Language Learning*, Oxford: Pergamon Press

Holec, H. (1985) 'On autonomy: some elementary concepts', in Riley, P. (ed.) (1985) *Discourse and Learning*, London: Longman, pp. 173–90

Holec, H. (2007) 'A brief historical perspective on learner and teacher autonomy', in Lamb, T. and Reinders, H. (eds) (2007) *Learner and Teacher Autonomy: Realities and Responses*, Amsterdam: Benjamins, pp. 3–4

Holliday, A., Hyde, M. and Kullman, J. (2004) *Intercultural Communication: An Advanced Resource Book*, London and New York, NY: Routledge

Hornberger, N. H. (2005) 'Heritage/community language education: US and Australian perspectives', *International Journal of Bilingual Education and Bilingualism*, Vol. 8, No. 2, pp. 101–8

Horton-Salway, M., Montague, J., Wiggins, S. and Seymour-Smith, S. (2008) 'Mapping the components of the telephone conference: an analysis of tutorial talk at a distance learning institution', *Discourse Studies*, Vol. 10, No. 6, pp. 737–58

Horwitz, E. (2001) 'Language anxiety and achievement', *Annual Review of Applied Linguistics*, Vol. 21, pp. 112–26

Horwitz, E. K., Horwitz, B. and Cope, J. (1986) 'Foreign language classroom anxiety', *The Modern Language Journal*, Vol. 70, No. 2, pp. 125–32

Horwitz, E. K. and Young, D. J. (eds) (1991) *Language Anxiety: From Theory and Research to Tutorial Implications*, Englewood Cliffs, NJ: Prentice Hall

Hoven, D. (2006) 'Communicating and interacting: an exploration of the changing roles of media in CALL/CMC', *Computer Assisted Language Instruction Consortium (CALICO) Journal*, Vol. 23, No. 2, pp. 233–56

Hurd, M. and Fernández-Toro, M. (2009) 'Affect in theory and practice: issues for learning and performance in independent language learning', 'Autonomy in a Connected World' conference paper, Milton Keynes, available from http://open2009.wordpress.com/details (accessed 25 May 2010)

Hurd, S. (2000) 'Distance language learners and learner support: beliefs, difficulties and use of strategies', *Links and Letters 7: Autonomy in Language Learning*, pp. 61–80, available from www.raco.cat/index. php/LinksLetters/article/view/22715/22549 (accessed 22 January 2010)

Hurd, S. (2005) 'Autonomy and the distance language learner', in Holmberg, B., Shelley, M. and White, C. (eds) (2005) *Distance Education and Language: Evolution and Change*, Clevedon: Multilingual Matters, pp. 1–19

Hurd, S. (2006) 'Towards a better understanding of the dynamic role of the distance language learner: learner perceptions of personality, motivation, roles and approaches', *Distance Education*, Vol. 27, No. 3, pp. 299–325

Hurd, S. (2008a) 'Affect and strategy use in independent language learning', in Hurd, S. and Lewis, T. (eds) (2008) *Language Learning Strategies in Independent Settings: Second Language Acquisition*, Bristol: Multilingual Matters, pp. 218–36

Hurd, S. (2008b) '*Second Language Learning at a Distance: Metacognition, Affect, Learning Strategies and Learner Support in Relation to the Development of Autonomy*' (unpublished PhD), Milton Keynes: The Open University available from http://oro.open.ac.uk/21280/ (accessed 7 May 2010)

Hurd, S., Beaven, T. and Ortega, A. (2001) 'Developing autonomy in a distance language learning context: issues and dilemmas for course writers', *System*, Vol. 29, No. 3, pp. 341–55

Hyland, F. (2001) 'Providing effective support: investigating feedback to distance language learners', *Open Learning*, Vol. 16, No. 3, pp. 233–47

ILEA (1990) *Language and Power*, Afro-Caribbean Language and Literacy Project in Further and Adult Education series, London: Harcourt Brace Jovanovich

Jansen, T. and van der Veen, R. (1996) 'Adult education in the light of the risk society', in Raggatt, P., Edwards, R. and Small, N. (eds) (1996) *The Learning Society: Challenges and Trends*, London: Routledge, pp. 122–35

Johnson, K. E. (2006) 'The sociocultural turn and its challenges for second language teacher education', *TESOL Quarterly*, Vol. 40, pp. 235–57

Johnson, K. E. and Golombek, P. R. (eds) (2002) *Teachers' Narrative Inquiry as Professional Development*, Cambridge: Cambridge University Press

Kao, S.-M. and O'Neill, C. (1998) *Words into Worlds: Learning a Second Language Through Process Drama*, London: JAI Press

Kemmis, S. and McTaggart, R. (1992) *The Action Research Planner*, Geelong, Victoria: Deakin University Press

Keogh, K. and Ní Mhurchú, J. (2009) 'Changing policy and an innovative response: teaching, learning and assessing Irish using mobile phones', in Keogh, K., Ní Mhurchú, J., O'Neill, H. and Riney, M. (eds) (2009) *Many Voices: Language Policy and Practice in Europe. Emerging Challenges and Innovative Responses*, Brussels: Consortium of Institutions for Development and Research in. Education in Europe/Department for Educational Development, Flemish Community of Belgium — Curriculum Division (CIDREE/DVO), pp. 127–40

Kiernan, P. J. and Aizawa, K. (2004) 'Cell phones in task based learning: are cell phones useful language learning tools?', *ReCALL*, Vol. 16, No. 1, pp. 71–84

Klapper, J. (2003) 'Taking communication to task? A critical review of recent trends in language teaching', *Language Learning Journal*, Vol. 27, pp. 33–42

Klippel, F. (1984) *Keep Talking*, Cambridge: Cambridge University Press

Kolb, D. A. (1984) *Experiential Learning: Experience as the Source of Learning and Development*, Englewood Cliffs, NJ: Prentice Hall

Krashen, S. D. and Terrell, T. D. (1983) *The Natural Approach: Language Acquisition in the Classroom*, Oxford: Pergamon Press

Kubanyiova, M. (2009) 'Possible selves in language teacher development', in Dörnyei, Z. and Ushioda, E. (eds) (2009) *Motivation, Language Identity and the L2 Self*, Bristol: Multilingual Matters, pp. 314–32

Kukulska-Hulme, A. and Traxler, J. (2007) 'Designing for mobile and wireless learning', in Beetham, H. and Sharpe, R. (eds) *Rethinking Pedagogy for a Digital Age: Designing and Delivering E-learning*, Abingdon, UK: Routledge

Kumaravadivelu, B. (1994) 'The postmethod condition: (e)merging strategies for second/foreign language teaching', *TESOL Quarterly*, Vol. 28, No. 1, pp. 27–48

Kumaravadivelu, B. (2003) *Beyond Methods: Macrostrategies for Language Teaching*, New Haven, CT: Yale

University Press

Kumaravadivelu, B. (2006) *Understanding Language Teaching, From Method to Postmethod*, Mahwah, NJ: Lawrence Erlbaum Associates

Lam, E. (2007) 'Digital literacies in negotiating local and translocal affiliations among migrant and multi-ligual youths', 2nd International Conference on Language, Education and Diversity (keynote speaker abstract) conference paper, University of Waikato, New Zealand

Lamb, T. and Reinders, H. (2008) *Learner and Teacher Autonomy: Concepts, Realities and Responses*, Association Internationale de Linguistique Appliquée (AILA) Applied Linguistics, Amsterdam: John Benjamins

Larsen-Freeman, D. (1991) 'Second language acquisition research: staking out the territory', *TESOL Quarterly*, Vol. 25, pp. 315–50

Lave, J. and Wenger, E. (1991) *Situated Learning: Legitimate Peripheral Participation*, Cambridge: Cambridge University Press

Lawton, B. L. and Logio, K. A. (2008) 'Teaching the Chinese language to heritage versus non-heritage learners: parents' perceptions of a community weekend school in the United States', *Language, Culture and Curriculum*, Vol. 22, No. 2, pp. 137–55

Levy, M. and Kennedy, C. (2005) 'Learning Italian via mobile SMS', in Kukulska-Hulme, A. and Traxler, J. (eds) (2005) *Mobile Learning: A Handbook for Educators and Trainers*, London: Taylor and Francis

Levy, M., Wang, Y. and Chen, N. (2009) 'Developing the skills and techniques for online language teaching: a focus on the process', *Innovation in Language Learning and Teaching*, Vol. 3, No. 1, pp. 17–34

Little, D. (1991) *Learner Autonomy 1: Definitions, Issues and Problems*, Dublin: Authentik

Little, D. (2001) 'How independent can independent language learning really be?', in Coleman, J.A., Ferney, D., Head, D. and Rix, R. (eds) (2001) *Language Learning Futures: Issues and Strategies for Modern Languages Provision in Higher Education*, London: The National Centre for Languages (CILT), pp. 30–43

Little, D. (2003) 'Learner autonomy and second language learning' *The Guide to Good Practice for Learning and Teaching in Languages, Linguistics and Area Studies*, available from www.llas.ac.uk/resources/gpg/1409 (accessed 21 January 2010)

Little, D. (2007) 'Language learner autonomy: some fundamental considerations revisited', *Innovation in Language Learning and Teaching*, Vol. 1, No. 1, pp. 14–29

Littlejohn, A. (2004) *Blended Learning: The 'Best of Both Worlds'?*, Strathclyde: University of Strathclyde, Centre for Academic Practice

Littlejohn, A. and Pegler, C. (2007) *Preparing for Blended E-learning*, Abingdon and New York: Routledge

MacCaluim, A. (2007) *Reversing Language Shift: The Social Identity and Role of Adult Learners of Scottish Gaelic*, Belfast: Cló Ollscoil na Banríona

McDermott, P. (2009) 'Acquisition, loss or multilingualism? Educational planning for speakers of migrant community languages in Northern Ireland', *Current Issues in Language Planning*, Vol. 9, No. 4, pp. 483–500

Macdonald, J. (2001) 'Exploiting online interactivity to enhance assignment development and feedback in distance education', *Open Learning*, Vol. 16, No. 2, pp. 179–89

Macdonald, J. (2004) 'The tutor's story. Blended learning in practice', *Solace Report*, Vol. 2, available from http://kn.open.ac.uk/sitewide/getfile.cfm?documentfileid=4232 (accessed 22 July 2010)

Macdonald, J. (2nd edn 2008) *Blended Learning and Online Tutoring: Planning Learner Support and Activity Design*, London: Gower Publishing

Macdonald, J. (2010) 'Online training course for moderators of asynchronous forums' (internal OU material), Milton Keynes, The Open University

Macdonald, S. (1997) *Reimagining Culture: Histories, identities and the Gaelic Renaissance*, Oxford: Berg

McGroarty, M. (ed.) (2005) 'A survey of applied linguistics', *Annual Review of Applied Linguistics*, 25

Maclellen, E. (2001) 'Assessment for learning: the different perceptions of tutors and students', *Assessment and Evaluation in Higher Education*, Vol. 26, No. 4, pp. 307–18

McLeod, W. (2006) 'Gaelic in contemporary Scotland: contradictions, challenges and strategies', available from www.arts.ed.ac.uk/celtic/poileasaidh/MCLEODCATALAN2.doc. (accessed 25 October 2010)

McLeod, W., Pollock, I. and MacCaluim, A. (2010) *Adult Gaelic Learning in Scotland: Opportunities, Motivations and Challenges, a research report for Bòrd na Gàidhlig*, Edinburgh: University of Edinburgh, School of Literatures, Languages and Cultures

McPake, J. and Sachdev, I. (2008) 'Community languages in higher education: towards realising the potential', available from www.routesintolanguages.ac.uk/community (accessed 10 October 2009)

Maslow, A. (1970) *Motivation and Personality*, New York: Harper and Row

Mills, J. (2005) 'Connecting communities: identity, language and diaspora', *The International Journal of Bilingual Education and Bilingualism*, Vol. 8, No. 4, pp. 253–74

Murphy, L. (2005) 'Critical reflection and autonomy: a study of distance learners of French, German and Spanish', in Holmberg, B., Shelley, M. and White, C. (eds) (2005) *Distance Education and Languages: Evolution and Change. New Perspectives on Language and Education*, Clevedon: Multilingual Matters, pp. 20–39

Murphy, L. (2007) 'Supporting learner autonomy: theory and practice in a distance learning context', in Gardner, D. (ed.) (2007) *Learner Autonomy 10: Integration and Support*, Dublin: Authentik Language Learning Resources, pp. 72–92

Murphy, L. (2008) 'Supporting learner autonomy: developing practice through the production of courses for distance learners of French, German and Spanish', *Language Teaching Research*, Vol. 12, No. 1, pp. 83–102

Murphy, L. (forthcoming) 'I'm not giving up! Maintaining motivation in independent language learning', in Morrison, B. (ed.) (forthcoming) *Independent Learning: Building on Experience, Seeking New Perspectives*, Hong Kong: Hong Kong University Press

Murphy, L., Hampel, R., Stickler, U. and Heiser, S. (2009) 'Learning through experience: developing distance teachers to support collaborative, autonomous language learning', paper delivered at the International Association of Teachers of English as a Foreign Language Autonomy Special Interest Group (IATEFL-SIG) Conference 'Autonomy in a Connected World', Milton Keynes, 11 December 2009, available from open2009.wordpress.com/details (accessed 25 May 2010)

Murphy, L., Hauck, M., Nicolson, M. and Adams, H. (2005) 'Reflection and self-evaluation', in Hurd, S. and Murphy, L. (eds) (2005) *Success with Languages*, Abingdon: Routledge, pp. 60–78

Naiman, N., Frohlich, M., Stern, D. and Todesco, A. (1978) *The Good Language Learner*, Toronto: Ontario Institute for Studies in Education

Neelands, J. (1990) *Structuring Drama Work: A Handbook of Available Forms in Theatre and Drama*, Cambridge: Cambridge University Press

Newcombe, L. P. (2002) '*The relevance of social context in the education of adult Welsh learners*', Cardiff: Cardiff University (unpublished PhD thesis)

Newcombe, L. P. (2007) *Social Context and Fluency: The Case for Wales*, Cleveland: Multilingual Matters

Newcombe, L. P. (2009) *Think Without Limits: You Can speak Welsh*, Llanrwst: Gwasg Carreg Gwalch

NicNeacail, M. and Maclomhair, M. (eds) (2007) *Foghlam Troimh Mheadhan na Gàidhlig*, Edinburgh: Dunedin Academic Press

Nicol, D., Minty, I. and Sinclair, C. (2003) 'The Social dimensions of online learning', *Innovations in Education and Training International*, Vol. 40, No. 3, pp. 270–81.

Nicol, D. and Macfarlane-Dick, D. (2004) 'Rethinking formative assessment in HE: a theoretical model and seven principles of good feedback practice', in Juwah, C., Macfarlane-Dick, D., Matthew, B., Nicol, D., Ross, D. and Smith, B. (eds) (2004) *Enhancing Student Learning through Effective Formative Feedback*, York: The Higher Education Academy, pp. 3–14

Nicolson, M. (1997) 'Sample telephone plan', in Hewer, S., Nicolson, M. and Stevens, A. (eds) (1997) 'Telephone tuition for language learning' (unpublished internal staff development pack), Milton Keynes: The Open University

Nicolson, M. (2003) 'Language and who we are: some Scottish student perspectives', *Scottish Educational Review*, Vol. 35, No. 2, pp. 121–34

Nicolson, M. (2010) 'Teaching through assessment' (internal induction pack for associate lecturers), Edinburgh: The Open University in Scotland

Nicolson, M. and Adams, H. (2008) 'Travelling in space and encounters of the third kind: distance language learner negotiation of speaking activities', *Innovation in Language Learning and Teaching*, Vol. 2, No. 2, pp. 105–16

Nicolson, M. and Adams, H. (2010) 'The languages classroom: place of comfort or obstacle course?' *The Language Learning Journal*, Vol. 38, No. 1, pp. 37–49

Nicolson, M. and Gallastegi, L. (2006) *2005 Research on TMA Feedback in Beginner Languages* (internal publication), Edinburgh: The Open University in Scotland

Nicolson, M. and MacIver, M. (eds) (2003) *Gaelic Medium Education*, Edinburgh: Dunedin Academic Press

Norbrook, H. and Scott, P. (2003) 'Motivation in mobile modern foreign language learning', in Attewell, J., Da Bormida, G., Sharples, M. and Savill-Smith, C. (eds) (2003) *MLEARN 2003: learning with mobile devices*, London: Learning and Skills Development Agency, pp. 50–1

Norton, B. (1997) 'Language, identity and the ownership of English', *TESOL Quarterly*, Vol. 31, No. 3, pp. 409–29

Norton, B. (2004) 'Non-participation, imagined communities and the language classroom', in Norton, B. and Toohey, K. (eds) *Critical Pedagogies and Language Learning*, Cambridge: Cambridge University Press, pp. 159–71

O'Dowd, R. (2006) *Telecollaboration and the Development of Intercultural Communicative Competence*, Munich: Langenscheidt-Longman

Oliver, M. and Trigwell, K. (2005) 'Can "blended learning" be redeemed?' *E-Learning*, Vol. 2, No. 1, pp. 17–26

O'Malley, J., Chamot, A. and Walker, C. (1987) 'Some applications of cognitive theory to second language acquisition', *Studies in Second Language Acquisition*, Vol. 9, pp. 287–306

Ó Murchú, H. (2008) *More Facts About Irish*, Dublin: Coiste Na hEirann den Bhuiro

Oxford, R. L. (1990) *Language Learning Strategies: What Every Teacher Should Know*, Boston, MA: Heinle and Heinle

Oxford, R. L. and Shearin, J. (1994) 'Language learning motivation: expanding the theoretical framework', *The Modern Language Journal*, Vol. 78, No. 1, pp. 12–25

Pellegrino Aveni, V. (2005) *Study Abroad and Second Language Use*, Cambridge: Cambridge University Press

Pennycook, A. (2004) 'Critical moments in a TESOL praxicum', in Norton, B. and Toohey, K. (eds) (2004) *Critical Pedagogies and Language Learning*, Cambridge: Cambridge University Press, pp. 327–45

Peters, H. (2008) 'An examination of the relationship between oral and written language development in second language learners, with particular reference to academic literacy' (internal publication), Milton Keynes: The Open University

Peters, H. and Shi, L. (2009) 'Report on the implications for teachers of grouping community and L2 learners together' (internal publication), London: The Open University

Pettit, J. and Kukulska-Hulme, A. (2007) 'Going with the grain: mobile devices in practice', *Australasian Journal of Educational Technology*, Vol. 23, No. 1, pp. 17–33

Powell, B. (2001) 'Understanding errors and mistakes', in Arthur, L. and Hurd, S. (eds) (2001) *Supporting Lifelong Language Learning: Theoretical and Practical Approaches*, London: CILT/The Open University, pp. 139–51

Prensky, M. (2001) 'Digital natives, digital immigrants', *On the Horizon*, Vol. 9, No. 5, pp. 1–6

Ramaprasad, A. (1983) 'On the definition of feedback', *Behavioural Science*, Vol. 28, pp. 4–13

Rao, P. V. and Hicks, B. L. (1972) 'Telephone based instructional systems', *Audiovisual Instruction*, Vol. 17, No. 4, pp. 18–22

Reece, I. and Walker, S. (6th revised edn 2007) *Teaching, Training and Learning: A Practical Guide*, Tyne and Wear: Business Education Publishers

Rekkedal, T. and Dye, A. (2007) 'Mobile distance learning with PDAs: development and testing of pedagogical and system solutions supporting mobile distance learners', *International Review of Research in Open and Distance Learning*, Vol. 8, No. 2, pp. 1–21

Richards, J. (1998) *Beyond Training: Perspectives on Language Teacher Education*, Cambridge: Cambridge University Press

Ridley, J. (1997) *Learner Autonomy 6: Developing Learners' Thinking Skills*, Dublin: Authentik

Robinson, P. (2001) 'Task complexity, task difficulty and task production: exploring interactions in a componential framework', *Applied Linguistics*, Vol. 22, No. 1, pp. 27–57

Rotheram, B. (2009) *Sounds good: quicker, better assessment using audio feedback*, Leeds: Leeds Metropolitan University, available from www.soundsgood.org.uk (accessed 6 December 2010)

Rowntree, D. 'Tips for providing feedback' (unpublished internal document), Milton Keynes: The Open University

Rüschoff, B. (2009) 'Web 2.0 tools to actively engage learners in output-oriented tasks', paper delivered at the International Association of Teachers of English as a Foreign Language Autonomy Special Interest Group (IATEFL-SIG) Conference 'Autonomy in a Connected World', Milton Keynes, 11 December 2009, available from www.learnerautonomy.org/open2009.html (accessed 5 August 2010)

Rutherford, J. (1990) 'The third space: interview with Homi Bhaba', *Identity: Community, Culture, Difference*, London: Lawrence and Wishart, pp. 207–21

Ryan, R. M. and Deci, E. L. (2000) 'Intrinsic and extrinsic motivations: classic definitions and new directions', *Contemporary Educational Psychology*, Vol. 25, No. 1, pp. 54–67

Sadler, D. R. (1989) 'Formative assessment and the design of instructional systems', *Instructional Science*, Vol. 18, pp. 119–44

St.John, E. and Cash, D. (1995) 'Language learning via email: demonstrable success with German', in Warschauer, M. (ed.) (1995) *Virtual Connections: Online Activities and Projects for Networking Language Learners*, Honolulu: University of Hawaii Press, pp. 191–9

Salaberry, M. R. (2001) 'The use of technology for second language learning and teaching: a retrospective', *The Modern Language Journal*, Vol. 85, No. 1, pp. 39–56

Salmon, G. (2nd edn 2003) *E-Moderating: The Key to Teaching and Learning Online*, London: Routledge Falmer

Samuda, V. (2005) 'Expertise in pedagogic task design', in Johnson, K. (ed.) (2005) *Expertise in Second Language Learning and Teaching*, Basingstoke: Palgrave, pp. 150–64

Schön, D. (1983) *The Reflective Practitioner*, London: Temple Smith

Schön, D. (1987) *Educating the Reflective Practitioner: Toward a New Design for Teaching and Learning in the Professions*, San Francisco, CA: Jossey-Bass

Sharma, P. (2010) 'Blended learning', *ELT Journal*, Vol. 64, No. 4, pp. 456–8

Shelley, M., White, C., Baumann, U. and Murphy, L. (2006) 'It's a unique role! Perspectives on tutor attributes and expertise in distance language teaching', *International Review of Research in Open and Distance Learning*, Vol. 7, No. 2, pp. 1–15

Shield, L. (2000) *Overcoming Isolation: The Loneliness of the Long Distance Language Learner*, keynote address at the European Association of Distance Teaching Universities (EADTU) Millennium Conference, Paris

Siemens, G. and Tittenberger, P. (2009) 'Handbook of emerging technologies for learning', available from www.umanitoba.ca/learning_technologies/cetl/HETL.pdf (accessed 20 January 2010)

Sinclair, B., McGrath, I. and Lamb, T. (2000) *Learner Autonomy, Teacher Autonomy: Future Directions*, Harlow: Longman in association with the British Council

Stacey, E. and Gerbic, P. (2008) 'Success factors for blended learning', proceedings of the Australasian Society for Computers in Learning in Tertiary Education (ascilite), Melbourne, available from www.ascilite.org.au/conferences/melbourne08/procs/stacey.pdf (accessed 29 January 2010)

Stevens, A. and Hewer, S. (1998) 'From policy to practice and back', 1st LEArn from Video Extensive Real Atm Gigabit Experiment (LEVERAGE) conference paper, 8 January 1998, Cambridge: University of Cambridge, available from http://greco.dit.upm.es/~leverage/conf1/hewer.htm (accessed 27 October 2010)

Stevick, E. (1999) 'Affect in learning and memory: from alchemy to chemistry', in Arnold, J. (ed.) (1999) *Affect in Language Learning*, Cambridge: Cambridge University Press, pp. 43–57

Stickler, U., Batstone, C., Duensing, A. and Heins, B. (2007) 'Distant classmates: speech and silence in online and telephone language tutorials', *European Journal of Open, Distance and E-Learning*, available from www.eurodl.org (accessed 4 December 2010)

Bibliography

Stickler, U. and St.John, E. (2001) 'News travels fast', in Lewis, T. and Rouxeville, A. (eds) (2001) *Technology and the Advanced Language Learner*, London: Association for French Language Studies / The National Centre for Languages (AFLS / CILT), pp. 173–207

Stockwell, G. (2007) 'Vocabulary on the move: investigating an intelligent mobile phone-based vocabulary tutor', *Computer Assisted Language Learning (CALL)*, Vol. 20, No. 4, pp. 365–83

Stork, A. (2006) 'Vokabellernen, nein danke? — Vokabellernstrategien, ja bitte! Vokabellernstrategien an Stationen kennenlernen und erbproben', *Fremdsprache Deutsch*, Vol. 35, pp. 48–53

Strake, E. (2007) 'Conflicting voices: blended learning in a German university foreign language classroom', in Miller, L. (ed.) (2007) *Learner Autonomy 9: Autonomy in the Classroom*, Dublin: Authentik, pp. 85–103

Sturges, P. (2002) 'Remember the human: the first rule of netiquette, librarians and the internet', *Online Information Review*, Vol. 26, No. 3, pp. 209–16

Tarone, E. (2004) 'Does social context affect second-language acquisition? The research evidence', conference paper, Iowa State University, 4 March 2004

The Open University (2007) 'Preparing assignments', booklet in the Skills for OU Study series, Milton Keynes: The Open University

The Open University (2009) 'Assessment and feedback', *in Learning Landscapes: Effective Learning in a Digital Age* (internal document), Milton Keynes: Centre for Open Learning of Mathematics, Science, Computing and Technology (COLMSCT), The Open University

The Open University (2010) *L314 A Buen Puerto: Advanced Spanish*, Milton Keynes: The Open University

The Open University (2010) 'Briefing notes for mentors' (internal website), Milton Keynes: The Open University

Thorton, P. and Houser, C. (2002) 'M-learning in transit', in Lewis, P. (ed.) (2002) *The Changing Face of CALL*, Lisse, The Netherlands: Swets and Zeitlinger, pp. 229–43

Thorton, P. and Houser, C. (2003) 'Using mobile web and video phones in English language teaching: projects with Japanese college learners', in Morrison, B., Green, C. and Motteram, G. (eds) (2003) *Directions in CALL: Experience, Experiments and Evaluation*, Hong Kong: English Language Centre, Hong Kong Polytechnic University, pp. 207–24

Thorton, P. and Houser, C. (2005) 'Using mobile phones in English education in Japan', *Journal of Computer Assisted Learning*, Vol. 21, pp. 217–28

Todd, R. W. and Tepsuriwong, S. (2008) 'Mobile mazes: investigating a mobile phone game for language learning', *CALL-EJ Online*, Vol. 10, No. 1, pp. 1–17

Tompkins, P. (1998) 'Role-playing/simulation', *The Internet TESL Journal*, Vol. IV, No. 8 available from http://iteslj.org (accessed 6 December 2010)

Torrance, H. (1995) *Evaluating Authentic Assessment: Problems and Possibilities in New Approaches to Assessment*, Buckingham: The Open University Press

Ushioda, E. (1996) *Learner Autonomy 5: The Role of Motivation*, Dublin: Authentik

Ushioda, E. (2007) 'Motivation, autonomy and sociocultural theory', in Benson, P. (ed.) (2007) *Learner Autonomy 8: Teacher and Learner Perspectives*, Dublin: Authentik, pp. 5–24

Valdés, G. (1995) 'The teaching of minority languages as academic subjects: pedagogical and theoretical challenges', *The Modern Language Journal*, Vol. 79, No. 3, pp. 299–328

Van Lier, L. (2008) 'Agency in the classroom', in Lantolf, J. P. and Poehner, M. E. (eds) (2008) *Sociocultural Theory and the Teaching of Second Languages*, London: Equinox Publishing

Van't Hooft, M. (2008) 'Emerging technologies for learning', Vol. 3, available from http://partners.becta.org.uk/upload-dir/downloads/page_documents/research/emerging_technologies08_chapter2.pdf (accessed 17 February 2010)

Vygotsky, L. S. (1978) *Mind in Society*, Cambridge, MT: Harvard University Press

Vygotsky, L. S. (revised edn 1986) *Thought and Language*, Cambridge, MT: MIT Press

Walker, M. (2007) *Improved Learning Through Improved Feedback on Assignments*, COLMSCT final report, Milton Keynes: The Open University, available from www.open.ac.uk/cetl-workspace/cetlcontent/documents/48bfaffd0ab8e.pdf (accessed 29 October 2010)

Walker, M. (2009) 'An investigation into written comments on assignments: do students find them usable?', *Assessment and Evaluation in Higher Education*, Vol. 34, No. 1, pp. 67–78

Wenger, E. (2000) *Communities of Practice: Learning, Meaning and Identity*, Cambridge: Cambridge University Press

White, C. (1999) 'Expectations and emergent beliefs of self-instructed language learners', *System*, Vol. 27, No. 4, pp. 443–57

White, C. (2003) *Language Learning in Distance Education*, Cambridge: Cambridge University Press

White, C. (2007) 'Innovation and identity in distance language learning and teaching', *Innovation in Language Learning and Teaching*, Vol. 1, No. 1, pp. 97–110

White, C. (2008) 'Language learning strategies in independent learning: an overview', in Hurd, S. and Lewis, T. (eds) (2008) *Language Learning Strategies in Independent Settings*, Clevedon: Multilingual Matters

White, D. (2008) '*Not "natives" & "immigrants" but "visitors" & "residents"* '; available from tallblog. conted.ox.ac.uk/index.php/2008/07/23/not-natives-immigrants-but-visitors-residents/ (accessed 12 October 2009)

Whitelock, D. (2004) *Blended Learning: Forget the Name But What About the Claims?*, PLUM Report No. 163, Milton Keynes: Institute of Educational Technology, The Open University

Wienroeder-Skinner, D. A. and Maass, S. G. (1997) 'Telefonkonferenz: mehr als ein Direktgespräch! Praktische Tips für ein erfolgreiches, interkulturelles Kommunikationsproject', *Die Unterrichtspraxis/Teaching German*, Vol. 30, No. 2, pp. 130–4

Wigfield, A. (1994) 'Expectancy-value theory of achievement motivation: a developmental perspective', *Educational Psychology Review*, Vol. 6, pp. 49–78

Wigfield, A. and Eccles, J. (1992) 'The development of achievement task values: a theoretical analysis', *Developmental Review*, Vol. 12, pp. 265–310

Willemsma, A. and Mac Póilin, A. (eds) (1997) *Irish: The Irish Language in Education in Northern Ireland*, Leeuwarden, The Netherlands: Mercator Education

Wilson, G. N. (2009) 'But the language has got children now: language revitalisation and education planning in the Isle of Man', *Shima: The International Journal of Research into Island Cultures*, Vol. 3, No. 2, pp. 15–31

Zhao, Y. (2005) 'The future of research in technology and second language education', in Zhao, Y. (ed.) (2005) *Research in Technology and Second Language Learning: Developments and Directions*, Greenwich, CT: Information Age Publishing, pp. 445–57

Zhao, Y. (2008) '*MSU newsroom special report*', Michigan State University; available from http://special. news.msu.edu/zon/release.php (accessed 28 October 2010)

Zuengler, J. and Miller, E. R. (2006) 'Cognitive and socio-cultural perspectives: two parallel SLA worlds?' *TESOL Quarterly*, Vol. 40, No. 1, pp. 35–58

Useful websites

(*urls correct at the time of writing*)

1Videoconference, free web conferencing tool: http://1videoconference.com

ACEN, Canolfan Iaith ac Adnoddau: www.acen.co.uk

ActiveWorlds: www.activeworlds.com

Alliance Française: www.alliancefrancaise.org.uk

Assessment for Learning Strategies: http://nationalstrategies.standards.dcsf.gov.uk

Asset Languages: www.assetlanguages.org.uk

Association for Language Learning (ALL): www.all-languages.org.uk

Athabasca University, English courses: http://eslau.ca/mlearning.php

Autonomous Language Learning (ALL) project: www.allproject.info

BBC Languages: www.bbc.co.uk/languages

British Association for Applied Linguistics (BAAL): www.baal.org.uk

Clì Gàidhlig: www.cli.org.uk

Conversation Exchange: www.conversationexchange.com

Dimdim free online meetings: www.dimdim.com

Elluminate Live! online conferencing: www.elluminate.com

Facebook: www.facebook.com

Faroes Project: www.faroes.ecs.soton.ac.uk

FlashMeeting: http://flashmeeting.open.ac.uk

Genesys Meeting Center: www.genesys.com

Goethe-Institut: www.goethe.de/ins/de/enindex.htm

Gomer Press: www.gomer.co.uk

Higher Education Academy (HEA): www.heacademy.ac.uk

Instituto Cervantes: http://londres.cervantes.es/en/default.shtm

International House Certificate in Teaching Languages with Technology (Blended CertICT): www.ihes.
  com/bcn/tt/cert-ict/cert-ict2.html

iLinc: www.ilinc.com

italki: www.italki.com

iTunes U: www.apple.com/education/itunes-u

Jing: www.techsmith.com/jing

Kaioo: www.kaioo.com

Language Exchange Community: www.mylanguageexchange.com

Language-Mobile (L-Mo) Project: http://research.nottingham.ac.uk/newsreviews/newsDisplay.
  aspx?id=303

Learnosity: www.learnosity.com

Livemocha: www.livemocha.com

LLAS (see Subject Centre)

MA in Online and Distance Education, The Open University: www3.open.ac.uk/study/postgraduate/
  qualification/f10.htm

Moodle for Mobiles: http://docs.moodle.org/en/Moodle_for_Mobiles

MySpace: www.myspace.com

National Centre for Languages (CILT): www.cilt.org.uk/home.aspx

Routes into Languages: www.routesintolanguages.ac.uk

Royds Languages Department: http://roydslanguagesdepartment.typepad.com

RTÉ Easy Irish: www.rte.ie/easyirish

Scotland's National Centre for Languages: www.strath.ac.uk/scilt

Scottish Association for Language Teaching: www.saltlangs.org.uk

Second Life: http://education.secondlife.com

Skype: www.skype.com

Subject Centre for Languages, Linguistics and Area Studies (LLAS): www.llas.ac.uk

Tool for Online and Offline Language Learning (TOOL) Project: www.toolproject.eu

Twitter: www.twitter.co.uk

Wimba: www.wimba.com

WordReference online dictionary: www.wordreference.com

Index

Note: **bold** page numbers denote glossary entries; *italics* denote figures or tables

Index

Littlejohn + Pegler

Space . Time

Media   Activity

- 'integrate' to blend.

- Use a text book as a 'bridge' on a distance course

- published photocopiable materials or own worksheets.

  ↓
  pitched at right level.

- email.

- You Tube itunes U.

- self assessment materials available for self-study tasks

Whitelock (2004)
greater learner satisfaction, less drop out, improved performance cf with entirely online.

Littlejohn & Pegler (2007) planning model for integrating variety of syn & asyn. online tools

tasks/activities, people & resources

programme, course module or part

teaching session

Garrison & Vaughan 4 phase model

powerpoint, wikis